D1482836

PRESIDENTIAL POWER

the politics of leadership

Richard E. Neustadt
Columbia University

John Wiley & Sons, Inc.
New York · London · Sydney · Toronto

To Bert and Roger

Preface

When we inaugurate a President of the United States we give a man the powers of our highest public office. From the moment he is sworn the man confronts a personal problem: how to make those powers work for *him*. That problem is the subject of this book. My theme is personal power and its politics: what it is, how to get it, how to keep it, how to use it. My interest is in what a President can do to make his own will felt within his own Administration; what he can do, as one man among many, to carry his own choices through that maze of personalities and institutions called the government of the United States.

This is not a book about the Presidency as an organization, or as legal powers, or as precedents, or as procedures. It is not about the politics of getting to the White House; nor is it a history of what has happened there. Least of all is it a list of what occurs there hour by hour. Fortunately, we have many books on all these other aspects of the Presidency: historical treatments, administrative surveys, nomination and election studies, contemporary commentaries, biographies galore. The reader who seeks background is referred to these; their contributions are not duplicated here.

The purpose here is to explore the power problem of the man inside the White House. This is the classic problem of the man on top in any political system: how to be on top in fact as well as name. It is a problem common to Prime Ministers and Premiers, and to dictators, however styled, and to those kings who rule as well as reign. It is a problem also for the heads of private "governments," for corporation presidents, trade union leaders, churchmen. But this book is not comparative, though possibly it may facilitate comparisons. This is an effort to look closely at the problem of one officeholder in one political system: the office is the Presidency, the system is American. The objects of this examination are our most recent Presidents. The problem for the man inside that office has not been the same at every time. We deal here only with the "present" time. This book does not compare historical periods any more than it compares political systems. Comparisons are not my present purpose.

The search for personal influence is at the center of the job of being President. To analyze the problem of obtaining personal power one must try to view the Presidency from over the President's shoulder, looking out and down with the perspective of *his* place. This is not the way that we conventionally view the office; ordinarily we stand outside it, looking in. From outside, or from below, a President is "many men," or one man wearing many "hats," or playing many "roles." Conventionally we divide the job of being President according to the categories such a view suggests, "Chief Legislator," "Chief Administrator," "Chief of Party," and the like, and analyze the job by treating chieftainships in turn. For many purposes this framework of analysis is valuable. For present purposes, however, it becomes a block to insight. The President himself plays every "role," wears every "hat" at once. Whatever he may do in one role is by definition done in all, and has effects in all. When he attempts to make his wishes manifest, his own will felt, he is one man, not many. To analyze this aspect of his job we need a frame of reference as unlike the usual categories as the view from inside out is unlike that from outside in.

Nothing has been harder in the writing of this book than the effort to escape from chiefs-of-this-and-that. Nothing may be harder in the reading. But the effort must be made if we are to explore the power problem of the man on top in our political system.

Because my purpose is analytical and my framework unconventional, I have illustrated every major step in the analysis with cases from the record of recent Administrations, mainly Truman's and Eisenhower's. To lighten the load of sheer description and to save the reader from dependence on my word alone, I have tried to meet two standards in selecting these cases: first, that they should have been widely publicized and much discussed when they occurred; second, that they should have been described elsewhere in studies to which readers can refer for more detail and for a judgment independent of my own. In the few instances when it has not been possible to meet the latter standard—lacking independent studies from another source—I have sought to compensate by relatively detailed treatment here. For the most part, however, at the start of my examples readers will find notes on other writings. These are noted with the hope they will be read.

My illustrations are designed to shed light on a problem, not to give a balanced view of recent Administrations. With one exception every major illustration in this book is in some sense the story of a failure; without exception every case turns on dramatic incidents. This does not mean that recent Presidents knew no successes, or that presidential business is invariably dramatic. It merely means that negative examples tend to be the most illuminating, and dramatic ones tend to be best remembered and recorded. These cases serve my purpose, but my aim is not historical. My treatment of events and men has no other objective than to clarify the nature of the search for personal power.

In several instances my illustrations have involved men and events still on the stage as I was writing. School integration at Little Rock is an example. Another example is the "new" Eisenhower of 1959. In instances like these I have not tried to bring the record up to date beyond July of 1959. My observations and conclusions rest on what occurred in that month and before. When one deals with contemporary matters one must stop somewhere; this is where I stopped. To help the reader place that point in time: the American economy had virtually recovered from the 1958 recession; a steel strike had just begun; the Little Rock high schools were soon to reopen; Congress was approaching adjournment; so was a Foreign ministers' conference on Berlin; the Vice-President was in the Soviet Union; the President was about to visit Western

Europe; the Soviet Premier had accepted an invitation to visit the United States. This book takes no account of what has happened since.

While writing, I have been aware that there will soon be rich additions to the literature concerning modern Presidents at work in modern government. The Inter-University Case Program, which pioneered depth case studies of policy decisions, is now preparing several studies focused in large part upon decisions at the White House. The Twentieth Century Fund, through its project on civil-military relations, is about to publish a notable series of case studies in foreign and military policy-making; these cases also reach into the White House. A comparable, complementary series has been undertaken by the Columbia University Institute of War and Peace Studies. In 1960 and in 1961, publications from these sources will provide detailed accounts of governmental action at the highest levels on a rather wide variety of foreign, military, budgetary, scientific, and economic policy decisions made in Roosevelt's time, and Truman's, and in Eisenhower's. I have been mindful of that prospect in preparing this book. Three of my major illustrations, most of my incidental illustrations, and the general organization of my argument were planned to provide links between the presentation here and that prospective case material. Students, I hope, will find it easy to move from the particular perspective of this book, focused on the President himself, to the wider focus of these forthcoming case studies.

It is a matter of regret to me that I have had personal contact with only one of the Presidents involved in my illustrations. In President Truman's instance I saw aspects of the man at work while I served on his staff and have had later opportunities to exchange views with him. His readiness in those exchanges to respect my scholarly purpose, regardless of our former association, was as kind as it was useful; I note it gratefully. In President Roosevelt's case I had a partial substitute: the recollections of my father's friends and of my own acquaintances who served in his Administration, and opportunities to talk with certain members of his family. In President Eisenhower's instance, on the other hand, although his aides were helpful and informative they felt

Preface

themselves unable to extend to me the privilege of direct contact with him or with their work. This is not noted in complaint but in acknowledgment of limits on my resources for personal observation. Recognizing these limits I have sought compensation in the usual way, by interviewing men who had the contacts I did not.

This book is my responsibility, of course, but many others have contributed to its development. I began it when I first returned to teaching at the close of the Truman Administration, after a decade of staff work in the Office of Price Administration, the Navy, the Budget Bureau, and the White House. During the seven years since then I have imposed on numbers of my former colleagues for access to their memories and their personal files. I have buttonholed assorted friends and strangers in the Washington press corps and at the Capitol. And I have interviewed officials in the Eisenhower Administration with the student's usual unconcern for other people's time. Everywhere I have been met with courtesy and candor, as well as information. I am profoundly grateful for all three. Many of my Washington informants were assured that there would be no attribution of their information. Since I cannot thank them all by name, I shall name none. But I can state the debt I owe them all: without their help this study could not have been done.

My work was aided, also, by financial grants in 1955 and 1957 from the Columbia University Council for Research in the Social Sciences. Research and writing were completed while I held an appointment from Columbia as Ford Research Professor in American Government. The University's help in these respects is noted with a great deal of appreciation.

While this book was in draft form, four friends and colleagues gave me detailed comments on the entire manuscript: Roger Jones, Wallace Sayre, Harold Stein, and David Truman. I am enormously obliged to them for criticisms and suggestions which have certainly made this a better book. I am equally obliged to several others who commented on portions of the draft: Daniel Bell, Douglass Cater, Violet Coffin, Herbert Deane, Henry Graff, Samuel Huntington, Frances Low, Warner Schilling, and Kenneth

Preface

Young. My thanks are due also to Everard Meade and Rose Marie O'Reilly of the Columbia Broadcasting System, and to George Gallup and John Fenton of the American Institute of Public Opinion, for their time and good counsel as well as for the data they so generously provided.

Finally, I owe more than I can readily express to Elinor Truman, who masqueraded as a typist but performed as an editor, to Bertha Neustadt, who joined in this enterprise not only as my wife but also as my research assistant, and to Rick and Betsy Neustadt who spent a whole year heeding the injunction, "Shhh—he's *writing.*"

RICHARD E. NEUSTADT

Morningside Heights
New York City
December, 1959

Contents

1
Leader or Clerk?   1

2
Three Cases of Command   9

3
The Power to Persuade   33

4
Professional Reputation   58

5
Public Prestige   86

6
Two Matters of Choice   108

7
Men in Office   152

8
The Sixties Come Next   181

Afterword: JFK   196

Notes   215

Index   239

Leader or Clerk? . 1

In the United States we like to "rate" a President. We measure him as "weak" or "strong" and call what we are measuring his "leadership." We do not wait until a man is dead; we rate him from the moment he takes office. We are quite right to do so. His office has become the focal point of politics and policy in our political system. Our commentators and our politicians make a specialty of taking the man's measurements. The rest of us join in when we feel "government" impinging on our private lives. In the third quarter of the twentieth century millions of us have that feeling often.

This book is an endeavor to illuminate what we are measuring. Although we all make judgments about presidential leadership, we often base our judgments upon images of office that are far removed from the reality. We also use those images when we tell one another whom to choose as President. But it is risky to appraise a man in office or to choose a man for office on false premises about the nature of his job. When the job is the Presidency of the United States the risk becomes excessive. Hopefully, this book can help reduce the risk.

We deal here with the President himself and with his influence on governmental action. In institutional terms the Presidency now includes 2000 men and women. The President is only one of them. But *his* performance scarcely can be measured without focusing on *him*. In terms of party, or of country, or the West, so-called, his leadership involves far more than governmental action. But the sharpening of spirit and of values and of purposes is not done in a vacuum. Although governmental action may not be the whole of leadership, all else is nurtured by it and gains meaning from it. Yet if we treat the Presidency as the President, we cannot measure him as though he were the government. Not action as an outcome but his impact on the outcome is the measure of the man. His strength or weakness, then, turns on his personal capacity to influence the conduct of the men who make up government. His influence becomes the mark of leadership. To rate a President according to these rules, one looks into the man's own capabilities as seeker and as wielder of effective influence upon the other men involved in governing the country. That is what this book will do.

"Presidential" on the title page means nothing but the President. "Power" means *his* influence. It helps to have these meanings settled at the start.

There are two ways to study "presidential power." One way is to focus on the tactics, so to speak, of influencing certain men in given situations: how to get a bill through Congress, how to settle strikes, how to quiet Cabinet feuds, or how to stop a Suez. The other way is to step back from tactics on those "givens" and to deal with influence in more strategic terms: what is its nature and what are its sources? What can *this* man accomplish to improve the prospect that he will have influence when he wants it? Strategically, the question is not how he masters Congress in a peculiar instance, but what he does to boost his chance for mastery in any instance, looking toward tomorrow from today. The second of these two ways has been chosen for this book.

II

To look into the strategy of presidential influence one must decide at whom to look. Power problems vary with the scope and scale of government, the state of politics, the progress of technology, the pace of world relationships. Power in the Nineteen-sixties cannot be acquired or employed on the same terms as those befitting Calvin Coolidge, or Theodore Roosevelt, or Grover Cleveland, or James K. Polk. But there is a real likelihood that in the next decade a President will have to reach for influence and use it under much the same conditions we have known since the Second World War. If so, the men whose problems shed most light on White House prospects are Dwight David Eisenhower and Harry S. Truman. It is at them, primarily, that we shall look. To do so is to see the shadow of another, Franklin D. Roosevelt. They worked amidst the remnants of his voter coalition, and they filled an office that his practice had enlarged.

Our two most recent Presidents have had in common something that is likely to endure into our future: the setting for a great deal of their work. They worked in an environment of policy and politics marked by a high degree of continuity. To sense the continuity from Truman's time through Eisenhower's one need only place the newspapers of 1959 alongside those of 1949. Save for the issue of domestic communists, the subject matter of our policy and politics remains almost unchanged. We deal as we have done in terms of cold war, of an arms race, of a competition overseas, of danger from inflation, and of damage from recession. We skirmish on the frontiers of the Welfare State and in the borderlands of race relations. Aspects change, but labels stay the same. So do dilemmas. Everything remains unfinished business. Not in this century has there been comparable continuity from a decade's beginning to its end; count back from 1949 and this grows plain. There even has been continuity in the behavior of our national electorate; what Samuel Lubell nine years ago called "stalemate" in our partisan alignments has not broken yet.

The similarities in Truman's setting and in Eisenhower's give their years a unity distinct from the War Years, or the Depression Era, or the Twenties, or before. In governmental terms, at least, the fifteen years since V-J Day deserve a designation all their own. "Mid-century" will serve for present purposes. And what distinguishes mid-century can be put very briefly: emergencies in policy with politics as usual.

"Emergency" describes mid-century conditions only by the standards of the past. By present standards what would once have been emergency is commonplace. Policy dilemmas through the postwar period resemble past emergencies in one respect, their difficulty and complexity for government. Technological innovation, social and political change abroad, population growth at home impose enormous strains not only on the managerial equipment of our policy-makers but also on their intellectual resources. The gropings of mature men at mid-century remind one of the intellectual confusions stemming from depression, thirty years ago, when men were also pushed past comprehension by the novelty of their condition. In our time innovation keeps us *constantly* confused; no sooner do we start to comprehend than something new is added, and we grope again. But unlike the Great Difficulties of the past, our policy dilemmas rarely produce what the country feels as "crisis." Not even the Korean War brought anything approaching sustained national "consensus." Since 1945 inumerable situations have been felt as crises inside government; there rarely has been comparable feeling outside government. In the era of the Cold War we have practiced "peacetime" politics. What else could we have done? Cold War is not a "crisis"; it becomes a way of life.

Our politics has been "as usual," but only by the standard of past *crises*. In comparison with what was once normality, our politics has been *un*usual. The weakening of party ties, the emphasis on personality, the close approach of world events, the changeability of public moods, and above all the ticket-splitting, none of this was "usual" before the Second World War. The symbol of mid-century political conditions is the White House in one party's hands with Congress in the other's—a symbol plainly visible in eight of the past fifteen years and all but visible in four of the remaining seven. Nothing really comparable has been seen in this country since the Eighteen-eighties. And the Eighties were not troubled by emergencies in policy.

As for politics and policy combined, we have seen some precursors of our setting at mid-century. Franklin Roosevelt had a reasonably comparable setting in his middle years as President, though not in his first years and not after Pearl Harbor. Indeed, if one excepts the war, mid-century could properly be said to start

with Roosevelt's second term. Our recent situation is to be compared, as well, with aspects of the Civil War. Abraham Lincoln is
much closer to us in condition than in time, the Lincoln plagued
by Radicals and shunned by Democrats amidst the managerial and
intellectual confusions of twentieth-century warfare in the nine-
teenth century. And in 1919 Woodrow Wilson faced and was
defeated by conditions something like our own. But save for these
men one can say of Truman and of Eisenhower that they were
the first who had to fashion presidential influence out of mid-century materials. Presumably they will not be the last.

III

We tend to measure Truman's predecessors as though "leadership" consisted of initiatives in economics, or diplomacy, or legislation, or in mass communication. If we measured him and his
successors so, they would be leaders automatically. A striking feature of our recent past has been the transformation into routine
practice of the actions we once treated as exceptional. A President
may retain liberty, in Woodrow Wilson's phrase, "to be as big a
man as he can." But nowadays he cannot be as small as he might
like.

Our two most recent Presidents have gone through all the mo-
tions we traditionally associate with strength in office. So will the
man who takes the oath on January 20, 1961. In instance after
instance the exceptional behavior of our earlier "strong" Presidents
has now been set by statute as a regular requirement. Theodore
Roosevelt once assumed the "steward's" role in the emergency
created by the great coal strike of 1902; the Railway Labor Act
and the Taft-Hartley Act now make such interventions mandatory
upon Presidents. The other Roosevelt once asserted personal responsibility for gauging and for guiding the American economy;
the Employment Act binds his successors to that task. Wilson and
F.D.R. became chief spokesmen, leading actors, on a world stage
at the height of war; now UN membership, far-flung alliances, prescribe that role continuously in times termed "peace." Through

both world wars our Presidents grappled experimentally with an emergency-created need to "integrate" foreign and military policies; the National Security Act now takes that need for granted as a constant of our times. F.D.R. and Truman made themselves responsible for the development and first use of atomic weapons; the Atomic Energy Act now puts a comparable burden on the back of every President. And what has escaped statutory recognition has mostly been accreted into presidential common law, confirmed by custom, no less binding: the "fireside chat" and the press conference, for example, or the personally presented legislative program, or personal campaigning in congressional elections.

In form all Presidents are leaders, nowadays. In fact this guarantees no more than that they will be clerks. Everybody now expects the man inside the White House to do something about everything. Laws and customs now reflect acceptance of him as the Great Initiator, an acceptance quite as widespread at the Capitol as at his end of Pennsylvania Avenue. But such acceptance does not signify that all the rest of government is at his feet. It merely signifies that other men have found it practically impossible to do *their* jobs without assurance of initiatives from him. Service for themselves, not power for the President, has brought them to accept his leadership in form. They find his actions useful in their business. The transformation of his routine obligations testifies to their dependence on an active White House. A President, these days, is an invaluable clerk. His services are in demand all over Washington. His influence, however, is a very different matter. Laws and customs tell us little about leadership in fact.

IV

Why have our Presidents been honored with this clerkship? The answer is that no one else's services suffice. Our Constitution, our traditions, and our politics provide no better source for the initiatives a President can take. Executive officials need decisions, and political protection, and a referee for fights. Where are these to come from but the White House? Congressmen need an agenda from outside, something with high status to respond to or react against. What provides it better than the program of the President? Party politicians need a record to defend in the next national campaign. How can it be made except by "their" Administration? Private persons with a public axe to grind may need a helping hand or they may need a grinding stone. In either case who gives more satisfaction than a President? And outside the United States, in every country where our policies and postures influence home politics, there will be people needing just the "right" thing said and done or just the "wrong" thing stopped *in Washington.* What symbolizes Washington more nearly than the White House?

A modern President is bound to face demands for aid and service from five more or less distinguishable sources: from Executive officialdom, from Congress, from his partisans, from citizens at large, and from abroad. The Presidency's clerkship is expressive of these pressures. In effect they are constituency pressures and each President has five sets of constituents. The five are not distinguished by their membership; membership is obviously an overlapping matter. And taken one by one they do not match the man's electorate; one of them, indeed, is outside his electorate. They are distinguished, rather, by their different claims upon him. Initiatives are what they want, for five distinctive reasons. Since government and politics have offered no alternative, our laws and customs turn those wants into his obligations.

Why, then, is the President not guaranteed an influence commensurate with services performed? Constituent relations are relations of dependence. Everyone with any share in governing this country will belong to one (or two, or three) of his "constituencies." Since everyone depends on him why is he not assured of everyone's support? The answer is that no one else sits where he sits, or sees quite as he sees; no one else feels the full weight of his obligations. Those obligations are a tribute to his unique place in our political system. But just because it is unique they fall on him alone. *The same conditions that promote his leadership in form preclude a guarantee of leadership in fact.* No man or group at either end of Pennsylvania Avenue shares his peculiar status in our government and politics. That is why his services are in de-

mand. By the same token, though, the obligations of all other men
are different from his own. His Cabinet officers have departmental
duties and constituents. His legislative leaders head *congressional*
parties, one in either House. His national party organization stands
apart from his official family. His political allies in the States need
not face Washington, or one another. The private groups that
seek him out are not compelled to govern. And friends abroad
are not compelled to run in our elections. Lacking his position and
prerogatives, these men cannot regard his obligations as their own.
They have their jobs to do; none is the same as his. As they perceive their duty they may find it right to follow him, in fact, or
they may not. Whether they will feel obliged *on their responsibility* to do what he wants done remains an open question. That
question serves to introduce this book.

Three Cases of Command . 2

In the early summer of 1952, before the heat of the campaign, President Truman used to contemplate the problems of the General-become-President should Eisenhower win the forthcoming election. "He'll sit here," Truman would remark (tapping his desk for emphasis), "and he'll say, 'Do this! Do that!' *And nothing will happen.* Poor Ike—it won't be a bit like the Army. He'll find it very frustrating."

Eisenhower evidently found it so. "In the face of the continuing dissidence and disunity, the President sometimes simply exploded with exasperation," wrote Robert Donovan in comment on the early months of Eisenhower's first term. "What was the use, he demanded to know, of his trying to lead the Republican Party . . . ." [1] And this reaction was not limited to early months alone, or to his party only. "The President still feels," an Eisenhower aide remarked to me in 1958, "that when he's decided something, that *ought* to be the end of it . . . and when it bounces back undone or done wrong, he tends to react with shocked surprise."

Truman knew whereof he spoke. With "resignation" in the place of "shocked surprise" the aide's description would have fitted Truman. The former senator may have been less shocked than the former general, but he was no less subjected to that painful and repetitive experience: "Do this, do that, and nothing will happen." Long before he came to talk of Eisenhower he had put his own experience in other words: "I sit here all day trying to

9

persuade people to do the things they ought to have sense enough
to do without my persuading them. . . . That's all the powers of
the President amount to."

In these words of a President, spoken on the job, one finds the
essence of the problem now before us: "powers" are no guarantee
of power; clerkship is no guarantee of leadership. The President of
the United States has an extraordinary range of formal powers, of
authority in statute law and in the Constitution. Here is testimony
that despite his "powers" he does not obtain results by giving
orders—or not, at any rate, merely by giving orders. He also has
extraordinary status, *ex officio*, according to the customs of our
government and politics. Here is testimony that despite his status
he does not get action without argument. Presidential *power* is
the power to persuade.

This testimony seems, at first glance, to be contradicted flatly by
events in the public record of Truman's own administration and
of Eisenhower's. Three cases, out of many, illustrate the seeming
contradiction. In 1951 Douglas MacArthur was ordered to relin-
quish his commands; he did as he was told. In 1952 Truman seized
the nation's steel mills; they remained in government possession for
some seven weeks until he ordered them released when the Supreme
Court held that he exceeded his authority. And in 1957 Eisenhower
ordered Federal troops to Little Rock; the mob was dispersed, and
the Negro children went to school. Evidently some commands
are effective; some results can be gained simply by giving orders;
some actions do get taken without argument. Truman's comments
seem to be belied by his own acts and those of his successor in
these instances, among others.

The contradiction is superficial. It exists if Truman's words are
stretched to mean that formal powers have no bearing upon influence. It disappears the moment one takes Truman to imply that
mere assertion of a formal power rarely is enough. Taken in that
second sense his words are actually *substantiated* by these cases of
command. For the recall of MacArthur, the seizure of the steel
mills, and the Federal troops at Little Rock go far to show how
special are the circumstances favoring command. They also show
how narrow may be its effective reach, how costly its employ-

ment. An analysis of presidential power must begin by marking out the limits upon presidential "powers." These examples tell us much about the limits.

II

Before I turn to what these cases show, let me review the facts in each of them. Chronologically, the MacArthur case comes first, the steel seizure second, and the Little Rock case third. For purposes of factual review it is convenient to discuss them in that order. Once the facts are stated, chronology can be ignored.

When the Korean War broke out in late June 1950 with a drive on South Korea from the North, MacArthur was in Tokyo, 600 miles away, as supreme commander for the allied occupation of Japan and as commander of American forces in the Far East, posts he had assumed five years before when he accepted Japanese surrender. To him and to his forces, necessarily, Truman first entrusted military aid for South Korea.[2] No other forces were at hand. When the United Nations made the war its own and gave command to the United States, Truman added to MacArthur's other titles a designation as the UN field commander.

By August the General had demonstrated both that he could keep a foothold in Korea and that he, personally, might have more in mind than throwing back the North Korean Communists. In the first days of the war Washington had "neutralized" Formosa, ordering the Seventh Fleet to interpose itself between the Communist regime in mainland China and the Nationalist regime which held the island. MacArthur soon met Chiang Kai-shek, and public statements by the two of them implied some sort of underwriting for Chiang's cause and some sort of involvement by the Nationalists in Korea. These statements were at variance with policy in Washington, to say nothing of its UN associates, and Truman, ultimately, had to tell MacArthur to withdraw a further statement he had sent the Veterans of Foreign Wars.

Within three weeks of this episode Washington was ready to forgive it and forget it in delight at the successes on the battlefield.

On September 15 MacArthur's forces landed at Inchon; thereafter, virtual victory came in a rush. A month later Truman met the General at Wake Island. They then agreed that they had no dispute about the Chinese Nationalists, and they looked forward confidently to an early end of fighting with the occupation of all North Korea.

Their confidence was not to last. In the first week of November it was shaken as the UN troops encountered Chinese Communists. In the last week of November it was shattered by a Chinese Communist attack that caught MacArthur unprepared and woefully deployed. To extricate his forces he was compelled to retreat two thirds of the way down the peninsula. Not until mid-January 1951 did Washington begin to feel assured that new lines could form, hold, and support real recovery. Meanwhile, MacArthur had announced the coming of a "new war." He had despaired of holding any part of the peninsula, and he had publicly blamed his defeat on Washington's insistence that the fighting should be confined to Korea. Immediately after Chinese intervention he began campaigning for war measures against the Chinese Communists on their home grounds.

Truman, and his advisers, and most allied governments had quite the opposite reaction to Peking's attack. Their eyes were fixed on Europe as the cold war's greatest stake. They hoped to minimize the risk of long involvement elsewhere, and especially the risk of World War III. If the original objective of the fighting, South Korea, could be salvaged without deepening those risks, they would be well content. By February General Ridgway, who commanded the ground forces in Korea, was assuring them it could be done. By March his troops were doing it. Before that month was out substantially the whole of South Korea was again in UN hands, and Ridgway's troops were reaching north toward natural defense lines past the border.

It now seemed likely that hostilities might end with restoration, roughly, of the situation as it had been at the start. To Washington and to its European allies this seemed the best of a bad bargain; to MacArthur, and to many fellow citizens at home, it seemed the worst. Rather than accept it he began a new barrage of public statements aimed, apparently, at pushing Washington to "win" the war. On March 7 in a statement to the press, he called for action to "provide on the highest international levels the answer to the obscurities [of] Red China's undeclared war . . . ."[3] On March 25 he published a demand for enemy surrender, undermining a planned presidential statement that would have expressed interest in negotiated settlement. On April 5 Joseph Martin, the Minority Leader of the House of Representatives, read into the record a letter from the General which deplored the policies of his superiors, and ended with the words "There is no substitute for victory."

By April 5 Truman's decision already had been taken; five days later MacArthur was relieved. An extraordinary burst of popular emotion heralded his homecoming. Emotion faded, and so did he, during the course of Senate Hearings which poked into every corner of official policy. Meanwhile the war remained limited. In July truce talks began; two years later these produced an armistice along a line the troops had reached by June of 1951.

So much for the facts of the MacArthur case. Next is the steel seizure case. On December 31, 1951, five months after the start of truce talks in Korea, contracts between the United Steelworkers and major steel concerns expired with a stalemate in collective bargaining.[4] At Truman's personal request the men continued work without a contract, while he referred their dispute to the Wage Stabilization Board, a body composed equally of labor, industry, and public members, which had charge of wage control and allied functions during the Korean War. Because this Wage Board still was hearing the case, the union twice postponed a strike, again at Truman's instance. Then, with the strike set for April 9, 1952, labor and public members of the Board agreed, March 20, on terms of settlement to recommend to the disputing parties. Industry members dissented. At first sight of these majority proposals the union embraced them, the companies denounced them, and in echelons above the Board officials thought them "high."

The Wage Stabilization Board was part of a complex administrative hierarchy established in the first six months of the Korean War. At the top was the Office of Defense Mobilization (ODM), headed by Charles E. (General Electric) Wilson whom Truman had entrusted with "direction," "supervision," and "control" of the entire home-front economic effort. ODM had been super-imposed on everything else in the immediate aftermath of Chinese intervention. Next in line was an Economic Stabilization Agency (ESA), which had been created before Wilson's appointment. On paper, this Agency administered discretionary powers over prices and wages conferred upon the President by the Defense Production Act. In fact, those powers were administered by two subordinate units: the Office of Price Stabilization, headed by Ellis Arnall, former governor of Georgia, and the Wage Board, itself. The Office was organized like a regular line agency. The Board was run like a regulatory commission with one of its public members in the chair. The Board had statutory authority by delegation through the ESA, to *set* maximum limits on wages. It also had a direct authorization from the White House to *recommend* solutions for nonwage issues in labor disputes. Both functions were involved in the steel case. Wage rulings by the Board were legally enforceable; its nonwage proposals were not. Theoretically, its wage ceilings were subject to revision by the Economic Stabilizer, or the Defense Mobilizer, or the President. But practically speaking, case by case, the Board's tripartite composition and quasi-judicial procedures made majority decisions irreversible on wages and not even reviewable on other issues. In comparison, the Office of Price Stabilization was an administrative unit with no more independence of its nominal superiors than it could win by bureau-cratic in-fighting, and with no nonprice duties to distract it from concern for price control. One thing, however, wage and price controllers had in common: they mistrusted those above them and were cool to one another.

The Wage Board proposals of March 20 precipitated a crisis in the steel case. The industry pronounced them unacceptable. The union termed them the least it would accept. The Administration could not disavow them without wrecking the machinery for wage stabilization. A strike was just three weeks away. According to the Pentagon the possibility of enemy offensives in Korea pre-cluded any loss of steel production. In these circumstances Wilson, as Director of Defense Mobilization, took personal charge. His answer for the crisis was a *price* concession to the companies sufficient to induce a settlement of wage and other issues before the strike deadline. After hurried consultation with the President, who was ending a vacation at Key West, Wilson sounded out the industry on price relief. Unfortunately, in an impromptu press conference he had exposed a private distaste for the Wage Board's terms of settlement. This ended union confidence in him and cast doubt on his claims to act for the Administration. Immediately after, Wilson was rebuffed by industry officials who wanted higher prices than he had in mind and made no promises to settle with the union. Immediately after that, Wilson's nominal subordinate Ellis Arnall, the Price Director, won support from Truman for a firmer stand on price controls. Concessions were to be allowed for cost increases in the normal course, but only *after* costs had been incurred. A labor-management agreement must come first. So Arnall argued. Truman sympathized. Wilson resigned on March 29.

In the remaining days before the strike the White House, now involved directly, tried to press the companies and union to a settlement without a price concession in advance. Collective bargaining was resumed and mediation was attempted. Much jockeying and many misadventures then ensued but not a settlement. Finally, to escape a shutdown of production Truman seized the industry two hours before the strike deadline. He ordered the Secretary of Commerce to administer the mills and called upon the men to work as government employees.

The union honored Truman's call; the companies accepted government control—and went to court. In ordering his seizure the President had acted without statutory sanction. Indeed, he had ignored a statute on the books, the Taft-Hartley Act, which gave him the alternative of seeking an injunction against union strike-calls for another eighty days. In these circumstances the steel companies asserted that his seizure was illegal. So they argued in the press and in a Federal District Court on April 9 and after. Government attorneys answered with appeals to the necessities of national defense. They also laid claims to unlimited, "inherent" presidential powers. The President, himself, repudiated these claims. The Court, however, was infuriated by them. The fury was shared by Congressmen and editors.

On April 29 the District Judge denied Truman's authority to seize the industry. A strike began at once. Three days later the order of that Judge was stayed by an Appeals Court decision which allowed the government to put its case before the Supreme Court. The men then straggled back to work. At Truman's request, company and union leaders went into the White House to bargain with each other then and there. On May 3 while bargaining was under way, the Supreme Court took jurisdiction of the case and pending its decision ordered that there be no change in wages. White House bargaining broke down at once; all parties turned, instead, to the Court.

On June 2 a Supreme Court majority upheld the District Judge with a set of opinions so diverse as to establish nothing but the outcome. The President at once returned the mills to private hands. Again there was a strike. This time the mills remained shut down for seven weeks until collective bargaining and White House promises of price relief produced a settlement on July 24. The men gained terms a shade less favorable than the Wage Board members had proposed; the companies gained considerably more price relief than Wilson once had offered.

Such was the outcome of steel seizure. Between it and the third 'case there are five years and Eisenhower's two elections. The Little Rock affair began in the first months of his second term.[5] In April 1957 a Federal Court of Appeals approved the integration plan prepared by school authorities in Little Rock, following the Supreme Court decision of 1954 that school segregation was unconstitutional. The Little Rock School Board announced that integrated schooling would begin at Central High School in September. It intensified its efforts to accustom the community to that prospect. So matters stood in August 1957, when a local citizen brought suit, successfully, in local court to halt the integration. The local court's injunction was declared void by a Federal Judge, and legally the way was cleared for integrated classes when the school reopened on September 3.

But on September 2, Orval Faubus, Governor of Arkansas, sent National Guardsmen to surround the school. These troops, at his instruction, kept all Negroes out in order to preclude the violent citizen reaction he announced might follow from their entry. Unable to carry out its integration plan, the School Board sought instruction from the Federal Judge. He ordered the Board to proceed as planned. Faubus's troops, however, barred compliance with his order. A petition to enjoin the Governor was put before the Judge September 10 with the United States Attorney General, among others, a petitioner. The next day Faubus asked Eisenhower for a conference; the President assented. He was then on vacation in Newport, Rhode Island, and a meeting was arranged there for September 14. But the meeting produced no action on either side.

On September 20, the Federal Judge enjoined the Governor from further interference with the School Board's plan. The Governor withdrew the National Guard and on the next school day, September 23, a noisy crowd broke through police lines and molested various bystanders. The Negro children who had come to school were taken home. That afternoon the President issued a proclamation to the citizens of Little Rock ordering "all persons" to cease the obstruction of justice. That night the White House and the Mayor of Little Rock held consultations. The next morning Eisenhower called the Arkansas National Guard into Federal service, thus removing it from Faubus's hands, and ordered regular Army troops to Little Rock. Order was restored and the Negro children returned to school. They remained in school, and federal troops remained on hand, through the school year until June 1958.

Thereafter, Little Rock's attempted integration entered a new phase. By school reopening in 1958, Faubus had proposed, received, and then invoked State legislation authorizing him to close the school if it were integrated. In 1959 the Federal courts struck down that legislation, and arrangements were made to open the school on roughly the same terms as in 1957. At the time of writing, the Governor had indicated an intention to set those terms aside if he could find a way to do it. This summary concludes without an ending.

III

The dismissal of MacArthur, the seizure of the steel mills, the dispatch of troops to Little Rock share a common characteristic: in terms of immediate intent the President's own order brought results as though his words were tantamount to action. He said, "Do this, do that," and *it was done.* From a presidential standpoint these three orders were self-executing. To give them was to have them carried out. Literally, no orders carry themselves out; self-executed actually means executed-by-others. But self-executing does describe the practical effect as it appeared to those who gave the orders. In the order-giver's eyes command amounted to compliance.

What lay behind "self-execution" of these orders? When troops were sent to Little Rock, Eisenhower's action took the form of an executive order which "authorized and directed" the Secretary of Defense to enforce the orders of the District Court in Arkansas, utilizing "such of the armed forces of the United States . . . as necessary." To implement this order there were successive delegations of authority from the Secretary of Defense through the Secretary of the Army down to units of the 101st Airborne Division and the Arkansas National Guard, the physical executors of Eisenhower's order. In form each delegation was discretionary. In fact, according to a White House participant, "The President decided which troops to use and how fast they should get there and what they should do when they arrived. That was worked out right here and all those fellows at the Pentagon had to do was turn the crank. They knew exactly what they were to do the minute the order was signed." They knew, also, that the President intended to address the nation justifying action *taken.* Under such circumstances, command and compliance are easy to equate.

In the MacArthur case the equation is even easier, for the circumstances were the simplest possible: Truman, as Commander-in-Chief, signed the order that relieved the General and the latter, himself, was its executor, transferring his commands to his designated successor. Misunderstanding was impossible; argument was precluded by publication of the order and by a presidential radio address explaining it.

As for seizure of the steel industry, Truman announced his action in a nationally televised address and at the same time, by executive order, he directed the Secretary of Commerce, Charles S. Sawyer, to take possession of the mills as government administrator. To carry out this order all that was initially required of Sawyer was a telegraphed notification to the managements and a delegation of authority to company executives, with a request that they stay on the job and fly the flag over the mills. Following the nationwide announcement the Secretary scarcely could do less and the government, thereby, was in possession without his having to do more.

This brief recital is enough to show what lay behind the ready execution of these orders. At least five common factors were at work. On each occasion the President's involvement was unambiguous. So were his words. His order was widely publicized. The men who received it had control of everything needed to carry it out. And they had no apparent doubt of his authority to issue it to them. It is no accident that these five factors can be found in all three instances. These are the factors that produce self-executing orders. Lacking any one of them the chances are that mere command will not produce compliance.

To see what happens in the absence of these favorable factors let me turn to incidents in the same factual setting as the three orders just described. These three were promptly executed. Preceding them, or following them, however, were many other orders that did not get carried out. Those others serve to illustrate what happens when a favorable factor is missing.

The first factor favoring compliance with a presidential order is assurance that the President has spoken. The three self-executing orders were given by the man himself, and not only in form but very much in fact. They were *his* orders in the double sense that they both came from him and expressed a definite decision by him personally. Recipients were left no room for doubt on either score; wording, timing, and publicity took care of that. To see what can occur when this factor is absent, one need but contrast the incident precipitating the dismissal of MacArthur: his publicized demand for enemy surrender on March 24, 1951.

The General's call for enemy surrender came at a moment when the President, in consultation with allied governments, was planning a statement that would virtually invite negotiated compromise to end the war. MacArthur got on record first with threats to spread the war. The White House statement then was set aside. To Truman, this action on MacArthur's part signified two things: deliberate sabotage of presidential policy and a deliberate violation of explicit orders. On the record there is no doubt that the President was right in both respects. For the General had been told through channels, in advance, of the impending White House initiative. And he had been under orders since the previous December to make no public statements on foreign or military policy without prior clearance from the Departments of State and Defense. "By this act," Truman writes, "MacArthur left me no choice—I could no longer tolerate his insubordination." [6]

Truman's comment implies what the record makes plain: he virtually invited this result by tolerating a long string of prior acts nearly as insubordinate. Since the Korean outbreak, as for years past, MacArthur had regularly used press statements to counter or to influence the views of his superiors. He had not previously used this means to stop their *acts*. But no penalties of consequence had been invoked for anything he had done short of that. To Truman this extension of the General's tactic was the final straw. MacArthur may have had no notion that the White House would react so strongly.

It is true that MacArthur violated an explicit order. But on its face the order seemed another form for form's sake. Dated December 6, 1950, it was addressed to all government departments and reached Tokyo routinely from the Pentagon. The order was expressed in terms more easily construed as the concoction of press attachés to hush Assistant Secretaries than as Truman's word to his Supreme Commander. In fact MacArthur *was* the target of this order; his press statements immediately after Chinese intervention were the cause of it. His conduct was of great concern to Truman personally. But how was the General to know? The order's widespread application and routine appearance were meant to spare him personal embarrassment (a fact which speaks volumes in itself). Their effect was to minimize its impact and to blur its source. Even had he recognized himself as addressee and Truman personally as sender, MacArthur may have noted that his press offensive at the start of the "new war" had drawn from Washington no more by way of a rebuke than this pale order. When stakes of policy and pride are high, convictions sharp (and political allies powerful), why should not a Supreme Commander try in March a somewhat bolder move than he had got away with in December?

A second factor making for compliance with a President's request is clarity about his meaning. If it helps to have respondents know that *he* wants what he asks, it also helps to have them know precisely what he wants. To shift the illustration, when the Governor of Arkansas met Eisenhower at Newport, a week before the troops were sent to Little Rock, there is no doubt that Faubus knew it was the President who wanted something done. But whether he was clear on what that something was remains uncertain; they met alone and the terms of their conversation left room for misunderstanding, apparent or real. According to an Eisenhower aide, "Faubus knew perfectly well what the President wanted: the order of the court complied with and the kids in school, peaceably . . . and he promised to produce. We were double-crossed, that's all." But Ashmore of the *Arkansas Gazette* records the impression that the Governor, believing he could "put off the dread day" until after his next gubernatorial campaign, "carried this illusion with him to Newport . . . and brought it home intact . . . ." [7]

A somewhat comparable piece of business marked the steel crisis of 1952 and led to resignation of the Mobilization Director, Wilson. At the outset of the crisis Wilson had conferred with Truman in Key West, talking at length and alone. But scarcely a week later, in exchanging letters upon Wilson's resignation, they recorded widely different notions of their Key West conversation. Wilson charged Truman with a change of tune; Truman charged Wilson with misconstruing orders. And both may have been right. For Wilson had returned from Key West with a mandate, as he saw it, to settle the dispute by price concessions if and as he could. This was a task demanding wide discretion for effective execution, and hence some open-endedness in its assignment. When a degree of ambiguity is inescapable, as in this case, it may take but a pinch of verbal imprecision or a dash of vacation atmosphere to produce misunderstanding. Both were in the recipe at Key West—and at Newport, five years later.

A third factor favoring compliance with a President's directive is publicity. Even when there is no need for ambiguity, no possibility of imprecision, no real discretionary leeway and nothing to misunderstand, compliance may depend not only on the respondent's awareness of what he is to do, but also on the awareness of others that he has been told to do it. In sending troops to Little Rock, in seizing the steel industry, in firing MacArthur, the whole country was taken into camp, informed of the President's commitment, invited to watch the response. But the circle of observers is rarely so broad. Often it may be entirely too narrow for presidential comfort. A case in point is Secretary Sawyer's interesting behavior in his first weeks as administrator of the seized steel industry.

Having seized the mills in desperation to avert production losses, the White House wanted to be rid of them as fast as possible—which meant as fast as it could gain assurance that production would continue once they were returned to private hands. This called for some settlement of the labor dispute whose lack of settlement had led to seizure in the first place. The circle could be broken only if continued government control were made so unattractive in the eyes of both disputants that they would prefer agreement with each other. To that end a tactic was devised: the Secretary of Commerce, as administrator of the mills, was to put into effect a *portion* of the union's wage demands to which the men were automatically entitled under the existing rules of wage control (a so-called cost-of-living adjustment). At the same time, he was to ask the price controllers for the amount of price relief to which the companies were automatically entitled under "pass through" provisions of existing legislation (the so-called Capehart Amendment). Secretary Sawyer then was to announce that he would do no more. Management and labor would be faced by a *fait accompli* that satisfied neither the union's wage demands nor the company's price demands but put some things beyond dispute and foreclosed better terms for the duration. With this prospect before them both sides might conclude that more was to be gained from settlement than from continued government direction. So, at least, the White House hoped.

Within a week of seizure Truman had decided to proceed along these lines. He asked that Sawyer act at once and planned to call for bargaining by companies and union with his Secretary's action in the background. The President's intent was clear. There were no ambiguities. But Sawyer did not act. The Secretary of Commerce spoke for business in the Cabinet. Officially and personally Sawyer had no liking for the seizure. He had not wanted to administer the mills, and he had taken the assignment with distaste. He was evidently unhappy at the prospect of his signature on wage orders and price requests committing the steel industry. Although he did not refuse to act, he managed to immerse himself in preparations. Presently the District Court relieved him of embarrassment (and the government of opportunity) by denying his authority to run the mills.[8] When the Appeals Court restored his powers, Sawyer reached the point of action only after he had won agreement from the President that in the public record his department should be seen to act on the advice of others. It was nearly four weeks after seizure when Truman brought the union and the companies together to bargain in his office. The Secretary's action was set for two days hence. By then it was too late. On the opening day of the bargaining session the Supreme Court barred changes in wages.

Had the President initially publicized his plan, Sawyer would have had to execute it promptly or resign. That was his choice upon the night of seizure. But Truman did not publicize this scheme of wage adjustments. Toward the end of the four weeks his pressure on the Secretary came to be an open secret. At the start, however, it was little known and Sawyer did not face so sharp a choice. When officials are reluctant to do as they are told, publicity spurs execution. But publicity performs this service at the risk of turning private reluctance into public defiance. Sometimes that may not matter very much, or may even promise some advantage, or the President may have no option. Here it mattered greatly. Truman had just lost his Director of Defense Mobilization (and he had just fired his Attorney General for reasons unrelated to steel). He could ill afford to lose his Secretary of Commerce, particularly on an issue involving the administration of the mills which he had just placed in the Secretary's hands. Truman had an option and he took it. He gave instructions privately and tolerated slow response.

A fourth factor favoring compliance with a President's request is actual ability to carry it out. It helps to have the order-taker in possession of the necessary means. In one respect Sawyer's situation after seizure paralleled his situation on the night of seizure: he had authority enough and resources enough to carry out the President's immediate intention. All that Sawyer needed was a staff to prepare papers, a pen with which to sign them, and access to the telegraph. Those resources were at his disposal. In this respect, on both occasions, Sawyer was in very much the same position as MacArthur when his last orders arrived, or the Secretary of the Army when the word came through on Little Rock. Each had the necessary means at *his* disposal. Without the wherewithal in his own hands a presidential agent may be unable to do as he is told no matter how good his understanding or honest his intention.

An example of a man without the means is Wilson, the Mobilization Director, in the preseizure phase of the steel crisis. Whatever Truman may or may not have said to him at Key West, it is reasonably clear that the President wanted the labor dispute settled without a strike, even at some cost to price control. But the moment Wilson tried to satisfy this want, two things became clear. The companies were in a mood to demand guarantees of price relief, but not to promise settlement. And the Price Director, Ellis Arnall, was in a mood to refuse *any* price increase save what the law would automatically require *after* settlement. In effect,

Arnall's stand became "play my way or fire me," and though Wilson ranked him bureaucratically, Arnall was a *presidential* appointee. Wilson actually controlled neither the companies nor the Price Director. He could not even bring much influence to bear upon them since his claims to speak for Truman had been clouded by a clumsy press remark about the Wage Board. Wilson had no recourse but to return to the President empty-handed. When Truman leaned toward Arnall, Wilson resigned. But even had the President renewed Wilson's mandate, it is not clear what he could have done.

Another illustration of the same point can be drawn from the act of seizure itself. I have described Truman's order in this instance as "self-executing" in effect, with Sawyer the executor in fact. But Sawyer had a silent partner, the United Steelworkers. The purpose of the seizure was production. Truman's order was effective upon issuance because the men honored their union's pledge that they would work if their employer were the government. Yet until just two hours before seizure was announced, the President had planned, simultaneously, to invoke the fact-finding procedure of the Taft-Hartley Act.[9] This plan was dropped upon the urgent plea that wild-cat strikes in protest, and thus losses of production, might result. In order to assure that Sawyer's silent partner could achieve the purpose of the presidential order, Truman had to modify it in advance.

A fifth factor making for compliance with a President's request is the sense that what he wants is his by right. The steelworkers assumed, as Truman did, that he had ample constitutional authority to seize and operate the mills. An interjection of the term "Taft-Hartley" might have altered their response, but in its absence they conformed to the convention that they would not strike against their government, accepting as *legitimate* the President's claim upon them. The sense of legitimate obligation, legitimately imposed, was present in MacArthur's transfer of his own commands and in the Army's response to its Little Rock directive, no less than in the union's action after seizure. Without a sense of that sort on the part of order-takers, those orders would not have been carried out so promptly. But judging by the illustrations offered up to now the obverse does not follow. There is no assurance that orders will be executed just because they seem legitimate to their recipients. In none of the instances cited—not even in the case of Faubus at Newport—was a President's request considered *illegitimate* by those who *failed* to carry it out.

Perhaps legitimacy exerts a stronger influence the more distinct is its relationship to some specific grant of constitutional authority. Truman's final order to MacArthur, for example, had a clearer constitutional foundation than Eisenhower's *tête-á-tête* with Faubus, where authority was shared and therefore blurred. But Truman's earlier order to MacArthur on the clearance of public statements had precisely the same constitutional foundation as dismissal did. That earlier order had no more effect upon the General than Eisenhower had upon the Governor. Whatever its source or its relative strength, a sense of legitimacy taken alone does not assure compliance with a President's request.

When MacArthur was dismissed, when the steel mills were seized, when troops were sent to Little Rock, five factors made command appear the equal of compliance. In each of these three instances an unambiguous directive from a determined and committed President was carried out by persons who were capable of prompt response and who accepted his authority. The appearance of self-execution was produced by all these things combined. And when in other instances there was no such combination, there was also no effect of automatic execution.

How often is that combination likely to occur? How much, then, can a President rely on sheer command to get him what he wants? It takes but a glance at the examples in this chapter to suggest the answers: not very often and not very much. "Do this, do that, and nothing will happen" was the rule in incidents surrounding the dismissal of the General, and the seizure of the steel mills, and the use of Federal troops at Central High School. Viewed in their surroundings these become exceptions to the rule. So it is with presidential business generally. Under mid-century conditions self-executing orders are anything but everyday affairs. Indeed, in the whole sweep of Truman's record and of

Eisenhower's, those three stand out precisely for that reason: what they represent is relatively rare.

IV

The recall of MacArthur, the steel seizure, and the dispatch of troops to Little Rock share still another notable characteristic: in each case, the decisive order was a painful last resort, a forced response to the exhaustion of all other remedies, suggestive less of mastery than failure—the failure of attempts to gain an end by softer means.

Truman records in his memoirs that in April 1951, after reading the Pentagon file, General Marshall "concluded that MacArthur should have been fired two years ago." [10] Not everything that Marshall read is on the public record, but quite enough is there to lend substance to the view that MacArthur's dismissal was remarkably long delayed. Even if one sets aside all pre-Korean matters, ignores all questions of *professional* performance after Inchon, and scans the record only for the insubordination that provoked the firing, one finds at least two earlier cases somewhat comparable in all respects *except* the President's response. These two are MacArthur's outcry after Chinese intervention (leading to the clearance order of December 1950), and, months earlier, his public dissent from Formosa policy.[11] The White House announcement of his recall in April 1951, could have been issued in August or December 1950, without changing a word. Yet Truman stayed his hand on those earlier occasions (though apparently dismissal crossed his mind) and tried to patch the damage, bridge the differences, without offense to anybody's dignity except his own. The record indicates that he definitely did not want to let MacArthur go. At every challenge, save the final one, before and during the Korean War, the President sought means to keep the General both contained and on the job. Whatever his reasons Truman's pursuit of this objective—at considerable risk to policy, real sacrifice of pride—seems as persistent as anything in his career.

In that sense the dismissal, when it finally came, marked failure.
And so it was with Eisenhower in the Little Rock affair. There
were few things he wanted *less* than federal troops enforcing the
desegregation of a Southern school. Indeed he may have helped
to set the stage for Faubus by observing in July of 1957:

> I can't imagine any set of circumstances that would ever induce
> me to send Federal troops . . . into any area to enforce the orders
> of a Federal Court, because I believe that common sense of America
> will never require it.
>
> Now there may be that kind of authority resting somewhere, but
> certainly I am not seeking any additional authority of that kind, and
> I would never believe that it would be a wise thing to do in this
> country.[12]

And when, as schools reopened in September, the Governor had
National Guardsmen interfere with execution of court orders, the
President made a determined effort to avoid the use of force, an
effort culminating in the inconclusive Newport conversation.
Eisenhower agreed to meet Faubus at Newport without exacting
advance guarantees. This is testimony to the President's desire
for a way out other than the one he finally chose. So is the sense
of "double-cross" that long persisted in the White House *after*
Newport, a natural result of wanting to believe there was another
way.

As for the steel seizure, the element of failure is self-evident.
Truman had sought to settle the labor dispute in order to insure
against a shutdown of production. When the union contract expired in December 1951, he tried to obtain settlement without a
shutdown by referring the dispute to the Wage Stabilization Board.
When the Board's report brought on a crisis instead, Wilson and the
President took up the search for settlement. Their disagreement
had to do with tactics, not the goal. After Wilson's resignation,
the search continued under White House auspices right up to the
day before the seizure. That drastic act was not even considered
as a serious alternative until the week before, nor chosen with
finality until the very day. The White House was so anxious for
a settlement that Truman cancelled plans to state his case on
television some days in advance of the strike deadline, lest there

be an adverse effect on last-minute collective bargaining. In consequence, when seizure came, he had to combine a grave announcement with a contentious argument—hardly the choice of a President bent on seizure in the first place. But he had no such bent. Truman did not try to prepare the country for that course, because, until the last, he was intent on an alternative.

In this instance, as in the others, command became a last resort; but save in very short-run terms, it was not "last" at all. Truman did not want the steel mills; he wanted steel production and reasonably strong price controls. Those aims could only be achieved by terms of settlement between the union and the companies not inconsistent with existing control policies. The President had no power—and seizure gave him none—to gain his ends by fiat. Seizure merely staved off their abandonment and changed the *context* of his efforts to *induce* a satisfactory settlement. Initially, the new context put new inducements at the President's disposal. But seizure produced complications also, and these ultimately cost him both of his objectives. Two months' production vanished with the strike that followed judicial invalidation of his seizure. And price controls were breached beyond repair in White House efforts to conclude the strike. Yet it does not require hindsight to perceive that seizure's nature, from the start, was that of an emergency expedient, powerfully affecting possible solutions but solving nothing of itself. This would have been the case had the outcome been happier from Truman's point of view. At best, not seizure *per se*, but the added leverage it gave to his persuasion might have brought the settlement he wanted.

The same point can be made regarding Little Rock, where Eisenhower's use of troops bought time and changed the context of his appeals to the "hearts and minds" of Southerners but solved no desegregation problems, not even the local one at Central High School. As for the MacArthur case, his removal certainly resolved command relationships in the Korean War, but these were scarcely the sole concern. What was at stake was nothing less than our strategic purpose in the conduct of the war. And Truman's order did not end MacArthur's challenge to Administration policy, however much it may have changed the context of their quarrel. The

General's threat to policy was ended by the Senate inquiry that followed his removal—and by the start of truce talks in Korea. Truman dug a grave, but that alone did not suffice to push Mac-Arthur in. Without the push administered by Senate hearings it is not entirely clear whose grave it might have been.

Not only are these "last" resorts less than conclusive, but they are also costly. Even though the order is assured of execution, drastic action rarely comes at bargain rates. It can be costly to the aims in whose defense it is employed. It can be costly, also, to objectives far afield.

When he dismissed MacArthur, for example, Truman had to pay at least one price in the coin of Korean policy. The price was public exposition, at the Senate hearings, of his regime's innermost thoughts about the further conduct of hostilities. Whatever its effect on subsequent events, Peking and Moscow thus were put on notice of American intentions through the rest of Truman's term, and at home the reading public was informed that Washington saw little point in a renewed attempt to conquer North Korea. Against this background there began the long ordeal of truce negotiations. The Chinese may not have been influenced by those disclosures; Americans certainly were. Henry Kissinger, among many others, has argued with considerable justice that ". . . by stopping [offensive] military operations . . . at the very beginning of armistice negotiations . . . we removed the only Chinese incentive for a settlement; we produced the frustration of two years of inconclusive negotiations." [13] But no one has suggested how we were to stay on the offensive after Washington officialdom had formulated for itself and then expressed in public an intense desire to have done as soon as Peking tired of hostilities. Belabored in the hearings to define a "way out" other than MacArthur's, the Administration crystallized its own responsiveness toward offers to negotiate before they were ever made. When offers came they were seized on as "vindication." Even without the whole MacArthur uproar, it would not have been easy to press the offensive as truce talks began. After Senate hearings it seems psychologically if not politically impossible.

Besides such costs as this, directly chargeable against the purpose he was trying to protect, Truman's dismissal of MacArthur involved other costs as well, charged against other policy objectives. These "indirect" costs are hard to isolate because causation is no single-track affair, but certainly they were not inconsiderable. Among others, it is possible that Truman's inability to make his case with Congress, Court, and public in the steel crisis of 1952 resulted from exhaustion of his credit, so to speak, in the MacArthur battle a year earlier. That there is something in this will be clear from later chapters.

Drastic action may be costly, but it can be less expensive than continuing inaction. Truman could no longer have retained MacArthur without yielding to him the conduct of the war. Eisenhower could no longer stay his hand in Little Rock without yielding to every Southern Governor the right—even the duty—to do what Faubus did. These consequences threatened for the obvious reason that the instant challenge openly discounted the position of the Presidency and bluntly posed the question, "Who is President?" In either case, a soft response would have been tantamount to abdication, so public was the challenge in these terms. When Truman seized the steel mills, the Pentagon was warning that a new Chinese offensive, even Soviet intervention, might be coming in Korea "as soon as the mud dries." The seizure proved a very costly venture. But on the information then available, an April shutdown of the mills could have been far more costly. By hindsight it appears that a strike instead of seizure was the cheapest course available. The Chinese did not move as forcefully as had been feared. If they had done so, seizure might have proved a notable success. Truman acted without benefit of hindsight.

Self-executing orders have their uses, however inconclusive or expensive they may be. In each of these three cases, even steel, the presidential order brought assurance that a policy objective would remain in reach just as its loss seemed irretrievable. This is a real accomplishment. But necessarily it is a *transitory* accomplishment. Even the last resorts turn out to share the character of all the softer measures they replace. They turn out to be incidents in a persuasive process whereby someone lacking abso-

lute control seeks to get something done through others who
have power to resist.

Truman is quite right when he declares that presidential power
is the power to persuade. Command is but a method of persuasion,
not a substitute, and not a method suitable for everyday
employment.

The Power to Persuade . 3

The limits on command suggest the structure of our government. The constitutional convention of 1787 is supposed to have created a government of "separated powers." It did nothing of the sort. Rather, it created a government of separated institutions *sharing* powers.[1] "I am part of the legislative process," Eisenhower often said in 1959 as a reminder of his veto.[2] Congress, the dispenser of authority and funds, is no less part of the administrative process. Federalism adds another set of separated institutions. The Bill of Rights adds others. Many public purposes can only be achieved by voluntary acts of private institutions; the press, for one, in Douglass Cater's phrase, is a "fourth branch of government."[3] And with the coming of alliances abroad, the separate institutions of a London, or a Bonn, share in the making of American public policy.

What the Constitution separates our political parties do not combine. The parties are themselves composed of separated organizations sharing public authority. The authority consists of nominating powers. Our national parties are confederations of state and local party institutions, with a headquarters that represents the White House, more or less, if the party has a President in office. These confederacies manage presidential nominations. All other public offices depend upon electorates confined within the states.[4] All other nominations are controlled within the states. The President and congressmen who bear one party's label are divided by dependence upon different sets of voters. The differences are sharpest at the stage of nomination. The White House has too small a share in nominating congressmen, and Congress has too little weight in nominating Presidents for party to erase their constitutional separation. Party links are stronger than is frequently supposed, but nominating processes assure the separation.[5]

The separateness of institutions and the sharing of authority prescribe the terms on which a President persuades. When one man shares authority with another, but does not gain or lose his job upon the other's whim, his willingness to act upon the urging of the other turns on whether he conceives the action right for him. The essence of a President's persuasive task is to convince such men that what the White House wants of them is what they ought to do for their sake and on their authority.

Persuasive power, thus defined, amounts to more than charm or reasoned argument. These have their uses for a President, but these are not the whole of his resources. For the men he would induce to do what he wants done on their own responsibility will need or fear some acts by him on his responsibility. If they share his authority, he has some share in theirs. Presidential "powers" may be inconclusive when a President commands, but always remain relevant as he persuades. The status and authority inherent in his office reinforce his logic and his charm.

Status adds something to persuasiveness; authority adds still more. When Truman urged wage changes on his Secretary of Commerce while the latter was administering the steel mills, he and Secretary Sawyer were not just two men reasoning with one another. Had they been so, Sawyer probably would never have agreed to act. Truman's status gave him special claims to Sawyer's loyalty, or at least attention. In Walter Bagehot's charming phrase "no man can *argue* on his knees." Although there is no kneeling in this country, few men—and exceedingly few Cabinet officers—are immune to the impulse to say "yes" to the President of the United States. It grows harder to say "no" when they are seated in his oval office at the White House, or in his study on the second floor, where almost tangibly he partakes of the aura of his physical surroundings. In Sawyer's case, moreover, the President possessed formal authority to intervene in many matters of concern to the Secretary of Commerce. These matters ranged from jurisdictional disputes among the defense agencies to legislation pending before Congress and, ultimately, to the tenure of the Secretary, himself. There is nothing in the record to suggest that Truman voiced specific threats when they negotiated over wage increases. But given his *formal* powers and their relevance to Sawyer's other interests, it is safe to assume that Truman's very advocacy of wage action conveyed an implicit threat.

A President's authority and status give him great advantages in dealing with the men he would persuade. Each "power" is a vantage point for him in the degree that other men have use for his authority. From the veto to appointments, from publicity to budgeting, and so down a long list, the White House now controls the most encompassing array of vantage points in the American political system. With hardly an exception, the men who share in governing this country are aware that at some time, in some degree, the doing of *their* jobs, the furthering of *their* ambitions, may depend upon the President of the United States. Their need for presidential action, or their fear of it, is bound to be recurrent if not actually continuous. Their need or fear is his advantage.

A President's advantages are greater than mere listing of his "powers" might suggest. The men with whom he deals must deal with him until the last day of his term. Because they have continuing relationships with him, his future, while it lasts, supports his present influence. Even though there is no need or fear of him today, what he could do tomorrow may supply today's advantage. Continuing relationships may convert any "power," any aspect of his status, into vantage points in almost any case. When he induces other men to do what he wants done, a President can trade on their dependence now *and* later.

The President's advantages are checked by the advantages of others. Continuing relationships will pull in both directions. These are relationships of mutual dependence. A President depends upon the men he would persuade; he has to reckon with his need or fear of them. They too will possess status, or authority, or both, else they would be of little use to him. Their vantage points confront his own; their power tempers his.

Persuasion is a two-way street. Sawyer, it will be recalled, did not respond at once to Truman's plan for wage increases at the steel mills. On the contrary, the Secretary hesitated and delayed and only acquiesced when he was satisfied that publicly he would not bear the onus of decision. Sawyer had some points of vantage all his own from which to resist presidential pressure. If he had to reckon with coercive implications in the President's "situations of strength," so had Truman to be mindful of the implications underlying Sawyer's place as a department head, as steel administrator, and as a Cabinet spokesman for business. Loyalty is reciprocal. Having taken on a dirty job in the steel crisis, Sawyer had strong claims to loyal support. Besides, he had authority to do some things that the White House could ill afford. Emulating Wilson, he might have resigned in a huff (the removal power also works two ways). Or emulating Ellis Arnall, he might have declined to sign necessary orders. Or, he might have let it be known publicly that he deplored what he was told to do and protested its doing. By following any of these courses Sawyer almost surely would have strengthened the position of management, weakened the position of the White House, and embittered the union. But the whole purpose of a wage increase was to enhance White House persuasiveness in urging settlement upon union and companies alike. Although Sawyer's status and authority did not give him the power to prevent an increase outright, they gave him capability to undermine its purpose. If his authority over wage rates had been vested by a statute, not by revocable presidential order, his power of prevention might have been complete. So Harold Ickes demonstrated in the famous case of helium sales to Germany before the Second World War.[6]

The power to persuade is the power to bargain. Status and authority yield bargaining advantages. But in a government of "separated institutions sharing powers," they yield them to all sides. With the array of vantage points at his disposal, a President may be far more persuasive than his logic or his charm could make him. But outcomes are not guaranteed by his advantages.

There remain the counter pressures those whom he would influence can bring to bear on him from vantage points at their
disposal. Command has limited utility; persuasion becomes give-
and-take. It is well that the White House holds the vantage points
it does. In such a business any President may need them all—
and more.

II

This view of power as akin to bargaining is one we commonly
accept in the sphere of congressional relations. Every textbook
states and every legislative session demonstrates that save in times
like the extraordinary Hundred Days of 1933—times virtually
ruled out by definition at mid-century—a President will often be
unable to obtain congressional action on his terms or even to halt
action he opposes. The reverse is equally accepted: Congress often
is frustrated by the President. Their formal powers are so intertwined that neither will accomplish very much, for very long,
without the acquiescence of the other. By the same token, though,
what one demands the other can resist. The stage is set for that
great game, much like collective bargaining, in which each seeks
to profit from the other's needs and fears. It is a game played
catch-as-catch-can, case by case. And everybody knows the game,
observers and participants alike.

The concept of real power as a give-and-take is equally familiar
when applied to presidential influence outside the formal structure
of the Federal government. The Little Rock affair may be extreme,
but Eisenhower's dealings with the Governor—and with the citizens—become a case in point. Less extreme but no less pertinent
is the steel seizure case with respect to union leaders, and to workers, and to company executives as well. When he deals with such
people a President draws bargaining advantage from his status
or authority. By virtue of their public places or their private
rights they have some capability to reply in kind.

In spheres of party politics the same thing follows, necessarily,
from the confederal nature of our party organizations. Even in

the case of national nominations a President's advantages are checked by those of others. In 1944 it is by no means clear that Roosevelt got his first choice as his running mate. In 1948 Truman, then the President, faced serious revolts against his nomination. In 1952 his intervention from the White House helped assure the choice of Adlai Stevenson, but it is far from clear that Truman could have done as much for any other candidate acceptable to him.[7] In 1956 when Eisenhower was President, the record leaves obscure just who backed Harold Stassen's effort to block Richard Nixon's renomination as Vice-President. But evidently everything did not go quite as Eisenhower wanted, whatever his intentions may have been.[8] The outcomes in these instances bear all the marks of limits on command and of power checked by power that characterize congressional relations. Both in and out of politics these checks and limits seem to be quite widely understood.

Influence becomes still more a matter of give-and-take when Presidents attempt to deal with allied governments. A classic illustration is the long unhappy wrangle over Suez policy in 1956. In dealing with the British and the French before their military intervention, Eisenhower had his share of bargaining advantages but no effective power of command. His allies had their share of counter pressures, and they finally tried the most extreme of all: action despite him. His pressure then was instrumental in reversing them. But had the British government been on safe ground *at home*, Eisenhower's wishes might have made as little difference after intervention as before. Behind the decorum of diplomacy— which was not very decorous in the Suez affair—relationships among allies are not unlike relationships among state delegations at a national convention. Power is persuasion and persuasion becomes bargaining. The concept is familiar to everyone who watches foreign policy.

In only one sphere is the concept unfamiliar: the sphere of executive relations. Perhaps because of civics textbooks and teaching in our schools, Americans instinctively resist the view that power in this sphere resembles power in all others. Even Washington reporters, White House aides, and congressmen are not immune to the illusion that administrative agencies comprise a single structure, "the" Executive Branch, where presidential word is law, or ought to be. Yet we have seen in Chapter 2 that when a President seeks something from executive officials his persuasiveness is subject to the same sorts of limitations as in the case of congressmen, or governors, or national committeemen, or private citizens, or foreign governments. There are no generic differences, no differences in kind and only sometimes in degree. The incidents preceding the dismissal of MacArthur and the incidents surrounding seizure of the steel mills make it plain that here as elsewhere influence derives from bargaining advantages; power is a give-and-take.

Like our governmental structure as a whole, the executive establishment consists of separated institutions sharing powers. The President heads one of these; Cabinet officers, agency administrators, and military commanders head others. Below the departmental level, virtually independent bureau chiefs head many more. Under mid-century conditions, Federal operations spill across dividing lines on organization charts; almost every policy entangles many agencies; almost every program calls for interagency collaboration. Everything somehow involves the President. But operating agencies owe their existence least of all to one another—and only in some part to him. Each has a separate statutory base; each has its statutes to administer; each deals with a different set of subcommittees at the Capitol. Each has its own peculiar set of clients, friends, and enemies outside the formal government. Each has a different set of specialized careerists inside its own bailiwick. Our Constitution gives the President the "take-care" clause and the appointive power. Our statutes give him central budgeting and a degree of personnel control. All agency administrators are responsible to him. But they *also* are responsible to Congress, to their clients, to their staffs, and to themselves. In short, they have five masters. Only after all of those do they owe any loyalty to each other.

"The members of the Cabinet," Charles G. Dawes used to remark, "are a President's natural enemies." Dawes had been Harding's Budget Director, Coolidge's Vice-President, and Hoover's Ambassador to London; he also had been General Pershing's chief

assistant for supply in the First World War. The words are
highly colored, but Dawes knew whereof he spoke. The men
who have to serve so many masters cannot help but be somewhat
the "enemy" of any one of them. By the same token, any master
wanting service is in some degree the "enemy" of such a servant.
A President is likely to want loyal support but not to relish trouble
on his doorstep. Yet the more his Cabinet members cleave to him,
the more they may need help from him in fending off the wrath
of rival masters. Help, though, is synonymous with trouble. Many
a Cabinet officer, with loyalty ill-rewarded by his lights and help
withheld, has come to view the White House as innately hostile to
department heads. Dawes's dictum can be turned around.

A senior presidential aide remarked to me in Eisenhower's time:
"If some of these Cabinet members would just take time out to
stop and ask themselves 'What would I want if I were President?',
they wouldn't give him all the trouble he's been having." But
even if they asked themselves the question, such officials often
could not act upon the answer. Their personal attachment to the
President is all too often overwhelmed by duty to their other
masters.

Executive officials are not equally advantaged in their dealings
with a President. Nor are the same officials equally advantaged
all the time. Not every officeholder can resist like a MacArthur,
or like Arnall, Sawyer, Wilson, in a rough descending order of
effective counter pressure. The vantage points conferred upon
officials by their own authority and status vary enormously. The
variance is heightened by particulars of time and circumstance.
In mid-October 1950, Truman, at a press conference, remarked
of the man he had considered firing in August and would fire the
next April for intolerable insubordination:

> Let me tell you something that will be good for your souls. It's
> a pity that you . . . can't understand the ideas of two intellectually
> honest men when they meet. General MacArthur . . . is a member
> of the Government of the United States. He is loyal to that Govern-
> ment. He is loyal to the President. He is loyal to the President
> in his foreign policy. . . . There is no disagreement between General
> MacArthur and myself . . . .[9]

MacArthur's status in and out of government was never higher than when Truman spoke those words. The words, once spoken, added to the General's credibility thereafter when he sought to use the press in his campaign against the President. And what had happened between August and October? Near-victory had happened, together with that premature conference on *post*-war plans, the meeting at Wake Island.

If the bargaining advantages of a MacArthur fluctuate with changing circumstances, this is bound to be so with subordinates who have at their disposal fewer "powers," lesser status, to fall back on. And when officials have no "powers" in their own right, or depend upon the President for status, their counter pressure may be limited indeed. White House aides, who fit both catagories, are among the most responsive men of all, and for good reason. As a Director of the Budget once remarked to me, "Thank God I'm here and not across the street. If the President doesn't call me, I've got plenty I can do right here and plenty coming up to me, by rights, to justify my calling him. But those poor fellows over there, if the boss doesn't call them, doesn't ask them to do something, what *can* they do but sit?" Authority and status so conditional are frail reliances in resisting a President's own wants. Within the White House precincts, lifted eyebrows may suffice to set an aide in motion; command, coercion, even charm aside. But even in the White House a President does not monopolize effective power. Even there persuasion is akin to bargaining. A former Roosevelt aide once wrote of Cabinet officers:

> Half of a President's suggestions, which theoretically carry the weight of orders, can be safely forgotten by a Cabinet member. And if the President asks about a suggestion a second time, he can be told that it is being investigated. If he asks a third time, a wise Cabinet officer will give him at least part of what he suggests. But only occasionally, except about the most important matters, do Presidents ever get around to asking three times.[10]

The rule applies to staff as well as to the Cabinet, and certainly has been applied *by* staff in Truman's time and Eisenhower's.

Some aides will have more vantage points than a selective memory. Sherman Adams, for example, as The Assistant to the

President under Eisenhower, scarcely deserved the appelation "White House aide" in the meaning of the term before his time or as applied to other members of the Eisenhower entourage. Although Adams was by no means "chief of staff" in any sense so sweeping—or so simple—as press commentaries often took for granted, he apparently became no more dependent on the President than Eisenhower on him. "I need him," said the President when Adams turned out to have been remarkably imprudent in the Gold-fine case, and delegated to him even the decision on his own departure.[11] This instance is extreme, but the tendency it illustrates is common enough. Any aide who demonstrates to others that he has the President's consistent confidence and a consistent part in presidential business will acquire so much business on his own account that he becomes in some sense independent of his chief. Nothing in the Constitution keeps a well-placed aide from converting status into power of his own, usable in some degree even against the President—an outcome not unknown in Truman's regime or, by all accounts, in Eisenhower's.

The more an officeholder's status and his "powers" stem from sources independent of the President, the stronger will be his potential pressure *on* the President. Department heads in general have more bargaining power than do most members of the White House staff; but bureau chiefs may have still more, and specialists at upper levels of established career services may have almost unlimited reserves of the enormous power which consists of sitting still. As Franklin Roosevelt once remarked:

> The Treasury is so large and far-flung and ingrained in its practices that I find it is almost impossible to get the action and results I want—even with Henry [Morgenthau] there. But the Treasury is not to be compared with the State Department. You should go through the experience of trying to get any changes in the thinking, policy, and action of the career diplomats and then you'd know what a real problem was. But the Treasury and the State Department put together are nothing compared with the Na-a-vy. The admirals are really something to cope with—and I should know. To change anything in the Na-a-vy is like punching a feather bed. You punch it with your right and you punch it with your left until you are finally exhausted, and then you find the damn bed just as it was before you started punching.[12]

In the right circumstances, of course, a President can have his way with any of these people. Chapter 2 includes three instances where circumstances were "right" and a presidential order was promptly carried out. But one need only note the favorable factors giving those three orders their self-executing quality to recognize that as between a President and his "subordinates," no less than others on whom he depends, real power is reciprocal and varies markedly with organization, subject matter, personality, and situation. The mere fact that persuasion is directed at executive officials signifies no necessary easing of his way. Any new congressman of the Administration's party, especially if narrowly elected, may turn out more amenable (though less useful) to the President than any seasoned bureau chief "downtown." *The probabilities of power do not derive from the literary theory of the Constitution.*

III

There is a widely held belief in the United States that were it not for folly or for knavery, a reasonable President would need no power other than the logic of his argument. No less a personage than Eisenhower has subscribed to that belief in many a campaign speech and press-conference remark. But faulty reasoning and bad intentions do not cause all quarrels with Presidents. The best of reasoning and of intent cannot compose them all. For in the first place, what the President wants will rarely seem a trifle to the men he wants it from. And in the second place, they will be bound to judge it by the standard of their own responsibilities, not his. However logical his argument according to his lights, their judgment may not bring them to his view.

The men who share in governing this country frequently appear to act as though they were in business for themselves. So, in a real though not entire sense, they are and have to be. When Truman and MacArthur fell to quarreling, for example, the stakes were no less than the substance of American foreign policy, the risks of greater war or military stalemate, the prerogatives of Presidents and field commanders, the pride of a pro-consul and his place in history. Intertwined, inevitably, were other stakes, as well: political stakes for men and factions of both parties; power stakes for interest groups with which they were or wished to be affiliated. And every stake was raised by the apparent discontent in the American public mood. There is no reason to suppose that in such circumstances men of large but differing responsibilities will see all things through the same glasses. On the contrary, it is to be expected that their views of what ought to be done and what they then should do will vary with the differing perspectives their particular responsibilities evoke. Since their duties are not vested in a "team" or a "collegium" but in themselves, as individuals, one must expect that they will see things *for* themselves. Moreover, when they are responsible to many masters and when an event or policy turns loyalty against loyalty—a day by day occurrence in the nature of the case—one must assume that those who have the duties to perform will choose the terms of reconciliation. This is the essence of their personal responsibility. When their own duties pull in opposite directions, who else but they can choose what they will do?

When Truman dismissed MacArthur, the latter lost three posts: the American command in the Far East, the Allied command for the occupation of Japan, and the United Nations command in Korea. He also lost his status as the senior officer on active duty in the United States armed forces. So long as he held those positions and that status, though, he had a duty to his troops, to his profession, to himself (the last is hard for any man to disentangle from the rest). As a public figure and a focus for men's hopes he had a duty to constituents at home, and in Korea and Japan. He owed a duty also to those other constituents, the UN governments contributing to his field forces. As a patriot he had a duty to his country. As an accountable official and an expert guide he stood at the call of Congress. As a military officer he had, besides, a duty to the President, his constitutional commander. Some of these duties may have manifested themselves in terms more tangible or more direct than others. But it would be nonsense to argue that the last *negated* all the rest, however much it might be claimed to override them. And it makes no more sense to think that anybody but MacArthur was effectively empowered to decide how he, himself, would reconcile the competing demands his duties made upon him.

Similar observations could be made about the rest of the executive officials encountered in Chapter 2. Price Director Arnall, it will be recalled, refused in advance to sign a major price increase for steel if Mobilization Director Wilson or the White House should concede' one before management had settled with the union. When Arnall did this, he took his stand, in substance, on his oath of office. He would do what he had sworn to do in *his* best judgment, so long as he was there to do it. This posture may have been assumed for purposes of bargaining and might have been abandoned had his challenge been accepted by the President. But no one could be sure and no one, certainly, could question Arnall's right to make the judgment for himself. As head of an agency and as a politician, with a program to defend and a future to advance, *he* had to decide what he had to do on matters that, from his perspective, were exceedingly important. Neither in policy nor in personal terms, nor in terms of agency survival, were the issues of a sort to be considered secondary by an Arnall, however much they might have seemed so to a Wilson (or a Truman). Nor were the merits likely to appear the same to a price stabilizer and to men with broader duties. Reasonable men, it is so often said, *ought* to be able to agree on the requirements of given situations. But when the outlook varies with the placement of each man, and the response required in his place is for each to decide, their reasoning may lead to disagreement quite as well— and quite as reasonably. Vanity, or vice, may weaken reason, to be sure, but it is idle to assign these as the cause of Arnall's threat or MacArthur's defiance. Secretary Sawyer's hesitations, cited earlier, are in the same category. One need not denigrate such men to explain their conduct. For the responsibilities they felt, the "facts" they saw, simply were not the same as those of their superiors; yet they, not the superiors, had to decide what they would do.

Outside the Executive Branch the situation is the same, except that loyalty to the President may often matter *less*. There is no need to spell out the comparison with Governors of Arkansas, steel company executives, trade union leaders, and the like. And when one comes to congressmen who can do nothing for themselves (or their constituents) save as they are elected, term by term, in districts and through party structures *differing* from those on which a President depends, the case is very clear. An able Eisenhower aide with long congressional experience remarked to me in 1958: "The people on the Hill don't do what they might *like* to do, they do what they think they *have* to do in their own interest as *they* see it . . . ." This states the case precisely.

The essence of a President's persuasive task with congressmen and everybody else, *is to induce them to believe that what he wants of them is what their own appraisal of their own responsibilities requires them to do in their interest, not his.* Because men may differ in their views on public policy, because differences in outlook stem from differences in duty—duty to one's office, one's constituents, oneself—that task is bound to be more like collective bargaining than like a reasoned argument among philosopher kings. Overtly or implicitly, hard bargaining has characterized all illustrations offered up to now. This is the reason why: persuasion deals in the coin of self-interest with men who have some freedom to reject what they find counterfeit.

IV

A President draws influence from bargaining advantages. But does he always need them? The episodes described in Chapter 2 were instances where views on public policy diverged with special sharpness. Suppose such sharp divergences are lacking, suppose most players of the governmental game see policy objectives much alike, then can he not rely on logic (or on charm) to get him what he wants? The answer is that even then most outcomes turn on bargaining. The reason for this answer is a simple one: most men who share in governing have interests of their own beyond the realm of policy *objectives*. The sponsorship of policy, the form it takes, the conduct of it, and the credit for it separate their interest from the President's despite agreement on the end in view. In political government, the means can matter quite as much as ends; they often matter more. And there are always differences of interest in the means.

Let me introduce a case externally the opposite of my previous examples: the European Recovery Program of 1948, the so-called Marshall Plan. This is perhaps the greatest exercise in policy *agreement* since the cold war began. When the then Secretary of State, George Catlett Marshall, spoke at the Harvard commencement in June of 1947, he launched one of the most creative, most imaginative ventures in the history of American foreign relations. What makes this policy most notable for present purposes, however, is that it became effective upon action by the 80th Congress, at the behest of Harry Truman, in the election year of 1948.[13]

Eight months before Marshall spoke at Harvard, the Democrats had lost control of both Houses of Congress for the first time in fourteen years. Truman, whom the Secretary represented, had just finished his second troubled year as President-by-succession. Truman was regarded with so little warmth in his own party that in 1946 he had been urged *not* to participate in the congressional campaign. At the opening of Congress in January 1947, Senator Robert A. Taft, "Mr. Republican," had somewhat the attitude of a President-elect. This was a vision widely shared in Washington, with Truman relegated, thereby, to the role of caretaker-on-term. Moreover, within just two weeks of Marshall's commencement address, Truman was to veto two prized accomplishments of Taft's congressional majority: the Taft-Hartley Act and tax reduction.[14] Yet scarcely ten months later the Marshall Plan was under way on terms to satisfy its sponsors, its authorization completed, its first-year funds in sight, its administering agency in being: all managed by as thorough a display of executive-congressional co-operation as any we have seen since the Second World War. For any President at any time this would have been a great accomplishment. In years before mid-century it would have been enough to make the future reputation of his term. And for a Truman, at this time, enactment of the Marshall Plan appears almost miraculous.

How was the miracle accomplished? How did a President so situated bring it off? In answer, the first thing to note is that he did not do it by himself. Truman had help of a sort no less extraordinary than the outcome. Although each stands for something more complex, the names of Marshall, Vandenberg, Patterson, Bevin, Stalin, tell the story of that help.

In 1947, two years after V-J Day, General Marshall was something more than Secretary of State. He was a man venerated by the President as "the greatest living American," literally an embodiment of Truman's ideals. He was honored at the Pentagon as an architect of victory. He was thoroughly respected by the Secretary of the Navy, James V. Forrestal, who that year became the first Secretary of Defense. On Capitol Hill Marshall had an enormous fund of respect stemming from his war record as Army Chief of Staff, and in the country generally no officer had come out of the war with a higher reputation for judgment, intellect, and probity. Besides, as Secretary of State, he had behind him the first generation of matured foreign service officers produced by the reforms of the 1920's, and mingled with them, in the departmental service, were some of the ablest of the men drawn by the war from private life to Washington. In terms both of staff talent and staff's use, Marshall's years began a State Department "golden age" which lasted until the era of McCarthy. Moreover, as his Under Secretary, Marshall had, successively, Dean Acheson and Robert Lovett, men who commanded the respect of the professionals and the regard of congressmen. (Acheson had been brilliantly successful at congressional relations as Assistant Secretary in the war and postwar years.) Finally, as a special undersecretary Marshall had Will Clayton, a man highly regarded, for good reason, at both ends of Pennsylvania Avenue.

Taken together, these are exceptional resources for a Secretary of State. In the circumstances, they were quite as necessary as they obviously are relevant. The Marshall Plan was launched by a "lame duck" Administration "scheduled" to leave office in eighteen months. Marshall's program faced a congressional leadership traditionally isolationist and currently intent upon economy. European aid was viewed with envy by a Pentagon distressed and virtually disarmed through budget cuts, and by domestic agencies intent on enlarged welfare programs. It was not viewed with liking by a Treasury intent on budget surpluses. The plan had need of every asset that could be extracted from the personal position of its nominal author and from the skills of his assistants.

Without the equally remarkable position of the senior Senator from Michigan, Arthur H. Vandenberg, it is hard to see how Marshall's assets could have been enough. Vandenberg was chairman of the Senate Foreign Relations Committee. Actually, he was much more than that. Twenty years a senator, he was the senior member of his party in the Chamber. Assiduously cultivated by F.D.R. and Truman, he was a chief Republican proponent of "bipartisanship" in foreign policy, and consciously conceived himself its living symbol to his party, to the country, and abroad. Moreover, by informal but entirely operative agreement with his colleague Taft, Vandenberg held the acknowledged lead among Senate Republicans in the whole field of international affairs. This acknowledgement meant more in 1947 than it might have meant at any other time. With confidence in the advent of a Republican administration two years hence, most of the gentlemen were in a mood to be responsive and responsible. The war was over, Roosevelt dead, Truman a caretaker, theirs the trust. That the Senator from Michigan saw matters in this light, his diaries make clear.[15] And this was not the outlook from the Senate side alone; the attitudes of House Republicans associated with the Herter Committee and its tours abroad suggest the same mood of responsibility. Vandenberg was not the only source of help on Capitol Hill. But relatively speaking, his position there was as exceptional as Marshall's was downtown.

Help of another sort was furnished by a group of dedicated private citizens who organized one of the most effective instruments for public information seen since the Second World War: the Committee for the Marshall Plan, headed by the eminent Republicans whom F.D.R., in 1940, had brought to the Department of War: Henry L. Stimson as honorary chairman and Robert P. Patterson as active spokesmen. The remarkable array of bankers, lawyers, trade unionists, and editors, who had drawn together

in defense of "internationalism" before Pearl Harbor and had joined
their talents in the war itself, combined again to spark the work
of this committee. Their efforts generated a great deal of vocal
public support to buttress Marshall's arguments, and Vandenberg's,
in Congress.

But before public support could be rallied, there had to be a
purpose tangible enough, concrete enough, to provide a rallying
ground. At Harvard, Marshall had voiced an idea in general terms.
That this was turned into a hard program susceptible of presentation and support is due, in major part, to Ernest Bevin, the British
Foreign Secretary. He well deserves the credit he has sometimes
been assigned as, in effect, co-author of the Marshall Plan. For
Bevin seized on Marshall's Harvard speech and organized a European response with promptness and concreteness beyond the State
Department's expectations. What had been virtually a trial balloon
to test reactions on both sides of the Atlantic was hailed in London as an invitation to the Europeans to send Washington a bill
of particulars. This they promptly organized to do, and the
American Administration then organized in turn for its reception
without further argument internally about the pros and cons of
issuing the "invitation" in the first place. But for Bevin there might
have been trouble from the Secretary of the Treasury and others
besides.[16]

If Bevin's help was useful at that early stage, Stalin's was vital
from first to last. In a mood of self-deprecation Truman once
remarked that without Moscow's "crazy" moves "we never would
have had our foreign policy . . . we never could have got a
thing from Congress." [17] George Kennan, among others, has deplored the anti-Soviet overtone of the case made for the Marshall
Plan in Congress and the country, but there is no doubt that this
clinched the argument for many segments of American opinion.
There also is no doubt that Moscow made the crucial contributions
to the case.

By 1947 events, far more than governmental prescience or open
action, had given a variety of publics an impression of inimical
Soviet intentions (and of Europe's weakness), and a growing urge
to "do something about it." Three months before Marshall spoke

at Harvard, Greek-Turkish aid and promulgation of the Truman Doctrine had seemed rather to crystallize than to create a public mood and a congressional response. The Marshall planners, be it said, were poorly placed to capitalize on that mood, nor had the Secretary wished to do so. Their object, indeed, was to cut across it, striking at the cause of European weakness rather than at Soviet aggressiveness, *per se*. A strong economy in Western Europe called, ideally, for restorative measures of continental scope. American assistance proffered in an anti-Soviet context would have been contradictory in theory and unacceptable in fact to several of the governments that Washington was anxious to assist. As Marshall, himself, saw it, the logic of his purpose forbade him to play his strongest congressional card. The Russians then proceeded to play it for him. When the Europeans met in Paris, Molotov walked out. After the Czechs had shown continued interest in American aid, a communist coup overthrew their government while Soviet forces stood along their borders within easy reach of Prague. Molotov transformed the Marshall Plan's initial presentation; Czechoslovakia assured its final passage, which followed by a month the take-over in Prague.

Such was the help accorded Truman in obtaining action on the Marshall Plan. Considering his politically straightened circumstances he scarcely could have done with less. Conceivably, some part of Moscow's contribution might have been dispensable, but not Marshall's, or Vandenberg's, or Bevin's, or Patterson's, or that of the great many other men whose work is represented by their names in my account. Their aid was not extended to the President for his own sake. He was not favored in this fashion just because they liked him personally, or were spellbound by his intellect or charm. They might have been as helpful had all held him in disdain, which some of them certainly did. The Londoners who seized the ball, Vandenberg and Taft and the congressional majority, Marshall and his planners, the officials of other agencies who actively supported them or "went along," the host of influential private citizens who rallied to the cause—all these played the parts they did because they thought they had to, in their interest, given their responsibilities, not Truman's. Yet they hardly would have found it in their interest to collaborate with one another, or with him, had he not furnished them precisely what *they* needed from the White House. Truman could not do without their help, but he could not have had it without unremitting effort on his part.

The crucial thing to note about this case is that despite compatibility of views on public policy, Truman got no help he did not pay for (except Stalin's). Bevin scarcely could have seized on Marshall's words had Marshall not been plainly backed by Truman. Marshall's interest would not have comported with the exploitation of his prestige by a President who undercut him openly, or subtly, or even inadvertently, at any point. Vandenberg, presumably, could not have backed proposals by a White House which begrudged him deference and access gratifying to his fellow-partisans (and satisfying to himself). Prominent Republicans in private life would not have found it easy to promote a cause identified with Truman's claims on 1948—and neither would the prominent New Dealers then engaged in searching for a substitute.

Truman paid the price required for their services. So far as the record shows, the White House did not falter once in firm support for Marshall and the Marshall Plan. Truman backed his Secretary's gamble on an invitation to all Europe. He made the plan his own in a well-timed address to the Canadians. He lost no opportunity to widen the involvements of his own official family in the cause. Averell Harriman the Secretary of Commerce, Julius Krug the Secretary of the Interior, Edwin Nourse the Economic Council Chairman, James Webb the Director of the Budget—all were made responsible for studies and reports contributing directly to the legislative presentation. Thus these men were committed in advance. Besides, the President continually emphasized to everyone in reach that he did not have doubts, did not desire complications and would foreclose all he could. Reportedly, his emphasis was felt at the Treasury, with good effect. And Truman was at special pains to smooth the way for Vandenberg. The Senator insisted on "no politics" from the Administration side; there was none. He thought a survey of American resources and capacity essential; he got it in the Krug and Harriman reports. Vandenberg expected advance consultation; he received it, step by step, in frequent meetings with the President and weekly conferences with Marshall. He asked for an effective liaison between Congress and agencies concerned; Lovett and others gave him what he wanted. When the Senator decided on the need to change financing and administrative features of the legislation, Truman disregarded Budget Bureau grumbling and acquiesced with grace. When, finally, Vandenberg desired a Republican to head the new administering agency, his candidate, Paul Hoffman, was appointed despite the President's own preference for another. In all of these ways Truman employed the sparse advantages his "powers" and his status then accorded him to gain the sort of help he had to have.

Truman helped himself in still another way. Traditionally and practically no one was placed as well as he to call public attention to the task of *Congress* (and its Republican leadership). Throughout the fall and winter of 1947 and on into the spring of 1948, he made repeated use of presidential "powers" to remind the country that congressional action was required. Messages, speeches, and an extra session were employed to make the point. Here, too, he drew advantage from his place. However, in his circumstances, Truman's public advocacy might have hurt, not helped, had his words seemed directed toward the forthcoming election. Truman gained advantage for his program only as his own endorsement of it stayed on the right side of that fine line between the "caretaker" in office and the would-be candidate. In public statements dealing with the Marshall Plan he seems to have risked blurring this distinction only once, when he called Congress into session in November 1947 asking both for interim aid to Europe *and* for peacetime price controls. The second request linked the then inflation with the current Congress (and with Taft), becoming a first step toward one of Truman's major themes in 1948. By calling for both measures at the extra session he could have been accused—and was—of mixing home-front politics with foreign aid. In the event no harm was done the European program (or his politics). But in advance a number of his own advisers feared that such a double call would jeopardize the Marshall Plan. Their fears are testimony to the narrowness of his advantage in employing his own "powers" for its benefit.[18]

It is symptomatic of Truman's situation that "bipartisan" accomodation by the White House then was thought to mean congressional consultation and conciliation on a scale unmatched in Eisenhower's time. Yet Eisenhower did about as well with opposition Congresses as Truman did, in terms of requests granted for defense and foreign aid. It may be said that Truman asked for more extraordinary measures. But it also may be said that Eisenhower never lacked for the prestige his predecessor had to borrow. It often was remarked, in Truman's time, that he seemed a "split-personality," so sharply did his conduct differentiate domestic politics from national security. But personality aside, how else could *he*, in his first term, gain ground for an evolving foreign policy? The plain fact is that Truman had to play bipartisanship as he did or lose the game.

V

Had Truman lacked the personal advantages his "powers" and his status gave him, or if he had been maladroit in using them, there probably would not have been a massive European aid program in 1948. Something of the sort, perhaps quite different in its emphasis, would almost certainly have come to pass before the end of 1949. *Some* American response to European weakness and to Soviet expansion was as certain as such things can be. But in 1948 temptations to await a Taft Plan or a Dewey Plan might well have caused at least a year's postponement of response had the "outgoing" Administration bungled its congressional, or public, or allied, or executive relations. Quite aside from the specific virtues of their plan, Truman and his helpers gained that year, at least, in timing the American response. As European time was measured then, this was a precious gain. The President's own share in this accomplishment was vital. He made his contribution by exploiting his advantages. Truman, in effect, lent Marshall and the rest the perquisites and status of his office. In return they lent

him their prestige and their own influence. The transfer *
his influence despite his limited authority in form an(
strength politically. Without the wherewithal to make th
Truman could not have contributed to European aid.

Bargaining advantages convey no guarantees. Influence remains
a two-way street. In the fortunate instance of the Marshall Plan,
what Truman needed was actually in the hands of men who were
prepared to "trade" with him. He personally could deliver what
they wanted in return. Marshall, Vandenberg, Harriman, *et al.*,
possessed the prestige, energy, associations, staffs, essential to the
legislative effort. Truman himself had a sufficient hold on presidential messages and speeches, on budget policy, on high-level appointments, and on his own time and temper to carry through all aspects
of his necessary part. But it takes two to make a bargain. It takes
those who have prestige to lend it on whatever terms. Suppose
that Marshall had declined the Secretaryship of State in January
1947; Truman might not have found a substitute so well-equipped
to furnish what he needed in the months ahead. Or suppose that
Vandenberg had fallen victim to a cancer two years before he
actually did; Senator Wiley of Wisconsin would not have seemed
to Taft a man with whom the world need be divided. Or suppose
that the Secretary of the Treasury had been possessed of stature,
force, and charm commensurate with that of his successor in
Eisenhower's time, the redoubtable George M. Humphrey. And
what if Truman then had seemed to the Republicans what he turned
out to be in 1948, a formidable candidate for President? It is unlikely that a single one of these "supposes" would have changed
the final outcome; two or three, however, might have altered it
entirely. Truman was not guaranteed more power than his
"powers" just because he had continuing relationships with Cabinet
secretaries and with senior senators. Here, as everywhere, the
outcome was conditional on who they were and what he was and
how each viewed events, and on their actual performance in response.

Granting that persuasion has no guarantee attached, how can a
President reduce the risks of failing to persuade? How can he
maximize his prospects for effectiveness by minimizing chances

that his power will elude him? The Marshall Plan suggests an answer: he guards his power prospects in the course of making choices. Marshall himself, and Forrestal, and Harriman, and others of the sort held office on the President's appointment. Vandenberg had vast symbolic value partly because F.D.R. and Truman had done everything they could, since 1944, to build him up. The Treasury Department and the Budget Bureau—which together might have jeopardized the plans these others made—were headed by officials whose prestige depended wholly on their jobs. What Truman needed from those "givers" he received, in part, because of his past choice of men and measures. What they received in turn were actions taken or withheld by him, himself. The things they needed from him mostly involved his own conduct where his current choices ruled. The President's own actions in the past had cleared the way for current bargaining. His actions in the present were his trading stock. Behind each action lay a personal choice, and these together comprised *his* control over the give-and-take that gained him what he wanted. In the degree that Truman, personally, affected the advantages he drew from his relationships with other men in government, *his power was protected by his choices.*

By "choice" I mean no more than what is commonly referred to as "decision": a President's own act of doing or not doing. Decision is so often indecisive and indecision is so frequently conclusive, that choice becomes the preferable term. "Choice" has its share of undesired connotations. In common usage it implies a black-and-white alternative. Presidential choices are rarely of that character. It also may imply that the alternatives are set before the choice-maker by someone else. A President is often left to figure out his options for himself. Neither implication holds in any of the references to "choice" throughout this book.

If Presidents could count upon past choices to enhance their current influence, as Truman's choice of men had done for him, persuasion would pose fewer difficulties than it does. But Presidents can count on no such thing. Depending on the circumstances, prior choices can be as embarrassing as they were helpful in the instance of the Marshall Plan. The incidents described in Chapter 2 include some sharp examples of embarrassment. Among others: Eisenhower's influence with Faubus was diminished by his earlier statements to the press and by his unconditional agreement to converse in friendly style at Newport. Truman's hold upon Mac-Arthur was weakened by his deference toward him in the past.

Assuming that past choices have protected influence, not harmed it, present choices still may be inadequate. If Presidents could count on their own conduct to provide them *enough* bargaining advantages, as Truman's conduct did where Vandenberg and Marshall were concerned, effective bargaining might be much easier to manage than it often is. In the steel crisis, for instance, Truman's own persuasiveness with companies and union, both, was burdened by the conduct of an independent Wage Board and of government attorneys in the courts, to say nothing of Wilson, Arnall, Sawyer, and the like. Yet in practice, if not theory, many of *their* crucial choices never were the President's to make. Decisions that are legally in other's hands, or delegated past recall, have an unhappy way of proving just the trading stock most needed when the White House wants to trade. One reason why Truman was consistently more influential in the instance of the Marshall Plan than in the steel case, or the MacArthur case, is that the Marshall Plan directly involved Congress. In congressional relations there are some things that no one but the President can do. His chance to choose is higher when a message must be sent, or a nomination submitted, or a bill signed into law, than when the sphere of action is confined to the Executive, where all decisive tasks may have been delegated past recall.

But adequate or not, a President's own choices are the only means *in his own hands* of guarding his own prospects for effective influence. He can draw power from continuing relationships in the degree that he can capitalize upon the needs of others for the Presidency's status and authority. He helps himself to do so, though, by nothing save ability to recognize the pre-conditions and the chance advantages and to proceed accordingly in the course of the choice-making that comes his way. To ask how he can guard prospective influence is thus to raise a further question: what helps him guard his power stakes in his own acts of choice?

Professional Reputation . 4

A President's persuasiveness with other men in government depends on something more than his advantages for bargaining. The men he would persuade must be convinced in their own minds that he has skill and will enough to *use* his advantages. Their judgment of him is a factor in his influence with them. The final question posed in Chapter 3 was how a President protects his power stakes in his own acts of choice. This question can be set aside until we have examined what he has at stake in judgments made by others.

The men who share in governing this country are inveterate observers of a President. They have the doing of whatever he wants done. They are the objects of his personal persuasion. They also are the most attentive members of his audience. These doers comprise what in spirit, not geography, might well be termed the "Washington community." This community cuts across the President's constituencies. Members of Congress and of his Administration, governors of states, military commanders in the field, leading politicians in both parties, representatives of private organizations, newsmen of assorted types and sizes, foreign diplomats (and principals abroad)—all these are "Washingtonians" no matter what their physical location. In most respects the Washington community is far from homogeneous. In one respect it is tightly knit indeed: by definition, all its members are compelled to watch the President for reasons not of pleasure but vocation. They need him in their business just as he needs them. Their own work thus requires that they keep an eye on him. Because they watch him closely his persuasiveness with them turns quite as much on their informed appraisals as on his presumed advantages.

In influencing Washingtonians, the most important law at a President's disposal is the "law" of "anticipated reactions," propounded years ago by Carl J. Friedrich.[1] The men who share in governing do what they think they must. A President's effect on them is heightened or diminished by their thoughts about his probable reaction to their doing. They base their expectations on what they can see of him. And they are watching all the time. Looking at themselves, at him, at the immediate event, and toward the future, they may think that what he might do in theory, he would not dare to do in fact. So MacArthur evidently thought before he was dismissed. They may think that the President has tied his hands behind his back, as Faubus thought, apparently, before and after Newport. They may conclude with Arnall that the President has more to lose than they do, should he not support them. Or they may conclude, as Sawyer evidently did, that they risk more than he does if they do not support him. A Marshall and a Vandenberg may decide that the President can be relied upon to put his "powers" and his status at their service. A Charles E. Wilson, after Key West, may decide the opposite.

What these men think may or may not be "true" but it is the reality on which they act, at least until their calculations turn out wrong. As the steel crisis loomed in 1952 many Washingtonians took it for granted that should matters reach the strike stage, Truman had too many other troubles to risk anything so controversial as seizure. By April that year he and his party faced a wide-open contest for the presidential nomination; the Governor of Illinois whom he had wanted to proclaim as heir apparent would not serve. In Congress fights impended on half a dozen fronts. Downtown he was entangled in abortive efforts, highly publicized, to oversee a "cleanup" of "corruption." That at this point he could "afford" to seize the whole steel industry was heavily discounted in the industry itself, at the Capitol, and even by some members of his Cabinet. It was their thought that he would have "no choice" but resort to Taft-Hartley. This thought may have re-duced management's incentive for a settlement; it almost certainly reduced the Pentagon's concern about the outcome.

Expectations often are much closer to the mark than were those views of Truman in the steel case. Ten months before the steel crisis, in June of 1951, he made an impassioned television plea to rally popular support for tighter price controls than Congress seemed about to grant as it renewed the authorizing legislation. Neither before his plea nor after were the anticontrol forces visibly impressed. A President's ability to "appeal to the people" may be chief among his vantage points, as all the textbooks say, but no one feared vast popular response to *Truman's* call for stiffer wartime regulation two months after his dismissal of MacArthur. In this instance, the expectation proved correct. "I never asked anybody to write to his congressman," Truman later told the press.[2] Hardly anybody did.

What other men expect of him becomes a cardinal factor in the President's own power to persuade. When men in government consider their relationships with him it does them little good to scan the Constitution or remind themselves that Presidents possess potential vantage points in excess of enumerated powers. Their problem never is what abstract Presidents might do in theory but what an actual incumbent will try in fact. They must anticipate, as best they can, his *ability* and *will* to make use of the bargaining advantages he has. Out of what others think of him emerge his opportunities for influence with them. If he would maximize his prospects for effectiveness, he must concern himself with what they think. To formulate his power problem in these terms is to illuminate the job of being President.

II

In a world of perfect rationality and unclouded perception it might turn out that Washingtonians could take the past perform-ance of a President as an exact, precise, definitive determinant of future conduct, case by case. The known and open record, wholly understood, could be ransacked for counterparts to all details of each new situation. His skill, or lack of it, in using comparable vantage points for comparable purposes in like conditions, could be gauged with such precision that forecasting his every move would become a science practiced with the aid of mathematics.

In the real world, however, nobody is altogether sure what aspects of the past fit which piece of the present or the future. As the illustrations in this book suggest, particulars of time, of substance, organization, personalities, may make so great a difference, case by case, that forecasting remains a tricky game and expectations rest upon perceptions of a most imperfect sort. This can both help a President and hurt him. It can help in the sense that almost everyone in government discounts, to some degree, the flaws in his performance at a given moment. But it can hurt in the sense that over time these may lead to discounting, in advance, of his ability at any future moment.

In every move a President may make there are bound to be numerous aspects beyond his immediate control. So many things can go wrong that almost always some things do. Accordingly, the men who watch a President professionally, so to speak, cannot afford to ground their expectations on the slippages and errors in his every effort. But these accumulate, and as they do men seek for the appearance of a *pattern*. Lacking a better base, they tend to rest their forecasts of the future on such patterns as they find. The greatest danger to a President's potential influence with them is not the show of incapacity he makes today, but its apparent kinship to what happened yesterday, last month, last year. For if his failures seem to form a pattern, the consequence is bound to be a loss of faith in his effectiveness "next time." The boy who cried "wolf" came to a sad end because nobody paid attention to his final cry.

The fine points of a President's "technique" in dealing with a given situation are not the only things men watch for signs of pattern. Whether he made the right phone call on the right day, or said the right words at the right time, or read the right report and drew the right conclusion may make all the difference at a given moment. If the same thing seems to happen at successive moments it will make a mark on expectations of his future conduct. But in the present, looking toward the future, most men have more to think about than his apparent mastery of such techniques. So long as they must keep in mind continuing relationships while they consider what he wants from them, they also have to think about how hard, persistently, determinedly, he seems to *try*. With will enough, even the clumsiest technician might manage to hurt enemies somehow, sometime, and to provide some sort of cover for his friends. Signs of tenacity count quite as much as signs of skill in shaping expectations of a President's behavior.

Were Washington observers confined to the evidence of personal experience, a President would shape their expectations as he dealt with each in turn. But those who watch a President because their work requires it do not see only what he chooses to disclose to them. They see some part of almost everything he does with almost everyone, and what they cannot see they try to hear. Everything reported in the press adds to their field of vision. Whatever happens to their neighbors amplifies their view. They ask each other questions. They tell each other stories. They read with care the news reports, and newsletters, and syndicated columns circulating "inside dope" drawn from men like themselves. Theirs is a most incestuous community. In consequence, their outlook on a President at any given moment will be affected by impressions of his will and skill then currently in vogue among observers like themselves. If he wants influence, therefore, he must concern himself with more than *tête-á-têtes* in person or by proxy; his problem is no less than what all Washington may think of him. He has to be concerned with his professional reputation as a governor among the men who share in governing.

The general reputation of a President in Washington will not reflect the views of every Washingtonian. There usually is a dominant tone, a central tendency, in Washington appraisals of a President. If one wants echoes of that tone at any time one reads Krock, Lippmann, Reston, and Rovere, and half a dozen others. (One gains forewarnings also; these columnists are read with care by those from whom they draw their information.) However, no matter what the fashionable impression of the moment, some of the men on whom a President depends will always be discounting it in favor of what they perceive themselves, by light of their own loyalties, jobs, and first-hand observations. White House aides, Cabinet officers, legislative leaders, and the like will know more about some things than most commentators do (or know them differently) and will appraise the President in light of what they know. This may move their impressions far from those held by their less advantaged neighbors.

Nevertheless, differences in view between the better and the less informed tend to be self-adjusting. For one thing, the "insiders," or their aides, are looked to for the tips and "steers" and "dope" stories which help their neighbors read the public record. For another thing, their own appraisals are not always proof against appearances outside the range of personal observation. Besides, the men best placed to gain an independent view are duty-bound to take into account what others think, no matter how mistaken. Department heads or congressional leaders may see the President as pure in heart, but if their followers are sullenly convinced that he is not, this is a datum to be weighed in their own calculations. His general reputation may not be conclusive for the best informed, but it is almost sure to be a factor in their thinking.

A President who values power need not be concerned with every flaw in his performance day by day, but he has every reason for concern with the residual impressions of tenacity and skill accumulating in the minds of Washingtonians-at-large. His bargaining advantages in seeking what he wants are heightened or diminished by what others think of him. Their thoughts are shaped by what they see. They do not see alone, they see together. What they think of him is likely to be much affected by the things they see alike. His look in "everybody's" eyes becomes strategically important for his influence. Reputation, of itself, does not persuade, but it can make persuasion easier, or harder, or impossible.

Ideally, any President who valued personal power would start his term with vivid demonstrations of tenacity and skill in every sphere, thereby establishing a reputation sure to stand the shocks of daily disarray until he was prepared to demonstrate again. This is no more than Franklin Roosevelt did in his first term. It is the

ideal formula for others. Unfortunately, F.D.R.'s successors have
not held the combination of advantages that helped him make his
first-term demonstration: the public memory of his predecessor, the
crisis of the Great Depression, the easy escape from foreign affairs,
the eagerness of intellectuals, the patronage for partisans, the
breadth of his experience in government (unmatched in this century save by the other Roosevelt). Nor is there anything to indicate that while mid-century conditions last, a future President is
likely to hold comparable advantages. Emergencies in policy with
politics as usual can hardly favor an effective use of Roosevelt's
formula.

A contemporary President may have to settle for a reputation
short of the ideal. If so, what then should be his object? It should
be to induce as much uncertainty as possible about the consequences of ignoring what he wants. If he cannot make men
think him bound to win, his need is to keep them from thinking
they can cross him without risk, or that they can be sure what
risks they run. At the same time (no mean feat) he needs to keep
them from fearing lest he leave them in the lurch if they support
him. To maximize uncertainties in future opposition, to minimize
the insecurities of possible support, and to avoid the opposite effect
in either case—these together form the goal for any mid-century
President who seeks a reputation that will serve his personal power.

How can a President accomplish this result? How does he build
his reputation? How does he protect it? Let me begin consideration of these questions with a classic instance of the ways in which
a reputation ought *not* to be guarded. This illustration deals with
the first year of Eisenhower's second term.

III

Early in 1958 a technician from the Bureau of the Budget testified before a subcommittee of the House on the provisions of a
pending bill within his field of expertise. As he concluded, he
remarked for emphasis that what he recommended was essential
"to the program of the President." Whereupon everybody

laughed. The hilarity was general and leaped party lines; to a man, committee members found the reference very funny.[3] This incident occurred only fifteen months after Eisenhower's smashing re-election victory. Yet it is perfectly indicative, so far as can be judged from the outside, of an impression pervading all corners of the Capitol (and most places downtown), as a result of what had seemed to happen at the White House in the months between. This impression was to change somewhat with subsequent events. In 1959 a "new" Eisenhower emerged. Still, early in the second legislative session of his second term that laughter well expressed what most men thought. And why they thought it is an object lesson in how not to guard professional reputation.[4]

On election night in 1956, knowing the dimensions of his personal triumph, but perhaps not yet aware that he had carried neither House of Congress, Eisenhower told a national television audience:

> . . . And now let me say something that looks to the future. I think that modern republicanism has now proved itself. And America has approved of modern republicanism.
>
> And so, as we look ahead—as we look ahead to the problems in front, let us remember that a political party deserves the approbation of America only as it represents the ideals, the aspirations and the hopes of Americans. If it is anything less, it is merely a conspiracy to seize power and the Republican party is not that!
>
> Modern republicanism looks to the future . . . .[5]

For a few weeks thereafter old Washington hands of both political persuasions engaged in speculation about what, if anything, that comment might portend. They did not have to wonder very long. On January 16, 1957, the President sent to Congress his budget for Fiscal 1958, a document marked very generally by "modern" Republican touches reminiscent of the past campaign. These were evident, particularly, in the budget's relatively generous handling of resource development and welfare programs (among them general aid for school construction), in its moderate increases for defense and foreign aid, and in its bland acceptance of a spending total close to 72 billion dollars. The total was 12 billion dollars higher than the oratorical objective of the first

Eisenhower campaign, four years gone but not forgotten; spending at this level heralded no further tax relief for at least two years more. Momentarily the budget seemed a clue to Eisenhower's views about the future of his party.

Then, the same day, Secretary of the Treasury George M. Humphrey held a press conference. His prepared statement struck a regretful note about the budget and its total but was mild compared to his response on being questioned. The *New York Times* account of that response is both accurate and concise:

> . . . if the government cannot reduce the "terrific" tax burden of the country, "I will predict that you will have a depression that will curl your hair, because we are just taking too much money out of this economy that we need to make jobs that you have to have as time goes on." . . . [Humphrey] said, "there are a lot of places in this budget that can be cut," and that he would be glad to see cuts "if Congress can find ways to cut and still do a proper job . . . ." [6]

"I may have gone overboard a bit this afternoon," Humphrey reportedly remarked, shortly thereafter, to the bemused Budget Director, Percival Brundage. To much of Washington that would have seemed an extraordinary understatement. Never in the history of executive budgeting since 1921 had there been anything to match the spectacle of a first-rank Cabinet officer publicly assailing the presidential budget on the very day it was sent down. Budget Bureau officials were furious; some of the aides within the White House were appalled. "Modern" Republicans in the Cabinet and their departmental staffs—and many a sharp-minded Pentagon official—took umbrage, as well they might, for obviously they were in the line of Humphrey's fire. At the Capitol and in the press corps, and among spokesmen for the private groups most vitally concerned, reactions were as unsure as the situation was unusual; everybody looked to see what Eisenhower would do.

Three days after his second inaugural, the President went before a packed press conference and, replying to the inevitable question, commented as follows:

> Well, in my own instructions to the Cabinet and heads of all offices, I have told them that every place that there is a chance to save a dollar out of the money that we have budgeted . . . every-

body that is examining the many details . . . ought to find some-place where they might save another dollar.

If they can, I think if Congress can, its committees, it is their duty to do it.

So with the thought behind the Secretary's statements I am in complete agreement, even though he made statements that I don't believe have a present and immediate application because, indeed, the outlook for the next few months in the economic field is very good indeed.[7]

When these words came across the news tickers there were few laughs in Congress, or downtown, but many stricken faces, some delight, a great deal of suspicion, and considerable scorn. "Old Guard" Republicans and like-minded associates across the aisle sensed prospects brighter than they had thought possible so soon after the Eisenhower re-election. "Modern" Republicans felt the ground opening beneath their feet just when they had thought themselves secure. Democrats, both "liberal" and "moderate," sensed a deliberate squeeze-play with the middle place reserved for them. On the one hand (as they saw it) the President proposed a budget big with borrowings from their traditional stock-in-trade; on the other hand he joined in dramatizing the traditional Republican attack on Federal spending; with both hands he pointed at Congress where their party held a nominal majority. That "modern" Republicans might be caught in a comparable squeeze was insufficient recompense for many Democrats.

Right or wrong, all of these first impressions seemed to be borne out by happenings in the weeks after Eisenhower's press conference. For one, congressional in-boxes promptly became crammed with protests against spending (and demands for tax relief). "But two weeks later," wrote a Senator in retrospect, "the protesting tide swelled into an organized torrent . . . [which] gave the impression of being largely stimulated by corporations."[8] Behind these "corporations" numbers of Washingtonians thought they perceived a prompter in the Secretary of the Treasury. On March 6 he was reported by the *New York Times* (a paper read with care in Washington) to have informed Detroit Republicans that "specific and substantial [budget] reductions were possible if the people of the country continued their 'insistence'. . . . [This] 'would not only take . . . pressure off prices . . . but would also lead the way toward another tax cut.' . . . high spending for security would be required for some time, but that is all the more reason why expenditures in other areas must be curtailed and postponed. . . ." [9] Those last words were read with particular attention by proponents of school aid, the largest new domestic item in the budget.

Executive officials publicly identified with major spending programs did not go unnoticed as the mail campaign progressed. The Budget Director, for one, got more than letters. "Brundage wants the shirt off your back" became the slogan of some businessmen— and laundry, clean or dirty, flooded in to him by parcel post.

At the same time the Executive Branch was in the throes of one of the most hectic episodes in the whole history of central budgeting, the out-of-season "budget season" of 1957. To prove the President's sincerity the Budget Bureau spent the months of February and March extracting from the agencies reductions in his January budget. Contemporary accounts vary: budget aides counted "about" two "overall" revisions of the budget; some weary officials thought they counted five. On March 1, half in fun and half in anger, a House majority resolved that Eisenhower should inform the Congress where to cut.[10] A week later, the Budget Director told a subcommittee of the House that at the President's behest he was already doing all he could to get an answer for them (a response so astonishing to practical politicians that some of them swore off political readings of Administration behavior). "You would have thought," remarked a legislative aide in private conversation, "that they had just come into office and were trying to clean up the outgoing crowd's budget. It was 1953 all over again, only odder."

So numbers of observers thought when, in mid-April, Eisenhower formally submitted the results of Brundage's endeavor. In a letter to the Speaker of the House, the President then proposed or accepted reductions of 1.3 billion dollars in his January request for new appropriations. He warned, however, that these would not have much effect on 1958 *expenditures* and that a "multibillion" saving in expenditures could be obtained "only at the expense of the national safety and interest." Taken alone, that warning spelled out a defense of the budget's central structure and the proffered cuts became no more than reasonable tidying by conscientious budgeteers. But in the light of what had gone before, the impact of this defense was diluted by the President's own opening remarks:

> I am sure many members of the Congress are as gratified as I am to note the growing awareness of private citizens that . . . Federal benefits are not free but must be paid for out of taxes collected from the people. It is good to see . . . widespread insistence that Federal activity be held to the minimum consistent with the national needs. . . .
> The evident responsiveness of the Congress to this attitude I find equally encouraging. I assure you . . . that the Executive Branch will continue to cooperate . . . .[11]

If his purpose was a defense of his budget—and a cover for the Congressmen who rallied to its cause—those remarks, as the saying goes, put Eisenhower's emphasis on the wrong syllable.

This letter of mid-April marked a late stage in White House equivocation after Humphrey's outbreak. When Eisenhower thus addressed the Speaker there were signs that he was concerned lest the assault on his budget go too far. Concern was certainly justified. By April, the Administration faced a real crisis of confidence in its own ranks and, simultaneously, a prospect of deep, indiscriminate appropriation cuts which would spare neither foreign aid nor national defense. Downtown the departmental staffs responsible for programs thought to be on Humphrey's "list," felt themselves victims of a backstairs *coup*. Under cover of the decorous behavior usual in Eisenhower's neighborhood their resentments ran deep, with the White House an object no less than Humphrey or Brundage. For Brundage's economy drive seemed to be strongly seconded at every turn by Sherman Adams and the President. At the Capitol, meanwhile, the sense of public pressure coupled to suspicions of Administration "strategy" left even friends of Pentagon programs—to say nothing of welfare or of aid abroad —increasingly inclined to show themselves more holy than the pope. Among the Democratic members of the House, especially, temptation grew to make a record out-economizing the economizers downtown. On April 11, no less a personage than Speaker Rayburn voiced the hope that by June revenue prospects and spending cuts, combined, would clear the way for tax relief. And on the Senate side Senator Byrd of Virginia, dean of the professional economizers, gained an unusually attentive audience for his retrenchment pleas which he embodied, late in March, in a 5 billion-dollar list of "feasible" appropriation cuts.

From the end of March until mid-April Eisenhower shifted back and forth between defense of his budget and good words for the economizers. On March 27, at his regular press conference, the President used stronger language on the budget's behalf than any since his January budget message. Stung, apparently, by Byrd's proposals and by talk of tax reduction, Eisenhower characterized as "futile" and as "fatuous" both sorts of claims. Without eliminating programs there could be no major savings, he asserted, and he entered a defense of programs such as foreign aid. In consequence, the claims for "piecemeal" cuts were fraudulent. ". . . to say you are going to save a few millions here and a few millions there, I think is the poorest kind of economy we can find." [12] As an acute observer noted at the time:

> The Congressional reaction to the President's strong attitude was unusually mixed. The "Eisenhower Republicans" were pleased and relieved . . . orthodox Republicans were glum and grumpy. The Democrats were not unhappy at the division . . . Sam Rayburn of Texas, Speaker of the House, pointed out that yesterday [March 26] House Republicans had passed a resolution unanimously calling for heavy budget cuts. The President's attack . . . "looks like a pretty good answer to what his own folks did up here yesterday." [13]

To concern over budget prospects, the White House had to add concern for the apparent disarray in Republican ranks. On two occasions in the week that followed, Eisenhower tried to formulate a budget stand that would both calm the "orthodox" and satisfy his "modern" followers.[14] The net effect was to reduce, somewhat, the force of his March 27 press statement. Then his letter in mid-April to the Speaker of the House blurred his position further.

Shortly thereafter Congress recessed for Easter and the White House gained a chance to collect its thoughts.

In early May the White House announced that Eisenhower would deliver two nationally televised addresses rallying the country to his budget. Visits home in recess had convinced many Congressmen that calls to cut the budget, reduce taxes, were beginning to bite deep into the consciousness of usually inattentive publics. Though these are tricky things to gauge, there is considerable evidence that consonant with Humphrey's invitation "public opinion," organized and not, grew more aroused about those issues during 1957 than at any time in Eisenhower's first term (a matter no doubt bearing some relation to the climb in living costs that had begun in 1956). And whatever the facts, it is apparent that by May a wide variety of bureaucrats and politicians *thought* this was the case, which is what counts in Washington. The President's decision to address the country is a tribute to that thought.

The first of Eisenhower's "fireside chats," a general roundup on the budget, came on May 14. It was judged fairly ineffectual in Washington, a view held on the Hill and by the press corps, and quite evidently at the White House. Some notion of its public impact can be gleaned from the fact that the President's press secretary would not comment upon rumors of an adverse mail response. And its impact upon politicians was reduced materially by Eisenhower's own appearance of ambivalence at a press conference the next day:

> I don't think it is the function of a President of the United States to punish anybody for voting what he believes. . . . I don't see how it is possible for any President to work with the Republican group in Congress, the whole Republican group, except through their elected leadership. . . . When these large sums are involved, there comes a chance for both the Executive and the Congress to do a squeezing process . . . there is some squeezing possible and I have never kicked about that.[15]

As Senators Knowland and Bridges, Republican leaders both, were just then in the van of the congressional economizers, those words were noted throughout Washington and appropriate conclusions drawn.

A week later all conclusions were shaken. The President's second televised address on May 21, dealt with defense and foreign aid. It was generally thought "effective" and the White House happily announced a strongly favorable mail response. Moreover at his next press conference, again the following day, his tone was confident, his fielding fast and his words relatively tough:

> Well, as long as I am in a fight, I never rest until [I get] . . . what . . . I believe to be necessary for the operation of this Government . . . . I shall never stop until a decision is reached . . . . I do believe this: when a political party gets together and agrees upon a platform . . . they should remain true to it. I believe they should stick with it through thick and thin . . . . I have no right and no desire to punish anybody. I just say this: I am committed to the support of people who believe, as I do, that the Republican platform of 1956 must be our political doctrine.[16]

"In what have probably been the two most effective days of his second administration," James Reston wrote of Eisenhower's performance, "he has regained the initiative over the opposition in his own and the Democratic party."[17] Most members of the Washington community seem to have shared that view, and it grew stronger as the initiative, once taken, was sustained. On May 22 a presidential message went to Congress outlining the plans for foreign aid which were to be supported by the dollars in the budget. The Secretary of State, John Foster Dulles, followed with an elaborate personal presentation to the Senate Committee on Foreign Relations. Both the message and his testimony emphasized Administration sponsorship of program innovations previously advanced by congressional study groups. Chief among them was a Development Loan Fund as a source of capital assistance for the less developed countries, with the implication that eventually loans would replace most outright grants abroad. The upshot of the Dulles presentation was a heartening reception for the foreign-aid program in Senate offices and a more general cordiality than had seemed possible a week before.

Two days later Eisenhower spoke by telephone to a Republican

Party conference in New Jersey and strongly urged the item veto as a way to "real" economies. His aim, apparently, was to turn the gaze of the economizers from his budget toward congressional initiatives on public works. At the same conference, his assistant, Sherman Adams, made a speech demanding party unity behind the President. Since Adams, twelve days earlier, reportedly had remarked on a television program that the budget could be cut 2 billion dollars without harm, his address in New Jersey seemed another sign in Washington of new determination at the White House.

Between the first and second presidential television talks, the Secretary of Defense, Charles E. (General Motors) Wilson, had held a press conference defending in detail the military budget which the House was threatening to cut by 1.2 billion dollars. Eisenhower in his second televised address had pressed the Secretary's case. A few days later, Minority Leader Martin was enabled to announce that as a party matter, House Republicans would now seek restoration of a fourth of the projected cut. When this was then attempted on the floor it was defeated by the Democrats. In the crucial roll-call all but eleven of them voted against the restoration, which three-quarters of the House Republicans supported.[18] Although this outcome seemed at first glance to repudiate the President's newly asserted leadership, the White House could take comfort from it nonetheless, and close observers gained from it a new respect for Eisenhower's potency. Congressional Republicans had closed ranks in a gesture to his cause, however short of his avowed objective. House Democrats had made a party record most embarrassing to defense-minded Senate colleagues. A base seemed surely laid for better fortune in the Senate and in conference.

Washingtonians quite generally responded with considerable respect to the "new" Eisenhower who had emerged in the month of May. Belatedly but definitely, he seemed to have accepted, now, the role reserved for Presidents in the time-honored play of legislative action on the budget. Downtown, men trying to rouse public support for their programs were encouraged. On Capitol Hill men trying to resist public pressure against spending were relieved. The President could now be praised or blamed for what they sought to do. Political interpretations of his conduct flourished once again, but these assigned him motives quite like those assigned in other years to other Presidents and the familiarity was reassuring to the politically minded. "Modern" Republicans were gratified. Democrats began to reassess. "Old Guard" Republicans prepared to give some ground. So far as I can ascertain, nobody laughed.

So matters stood by June of 1957. The President's own actions for the past five months, along with those of his associates, now seemed to show contrasting patterns, and the latest signs seemed to belie the relevance of what had gone before. Momentarily, a host of expectations throughout Washington were tempered or revised to suit.

In the month of June, however, there came some harbingers of new developments. For one thing, the Comptroller of the Pentagon testified on June 4 to a House subcommittee that military expenditures were running at an annual rate of 4 billion dollars above January estimates—the result of rising costs and (paradoxically) of improved paper work—and that, in consequence, directives had come down from Wilson and from Brundage, late in May, to slow current spending to the rates originally projected. On the same day as this testimony, at the other end of Pennsylvania Avenue, the chairman of the Republican National Committee told the press that Eisenhower had been briefed on the adverse reaction of Republican contributors to current White House views about the budget. Three weeks later a Young Republican convention voted almost two-to-one, in Washington, against support for the Administration's proposed aid to schools. A week after that, the President in a letter to one of his most ardent House supporters said he could not "pass judgment on all the details" of the pending school aid bill, a response described by its recipient as "disappointing." [19]

Such miscellaneous occurrences as these gained pattern retrospectively for many Washingtonians when the Administration found itself embarrassed on three notable occasions in July. Early that month the Senate passed a military appropriation bill restoring most of the funds cut by the House, as Wilson and the President had urged. With confidence, the Senate conferees prepared to battle for their version. Then on July 18, while the conference committee was in session, a letter from the Secretary of Defense announced that to hold spending at the rate of January's estimate (under his May directive from Brundage) 100,000 men would be dropped by the army and a portion of the Senate increase would be saved. That announcement not only made senators look silly —and forced the Senate conferees to drop their base for bargaining —it also seriously hampered Senate advocates of foreign aid on which debate had just begun. Nine months later, Wilson's letter still caused scathing comment on the Senate floor, and there were no defenders in the chamber.[20]

On July 25 general aid for school construction came to a vote in the House. The measure as reported from committee compromised Administration plans for grants to states on grounds of need alone with plans by the bill's sponsors for grants proportional to school-age population. Eisenhower had not blessed the compromise, exactly. Although he had called repeatedly for action on the measure, he had evaded opportunities to put his own stamp of approval on its grant provisions. Even so, the Secretary of Health, Education and Welfare, Marion Folsom, had never ceased to represent the White House as firmly behind the bill. On the House floor, however, the Republican leadership failed to support it, even at the crucial moment when its Democratic sponsors offered to accept Administration terms for grants-in-aid. Thereupon the bill was killed in parliamentary circumstances so complex that this offer was scarcely mentioned by most press reports, while members made a record for each party on which blame could be heaped from across the aisle.[21] But the interested lobbyists, officials, and reporters were aware, of course, that there had come a point in the debate when the Administration *might* have gained its grant provisions and secured the bill. In consequence the President was asked at his next press conference to comment on the lack of response from Republican leaders. He replied: "I never heard . . . . If that is true, why you are telling me something I never heard." [22]

The impact of that comment in the Washington community was heightened by the fact that just three weeks before the President had responded somewhat similarly on a matter even closer to the heart of his program. In the first week of July, Senator Russell of Georgia had charged the Administration with a tricky, hidden intent in provisions of the civil rights bill that it had sponsored and that the House had passed. The bill was in the front rank of Administration measures; its drafting had been done by the Department of Justice; those provisions were included from the first. Yet the President, on being asked about them in press conference had said:

> Well, I would not want to answer . . . in detail because I was reading part of that bill this morning, and I—there were certain phrases I didn't completely understand. So, before I made any more remarks on that, I would want to talk to the Attorney General and see exactly what they do mean. . . . Naturally I'm not a lawyer and I don't participate in drawing up the exact language of proposals. . . .[23]

These three occurrences in July furnished considerable food for thought to those who watch a President professionally, but it cannot be said that there was a consensus, all at once, on their interpretation. For during August Eisenhower led a renewed White House effort on behalf of foreign aid. Reportedly, he also intervened to assure enactment of a useful compromise on civil rights. By late August when Congress adjourned, its record, although mixed, seemed no disaster for the Administration, not even on the budget (when one sets aside the cuts that Eisenhower had endorsed). In light of that outcome there were numbers of Washingtonians, especially downtown, who thought they saw the likelihood of more consistency and more determination from the White House in the year ahead. For one thing, Humphrey had left office in July. For another, as one high official told me hopefully: "I think the President knows some things now he didn't have to learn in his first term." Again, as in late May, although less markedly, there was a tendency to read two patterns into Eisenhower's past behavior and to hedge, somewhat, the expectations based on either one of them.

Then, in September, came the Little Rock affair. Immediately afterward, the first Soviet sputniks went aloft. American egos were

badly bruised, as all the world found out, and defense-minded
citizens of every sort were jarred by contemplation of the thrust
required to put Sputnik II in orbit. Moreover, as the sputniks rose
there came the first sharp signs of a decline in the American economy, heralding the 1958 recession and rendered the more disturbing by continued increases in living costs. By December 1957
needs, lags, and lacks of national "preparedness" to meet the Russian "challenge" had become *the* Washington preoccupation, in
terms ranging all the way from military hardware to science in
our schools. As for the question posed by lessening production,
many Washingtonians assumed that a response to sputnik held the
answer.

The President's forthcoming budget and his legislative program
thus became the focus of a new concern, at odds with—and in
many quarters overriding, for a time—the "swollen" budget and
high tax preoccupations of the spring. The congressmen who six
months earlier had championed economy, the Pentagon officials
who had worked throughout September to cut active forces to
a level consonant with programmed spending rates; a whole array
of experts, editorial writers, commentators, spokesmen for assorted
interest groups—all these now called for governmental action,
"leadership," "a sense of urgency," to meet the threats of Russian
technological superiority and of American economic instability.
And lest the presidential program fail to satisfy the urgent activists,
the Senate leader, Johnson of Texas, made it plain that Democrats
would do their utmost to make up the lack. As early as November he had convened a bipartisan Preparedness Subcommittee which
gave the activists a forum in the weeks before Congress returned
to Washington.

The President, himself, had spent much of November incapaci-
tated by a cerebral spasm. Pushing his recovery, he had spent
part of December in Paris at a post-sputnik rally of the North
Atlantic Treaty Organization. The concern and curiosity about his
coming program were heightened by his illness, by his absence, and
by a long suspension of press conferences. He was, therefore, the
center of attention in a transformed situation when his annual

messages for 1958 went to the new session of Congress. The situation seemed so different that the patterns of the past appeared no guide; expectations, momentarily, were in suspense.

Eisenhower's State of the Union address in 1958 was strong in tone and vigorously delivered. It was also rather unspecific. But it won him a good deal of praise as Washington awaited the specifics of the budget. Speaker Rayburn, for one, called it the "strongest" speech the President had ever made to Congress.[24] This rendered all the more astonishing the Eisenhower budget (fiscal 1959) that Congress received on January 13. For congressmen and interest groups soon found, as department staffs already knew, that save for minimal response to sputnik, it was just the sort of budget Humphrey had desired but had failed to gain before his public outburst a year earlier.

On the domestic side, the new budget requested *program* changes to reduce the spending base in future years. Technically this was a realistic route toward major savings. Politically, it was a way of irritating interest groups of every sort and all at once. The President proposed a ban on all new starts for power, flood control, and reclamation. He urged a sharp downward revision of farm subsidies. He asked a narrowing of legal limits upon grants to states for hospital construction, urban redevelopment, and public welfare programs, among others. He hinted at reduction of the base for veterans' benefits and urged an increase in the interest rate on G.I. mortgages. He abandoned aid for school construction on the plea that funds were limited and aid for science training now deserved priority.

As Truman once used budgets to project his Fair Deal aims beyond his current prospects, Eisenhower now presented an ideal projection for conservative Republicans. "Politically," as William S. White put it, "his domestic program involves an effort to return to the spirit of a traditional Republicanism never before seen in the current White House and not in years manifested in Congress itself, save by a comparative handful of beleaguered orthodox Republicans." [25]

The reaction among Democrats was sharp and scornful. "What does he want," one Senator is said to have asked an executive official, "every lobby in the country ganging up on foreign aid?" As for Republicans, to quote White once again, "They see the impact of the Eisenhower domestic policy as heavy all over the country for Republican members of Congress—damaging in urban areas . . . and simultaneously very bad news indeed in the farm belt . . . . Thus as not before in his Presidency has Eisenhower challenged the vital political interests of both wings of his congressional party at the same time." [26] As no one in Congress could forget, there would be an election in November.

Had the domestic policy been coupled to a massive build-up on the military side, it might have had a kindlier reception from the politically minded. Certainly they would have understood it better. But Eisenhower's budget for defense did little more than return Pentagon expenditures to rates achieved six months before (allowing for price changes in the interim), while increased emphasis on missiles and research was compensated, to a large degree, by reduced emphasis on active forces. The most striking of Eisenhower's own proposals in the defense sphere was not a budget increase but a Pentagon reorganization to "end" interservice rivalries. "America," he said in his initial address, "wants them stopped." Thereupon he pledged himself to find a way to do it: "Soon my conclusions will be finalized. I shall promptly take such executive action as is necessary and . . . present appropriate recommendations to the Congress." [27]

This pledge, at least, emerged unscathed from critical reactions to his budget. But in mid-January, when asked by the press how hard he meant to fight for Pentagon reform, his response struck a rather different note:

> . . . my personal convictions, no matter how strong, cannot be the final answer. There must be a consensus reached with the cab— with the Congress, with the people that have the job of operating the services . . . I am certainly hopeful that it goes in the direction of what I believe. But . . . organization has got to be effective after . . . [I have] passed from the scene . . . .[28]

A few days later, obviously mindful of reactions to this statement, Eisenhower announced that he "would participate personally" in the reorganization "until the job was done," and he journeyed to the Pentagon to emphasize the point.[29] But many Washingtonians were left unsure which Eisenhower to believe. Their puzzlement was not confined to this one issue.

Late in January 1958 there came the episode with which this story started: a Budget Bureau aide evoked "the program of the President" in testimony on the Hill and all his hearers laughed. It is scarcely to be wondered why they did.

IV

The professional reputation of a President in Washington is made or altered by the man himself. No one can guard it for him; no one saves him from himself. His office has been institutionalized to a degree unknown before the Second World War, but as a reputation-builder he is no mere "office manager." On the contrary, everything he personally says and does (or fails to say, omits to do), becomes significant in everyone's appraisals regardless of the claims of his officialdom. For his words, his own actions, provide clues not only to his personal proclivities but to the forecasts and asserted influence of those around him. What Humphrey says gains weight as Eisenhower seems not to oppose him. What Folsom says becomes a joke as Eisenhower seems not to support him. Press secretariats and "chiefs of staff" and other aides aside, in fashioning his Washington reputation a President's own doings are decisive.

As these Eisenhower episodes make plain, a President runs risks by being personally responsible for his own reputation. In the fifteen months after his re-election Eisenhower managed to reverse the reputation-builder's goal: he increased the insecurities attendant on supporting him and lessened the apparent risks of openly opposing him. He managed this by seeming both unsure of his objectives and unwilling to persist, for long, in any given course. His words and actions cast increasing doubt not only on his skill but on his will. Both came to be discounted in the Washington community. The impact on his influence was marked.

Not all of Eisenhower's troubles were avoidable; some of them are native to the presidential job. In concrete cases any President may feel he must support, or rationalize, what his associates have done, as Eisenhower felt when Humphrey spoke out to the press. If he disavows their doings he may cast more doubt on his own will and capability than on theirs. And any President is judged in part by standards of behavior very different from his own. The impression that he makes by what he does depends not only on the content of his action but on the events surrounding it, as these events are understood by men who watch him work. Their notions of what they would do if they were in his place may count as much as what he does in shaping their impressions. When Eisenhower urged his program cuts in January 1958, politically minded members of the Washington community found his stand incredible in their terms of reference. Since they could not imagine themselves acting so, they would not take him seriously; what he meant to be decisive seemed instead to be equivocal or perverse. Yet there are so many different terms of reference in the Washington community that White House action rarely will be taken at face value by every part of Washington at once. Eisenhower suffered from a general lack of credit. This condition might have been avoidable. But nothing that he could have said or done would have made sense to every Washingtonian.

A President's decisive role in reputation-building is a source of opportunity as well as risk. In a government where Secretaries of the Treasury may go astray at press conference, where Secretaries of Defense may choose the poorest time to make announcements, where Presidents may not be briefed on legislative drafts—and ours is such a government no matter who is President—the fact that his own conduct will decide what others think of him is precious for the man inside the White House. He can steal scenes from his subordinates. He can switch roles or even open a new play. In May of 1957 when Eisenhower made and pressed a vigorous appeal for portions of his budget, he very nearly managed to switch roles himself. He also turned attention from what Humphrey, Brundage, Adams, and the like had seemed to say or do up to that time. A President can *change* his reputation. This is the essence of his opportunity. "I always must remind myself," a very senior bureaucrat once told me, looking at the White House from his office window, "that the power of that fellow over there is never the same two weeks in a row; it fluctuates almost from day to day." Had "everybody's" laughter in the early days of 1958 expressed a fixed, immutable impression, Eisenhower's own prospects for influence would have been less than actually became the case in the years after.

Few single actions on a President's part will either set or totally transform what Washington perceives of him. Eisenhower's program did not become laughable the moment he first seemed to sanction Humphrey's attack on his budget. The laughter followed a year later when that incident appeared the key to a whole pattern of equivocation. Nothing short of a contrasting pattern, equally substantial and sustained, could have transformed the view induced by the occurrences of 1957. In 1958 amidst recession difficulties, defense dilemmas, vicuña coats, hard deseg-regation problems, and a host of troubles overseas, Eisenhower managed no such transformation. But in 1959 he did achieve it; a "New Eisenhower" emerged that year. The newness was sus-tained for months on end. Impressions of equivocation were replaced by visions of tenacity and not a little skill. In his seventh year this President apparently won more respect from Washington on both these scores than he had been accorded since the time of his belated honeymoon in 1955, after the eclipse of Senator McCarthy and before the Denver heart attack. That Eisenhower could look "new" in 1959 despite his look in 1957 is a tribute to the opportunity presented by a President's own role in reputation.

How did Eisenhower manage to transform his reputation? He did it by defending a restrictive budget, of the sort he had pro-posed in 1958, against congressional attempts to add new programs of the sort he had endorsed in 1957. This oversimplifies to a degree: the Eisenhower budget for 1959 was rather more restric-tive than had been the case before, and some of the congressional additions he disputed went beyond his own proposals two years earlier. But in education, housing, public works, and foreign aid, the parallels are close.[30] He changed his reputation by *consistently* opposing what he once had urged equivocally. He made his opposition manifest by threatening the veto and by using it. He made his purpose plain by his demeanor at press conference and he used the conference freely to expound his case in public. From the start of 1959 up to the time of writing (in July), Eisenhower's words and actions were consistent—and his vetoes were sustained. The public record in those months presents a striking contrast with the comparable period of 1957. His success was largely negative but it was still success. His reputation fed on his consistency and on accomplishment. The "new" Eisenhower was not universally approved by any means. Interpretations of his conduct were not always flattering. Both at the Capitol and near the White House some men saw him as the victim of an *idée fixe*. But those who held this view were all the more respectful of his will, at least within the range of his presumed fixation.

A President's opportunity to change his reputation is not un-limited. The circumstances of this Eisenhower transformation will suggest the limits. For one thing his display of will and skill was managed from the strongest ground a President can occupy late in his final term: the ground of opposition to congressional initiatives when Congress does not bear his party's label. Upon this ground his vantage points of "powers" and of status suffered nothing from the Twenty-second Amendment. For another thing, when Eisen-hower occupied that ground his setting lent his actions weight in Washington. From early 1959 production and employment indices rose rapidly; his popularity appeared to move in train. By May he spoke and acted in a setting reminiscent of 1957. Psycho-logically, and in most economic terms, the recession was over. Sputniks had long since become routine. Popular concern about inflation and taxation reappeared as fears of a depression vanished. Eisenhower's legislative program had seemed laughable to congress-men in 1958; it was no laughing matter in 1959. The congressional elections of 1958 had produced heavy Democratic majorities, but with the economic upturn these majorities were as susceptible to pressures for economy as Democrats had been in 1957. Besides, throughout the spring of 1959 a threat of Soviet action in Berlin warned Washingtonians that they might have to rally around the White House on short notice. Eisenhower's critics grew relatively quiet as the year advanced. His new look was the product, partly, of the quietude around him. It left him free to stand on the offensive and it limited awareness of the flaws in his performance. A President can change the way he looks, but first he has to find some actions suited to the purpose, and then he has to hope that other men respect the change. His action does not dictate their reaction. His situation and their own, as *they* interpret both, decide what they will think of his new look. These are the limits on his opportunity.

Granting the limits, acknowledging the risks, how does a President exploit his opportunity? How does he make the most he can of his own reputation? The answer returns us to his choices. His general reputation will be shaped by signs of pattern in the things he says and does. These are the words and actions he has chosen, day by day. His choices are the means by which he does what he can do to build his reputation as he wants it. Decisions are his building-blocks. He has no others in *his* hands. The point we reached in Chapter 3 we reach again.

The President of the United States can rarely make a choice with nothing more in mind than his professional reputation. Franklin Roosevelt sometimes asked his aides for "something I can veto" as a lesson and a reminder to congressmen.[31] But chances for decision in these terms alone will not come often to a President. Most choices will involve him also in the institutional imperatives of being President, in the extensive duties of his clerkship. Through the first half of 1957 Eisenhower's troubles turned upon the fact that whatever he might want to be or seem, he could not escape authorship and advocacy of a budget. Both were required of the President-as-clerk in order that congressional and agency officials could carry on their jobs. Moreover. many choices will involve the President's own sense of right and wrong. Eisenhower, as we have seen, argued for economy amidst the outcry over sputniks and recession; Truman stuck to advocacy of his Fair Deal measures in the hardest months of the Korean War. Besides, each choice involves not only general reputation but particular relationships. The two considerations often clash. Although a President lacks other means to guard the way he looks, his choice-making involves

him in *competing* considerations. The choice that started Eisenhower's reputation toward its downward slide in 1957 was his
personal approval of a Treasury press conference on Budget Day.
The grounds for that approval illustrate the competitions in a
presidential choice. The story of that choice is told in Chapter 6.

At the start of this discussion of professional reputation I postponed consideration of choice-making. Now let me postpone it
once again. The men who judge a President in Washington watch
more than his performance and their neighbor's reaction. They
also keep an eye upon reactions from his audience outside their
own community; they watch the way he looks to that residual
cross-section of constituents, his public at large. His power stakes
are not confined to his relationships and reputation inside Washington; his influence depends, as well, on his apparent popular
prestige. This factor in his influence remains to be explored.

Public Prestige . 5

The Washingtonians who watch a President have more to think about than his professional reputation. They also have to think about his standing with the public outside Washington. They have to gauge his popular prestige. Because they think about it, public standing is a source of influence for him, another factor bearing on their willingness to give him what he wants.

Prestige, like reputation, is a subjective factor, a matter of judgment. It works on power just as reputation does through the mechanism of anticipated reactions. The same men, Washingtonians, do the judging. In the case of reputation they anticipate reactions from the President. In the instance of prestige they anticipate reactions from the public. Most members of the Washington community depend upon outsiders to support them or their interests. The dependence may be as direct as votes, or it may be as indirect as passive toleration. Dependent men must take account of popular reaction to *their* actions. What their publics may think of them becomes a factor, therefore, in deciding how to deal with the desires of a President. His prestige enters into that decision; their publics are part of his. Their view from inside Washington of how outsiders view him thus affects his influence with them.

A President's prestige is not a very precise thing to keep in view. "The" presidential public is actually an aggregate of publics as diverse and overlapping as the claims Americans and allied peoples press on Washington. Members of "the" public are divided not alone by differently felt needs and wants but by degrees of difference in attention paid a President. Some of them may make an avocation of the watchfulness vocationally imposed on Washingtonians. But the responses of the great majority shade all the way to general inattention broken only as a private share in public trouble makes men lift their eyes. Presidential standing outside Washington is actually a jumble of imprecise impressions held by relatively inattentive men.

This is a factor operating mostly in the background as a conditioner, not the determinant, of what Washingtonians will do about a President's request. Rarely is there any one-to-one relationship between appraisals of his popularity in general and responses to his wishes in particular. The Hundred Days of 1933 remain as exceptional as they were memorable. Even then, as careful commentators have made plain, both skill and energy were needed to maintain the link.[1] After Roosevelt's *second* inaugural came the legislative storms of 1937. After Eisenhower's re-election came the House revolt against his military budget. Yet the prevalent impression of a President's public standing tends to set a tone and to define the limits of what Washingtonians do for him, or do to him. In the background of MacArthur's insubordination and the cheering that accompanied it on Capitol Hill was a prevailing view of Truman as decidedly unpopular. One finds this also in the background of the steel case, a year later. In 1958 the laughter heard in Washington became the louder as impressions spread that Eisenhower's popularity was falling. In 1959 the first signs of respect for the "new" Eisenhower coincided with reports that his prestige was on the rise again.

In conditioning responses to a President, the quality of his prestige can matter quite as much as any quantitative notion of his popularity. When men make judgments in the Washington community they are no less concerned with what he is liked *for*, than with how many like him. In 1949, to take a sharp example, Air Force and Navy "brass" fought openly, in turn, against the Truman budget for defense.[2] In 1954, armed with a technically better case, the Army swallowed hard and did not battle publicly against the "New Look" Eisenhower was presenting as his own.[3] Even in 1958, the year of Lebanon, when the Army's plight was worse but its case as good as ever, there came no "revolt of the generals." [4] Truman had been challenged within months of his surprise election. Eisenhower seemed less popular in 1958 than ever before. Truman, of course, had not gone to Annapolis; Eisenhower was a certified West Pointer. This may account for some part of the difference between Navy "revolt" and Army quiescence. But also Truman was not popularly thought to be among the country's greatests experts in military affairs; his successor was accorded that distinction. No doubt a factor in the Army's conduct was the difficulty of conceiving how to win a shouting match with *General* Eisenhower.[5]

The public standing of a President in the United States may be quite different from his standing with constituents abroad. Apparently, the President's position overseas was higher than at home in most of Truman's years and lower than at home in most of Eisenhower's. Those Washingtonians who are themselves dependent on a foreign public have to think about the quality of his prestige in both these spheres at once. But even Washingtonians whose publics are American will think, from time to time, of how he stands abroad. Members of Congress, for example, are increasingly aware that his position overseas can be a national asset and that their behavior toward him can enlarge it or diminish it. Their publics sometimes seem to be aware of this as well. Most men at the Capitol are anxious not to jeopardize American advantages, and no one wants the accusation flung at him from his own state or district. Except in Truman's final years, consideration for the President's prestige abroad has tended to inhibit congressional behavior ever since the Second World War. In 1959 the presence of Berlin, as an *impending* crisis through the whole length of the session, contributed to the respectfulness shown Eisenhower by a Congress that was advertised as certain to oppose him. However, even though a President's position overseas affects all sorts of judgments made in Washington, his standing with home publics is a matter of more moment to most Washingtonians most of the time. Accordingly, this chapter deals with the domestic side alone.

How do members of the Washington community assess a President's prestige with the American public? They talk to one another and to taxi drivers. They read the columnists and polls and news reports. They sample the opinions of their visitors and friends. They travel in the country and they listen as they go. Above all, they watch Congress. Generally speaking, only national party politicians, legislative leaders, congressmen in unsafe seats, and lobbyists in trouble wet their fingers every day to gauge winds blowing toward the White House from the public. Most others, and especially most bureaucrats, concentrate on the winds blowing from the Capitol. If an agency's careerists fail to challenge an Eisenhower, as in the Army case, their usual calculation is not that the public supports him but that Congress, fearing so, will not support them. Congressional sentiment tends to be official-dom's pragmatic substitute for "public opinion" because it is on Congress, not the general public, that officials must depend, day after day, for legislation and for funds to keep programs and personnel alive. And bureaucrats are not the only ones who make that substitution. For comparable reasons it is made, much of the time, by diplomats of many countries, officers of every state, representatives of private interests, local party leaders, and even congressmen themselves.

Congress is a distorting mirror for a President's prestige. Congressional constituencies differ from his own. What happens at the Capitol rarely will reflect the full extent of his apparent popularity. Eisenhower found this out in his first term. Neither is it likely to reflect the full extent of his unpopularity. Congressmen must live with presidential "powers." Truman's last Congress was often in an ugly mood; the mood of the country sometimes seemed uglier. Distortions are as likely to assist a man as hurt him.

Since the general public does not govern, presidential influence is shielded from the vagaries of shifting sentiment. Truman could not keep his Admirals from revolting in 1949, but as Commander-in-Chief he could retaliate and did: the Chief of Naval Operations was retired; other officers were transferred overseas. That year he could not keep the Air Force from demanding and obtaining an appropriation bigger than its budget but he could and did keep extra funds unspent, "impounding" them (by the device of not apportioning them) as statutes on the books allowed. When he seized the steel mills, press denunciations could not make him give them up, unless it can be said that the Supreme Court followed the newspapers. When he dismissed MacArthur, public outcries could not put the General back. With "powers" and with status—and sufficient show of will—a President of the United States can wield effective influence in many situations even though he has a balky Congress and seems short on popular appeal. Obviously, though, the less his demonstrated power at the Capitol, the more he is confined, downtown, to realms where sheer command proves workable. The weaker his apparent popular support, the more his cause in Congress may depend on negatives at his disposal like the veto, or "impounding." He may not be left helpless, but his options are reduced, his opportunities diminished, his freedom for maneuver checked in the degree that Washington conceives him unimpressive to the public.

Leeway is the term that best describes the presidential stake in Washington appraisals of prestige—leeway as opportunity, leeway in the sense of chances to be taken. This is what Truman gained from the prestige he borrowed during 1947 for the early, crucial stages of the Marshall Plan. This is what Eisenhower gained in 1959 when, contrary to expectations, Washington discovered that his popularity was rising. Leeway is no guarantee of governmental action. Popularity may not produce a Washington response. But public disapproval heartens Washington's resistance. Leeway guarantees one thing: avoidance of the trouble that can follow from its absence. Prestige counts in power by establishing some checks upon resistance from the men engaged in governing.

Not only does prestige check Washingtonians, it also often checks those members of the public who are called upon to act as agents for a President. Some chores of governing are not done in the Washington community. Some things are done directly by a portion of the public. Presidential influence on government becomes, in part, a matter of direct relationships with special-purpose publics. And the members of a special public, quite like

Washingtonians, are often swayed by what they think the general public thinks of him.

What may a President desire from some portion of his public? One thing he may desire is an alteration of the Washington community to aid him in attaining policy objectives. In short, he may want votes. To be sure, votes are not a guarantee of any policy objective. But election outcomes obviously bear upon his chances to obtain his policy ends by other means. Since 1938 a consequence of each mid-term congressional election (with the possible exception of 1954) has been elimination, practically speaking, of prospects for some policy departures wanted by the White House. In 1952 the presidential election had the same effect on numbers of objectives urged by the retiring Administration.

Aside from votes, a President's objectives are affected by the willingness of special publics to use *private* means as substitutes for an official action. There are all sorts of concrete situations where a presidential policy or preference seems beyond accomplishment by acts of formal government, or would be better served by private action. Remember Truman's efforts to achieve a settlement in steel without a seizure. Recall that Eisenhower sent no troops to Little Rock until the mob had failed to heed his proclamation urging citizens to cease the obstruction of justice. On both occasions, failing private action, these Presidents were able to find official stop-gaps. But private action was what they required if their policy objectives were to be achieved. Moreover, in steel seizure, there was Sawyer's silent partner, the trade union. Even as a stop-gap, official action was contingent on collaboration from its members in the mills.

When a President appeals for votes or private action, the men whom he addresses will have more in mind than notions of his national prestige. As in the case of Washington, one rarely finds a one-to-one relationship between appraisals of his general popularity and responses from some public in particular. In 1954 and 1956 when Eisenhower was conceded to be high in public favor, he appealed in vain for a Republican Congress. In 1957 when he still seemed very popular, his unsupported word did not disperse the mob in Little Rock. Truman, on the other hand, was widely thought unpopular in 1952 when the men honored his call to stay at work in the steel mills. Yet the closer one looks at instances like these, the clearer are the signs that prestige was a factor in the background of behavior. Eisenhower did not get the Congresses he wanted, but the Democrats he got instead were pledged to treat him well, and Democratic leaders in both Houses had worked hard to lend those pledges substance in advance. At Little Rock he had to call upon the Army; bayonets dispersed the mob. It is notable, however, that mobs did not assemble elsewhere in the South and did not reassemble around Central High School. One cannot know to what extent the men who might have led such mobs were influenced by thoughts about the President's prestige. But had Eisenhower worn the look of Truman in the South, local leaders might have hastened to defy him. In the steel case the workers supported Truman when his course suited their purposes; they did not hesitate to overthrow his object, steel production, the moment that he ceased to be of concrete use to them.

With special publics as with Washingtonians, the President's supposed prestige can set a tone and may prescribe the limits of response to his appeals. Prestige can have great impact on behavior when the special public is self-consciously endeavoring to court "public opinion." On the other side of steel seizure were those most unhappy presidential "agents," the company executives. As an adjunct of their appeal to the courts they mounted an extraordinary attack on Truman personally. No doubt they were spurred on by a presumption of his lack of popularity. Had Truman worn the look of Eisenhower, one cannot conceive that they would have denounced him in such personal terms. Larger, looser publics than an industry's executives, and publics farther removed from the Washington community, may be much less concerned about the general public. For voters in a congressional district, or for workers in a steel mill, or for men on the streets of Little Rock, a sense of how the President is viewed outside their neighborhood may be a minor factor in deciding their behavior. But it rarely will be absent altogether from the thoughts of those who lead within the neighborhood.

A President's prestige is thus a factor in his influence of roughly the same sort as his professional reputation: a factor that may not decide the outcome in a given case but can affect the likelihoods in every case and therefore is strategically important to his power. If he cares about his prospects for effectiveness in government, he need be no less mindful of the one than of the other. Granting the importance of his popular prestige, how is a President to keep it under guard?

This question parallels my inquiry in the last chapter, but the two are not the same. Professional reputation is not popularity. Guarding the one, therefore, is not equivalent to guarding the other. Prestige will have a bearing upon reputation, certainly, and professional appraisals by attentive Washingtonians unquestionably trickle down to those outside. The interaction is continuous, but it is interaction between very different things. In Eisenhower's instance, for example, polls and press reports agree that his sharpest loss of popularity occurred in the recession year of 1958. But this loss corresponded neither in severity nor timing to the damage done his Washington reputation during 1957. Truman, on the other hand, undoubtedly got higher marks in Washington for capability and will than he obtained in public through his last two years of office, after Chinese intervention lengthened the Korean War. Like reputation, prestige is a matter to be judged, not "known." The judging, for the most part, will be done by Washingtonians. Judgments of prestige may be distorted inside Washington, but what is being judged remains outside. To question how a President can guard prestige is not to deal in disguise with his Washington reputation. Prestige must be guarded at its source.

II

If it were clear that publics outside Washington perceived a President in terms of personality alone, the guarding of prestige might be—as sometimes it is thought to be—a matter for Madison Avenue. But there have been sharp changes in the popularity of men whose public manners were substantially unaltered. The

Truman of 1951 looked and sounded very much like Truman on Election Day in 1948. Allowing for age and illness (which millions of Americans were happy to do in 1956), Eisenhower seems to have projected the same human qualities throughout his time in office. To guard one's look in human terms is not enough.

Personality is a factor in prestige but not a very dynamic factor. Recent experience suggests that an impression of the presidential personality, a "public image" as the term is commonly, non-technically employed, takes shape for most constituents no later than the time they first perceive him being President (a different thing from seeing him as candidate). And save within the Washington community where White House personalities are reassessed each day, such images, once formed, appear to change but slowly, if at all. Louis Harris, among others, has suggested that public perceptions of the Eisenhower personality shifted between 1952 and 1956 from "father" to "grandfather." [6] But this is to compare perceptions of the man as a *prospective* President with those of him in office. The "grandfather" image Harris traces as of 1956 seems in no way inconsistent with prevailing views reported by the press as early as 1954 and as late as 1959. In Truman's instance, an impression of the "little man" in Roosevelt's shoes, courageous and hard-working but not "big enough" was probably pervasive within days of his succession. Perhaps, for a time, he shared it himself; he certainly helped to spread it. "Boys, if you ever pray, pray for me now," he told the press with national attention focused on his takeover, ". . . when they told me . . . what had happened I felt like the moon, the stars, and all the planets had fallen on me." [7] Three years later, his campaign for election and his victory highlighted very different human qualities. The "little man" may not have disappeared, but now, in Jonathan Daniels's allusive phrase, he had become "The Man of Independence." Although we lack evidence on which to base conclusions about just whose views were changed by just how much, there seems no doubt that 1948 did have a marked effect on widely shared ideas about the Truman personality.[8] This is testimony rather to the impact of exceptional events than to the instability of public images. To judge from what occurred in his last years, the older image was not driven far below the surface.

An image of the office, not an image of the man, is the dynamic factor in a President's prestige. Impressions of the person will form early and last long, but the values men assign to what they see can alter rather quickly. "Decisiveness" may turn into irascibility; "cleverness" may come to seem deceitfulness; "open-mindedness" to seem soft-headedness; "courage" to seem rashness. Truman, the "master-politician" of 1948 was the "mere" politician of 1951. The very sharpness of impressions driven home by his election made him suspect at the height of the Korean War. Two years after Eisenhower's smashing re-election, every poll behaved as though considerably fewer citizens welcomed what he represented at the White House. In his case, as in Truman's, the sense of what he *was* does not seem to have changed. Rather, the sense of what he *ought* to be had changed. Not personality perceptions but these "oughts" of office underlie most short-run shifts in popular prestige.

Why do the "oughts" of office vary as they do? Why are perceptions of the *job* so changeable? The answer, evidently, is that what a President should be is something most men see by light of what is happening to *them*. Their notions of the part a President should play, their satisfaction with the way he plays it, are affected by their private hopes and fears. Behind their judgments of performance lie the consequences in their lives. What threatens his prestige is their frustration.

For more than two decades the Gallup Poll has sampled nationally, at monthly intervals or thereabouts, "approval" of the President's performance on the job. The question asked has been almost unvarying: "Do you approve or disapprove of the way [the incumbent] is handling his job as President?" Unlike a pre-election poll, this inquiry does not relate to any concrete action by respondents. Unlike a query on specific issues, it does not relate to any concrete information. The question is unfocused; so is the response, which tells us anything or nothing about what respondents meant by what they said. The timing, however, provides a clue to what they saw around them when they said it. Approval figures in the poll results change almost every month. Minor variations and wild swings in narrow time-spans need be treated with reserve. But large and relatively lasting changes come at the same times as great events with widespread consequences. These major changes illustrate what threatens popularity.

Two of the largest changes ever traced by Gallup Polls came at the start of 1951 and in the spring of 1958. All through 1950 Truman's conduct was approved by a sample of his countrymen in proportions varying from 46 to 37 per cent.[9] (His first-term "low" had been 32 per cent in 1946.) After 1950 through the balance of his term, approval fluctuated in a range of 32 to 23 per cent.[10] For almost a year following the 1956 election, approval of Eisenhower's conduct ranged above 62 per cent; at the time of his inauguration it touched 79 per cent. (His first-term "low" had been 57 per cent in 1954.) In 1958, however, approval fell to 49 per cent in one month, April, and only once, in August, rose as high as 58 per cent; most of the year it moved within the narrow range of 52 to 56 per cent.[11] In 1959 a rise began that brought approval up one point a month to 62 per cent in June, the last figure available at this writing.[12] Assuming a continuation of the trend, Eisenhower's instance, unlike Truman's, will end with a recovery of range.

In looking at these figures, one can and probably should ignore the variations month by month; what cannot be ignored is the sharp shift of range. Such shifts do not disclose whose views were changed, in what direction, when. These figures may hide crosscurrents; they certainly hide regional differentials. But assuming an adequate sample, or at least a constant error, when Truman shifted from the "forties" to the "twenties," when Eisenhower shifted from the "sixties" to the "fifties," and when the figures stabilized for many months thereafter, public standing certainly had changed. And what must have contributed to changing it is not hard to discover.

In both these cases popular approval tumbled at a time when governmental action (or inaction) was associated with extraordinary disturbance in the private lives of millions of Americans.

What happened between 1957 and 1958? "Prosperity" gave way to recession *and* inflation; "peace" gave way to an intensified cold war, with troops in Lebanon and fighting on the China Coast. A sense of social calm gave way before the struggles over school desegregation. "Complacency" in science, education, and defense was shaken, at the least, by outcries after sputnik. What happened between 1950 and 1951? Above all else, inflation and taxation and lost lives in "Truman's War," which had become interminable war with the Chinese.[13]

It scarcely is an accident that Truman's popularity, according to the polls, was never lower than in 1951. It scarcely is an accident that polls show Eisenhower more unpopular in 1958 than ever before or since. Such happenings as these are bound to threaten or upset the private prospects of great numbers of Americans. As these prospects are seen to change, the outlook on the Presidency cannot help but change. That marvelous rummage bag sometimes called our "belief system" is crammed with alternate and contradictory images of office ready for instant use. Eisenhower, once so satisfying as a "man above the struggle," apparently collided during 1958 with yearnings for a President who made his presence *felt*.[14] Truman, on the other hand, while very much in evidence some seven years before, seems to have run afoul of the twin notions that a wartime Chief Executive ought to be "above politics" and that he ought to help the generals "win." As private prospects are upset, men change their expectations of the President. As images of office change, appraisals of performance change to suit. It is no wonder that "approval" dropped in 1951 and 1958. Nor is it any wonder that there seemed to be recovery in 1959 but not in 1952.

This is not to suggest that members of the public act like Washingtonians, attending and reacting to a President at every stage of all proceedings. One never should underestimate the public's power to ignore, to acquiesce, and to forget, especially when the proceedings seem incalculable or remote from private life. Unless the shooting starts a Lebanon may be remote, a Berlin seems incalculable, sputniks overhead become routine. But paychecks, grocery bills, children's schooling, sons at war are quite distinctly matters of real life. No happenings in Eisenhower's whole first term brought him more public credit, it appears, than the truce in Korea and the "spirit of Geneva." Apparently, no happening in 1958 bit deeper than the juncture of recession with inflation.[15] One doubts, for instance, that the indiscretion of a Sherman Adams would have mattered much to voters (as the White House clearly thought it did) save for its symbolism at a time when "life" was not as advertised.[16] In 1951 there is no reason to suppose that lacking the hard, unexpected stretch-out in Korea either "communism" or "corruption" could have caused such deep frustrations as were evident when MacArthur came home.[17]

Personality is not without effect upon prestige. Impressions of the *man* can be a cushion and a prop. Judged by percentage points in Gallup polls, Eisenhower's lost approval during 1958 was not much less than Truman's after 1950. Still, one was left with better than majority approval and the other with approval half as large. Judged not in terms of figures but in terms of trend, these polls trace somewhat comparable patterns for both Presidents throughout their earlier years. But Truman's variations are much larger and much sharper, with much lower "lows" than Eisenhower's.[18] Such differences display the cushioning and bolstering effects of personality on expectations. Eisenhower was a hero *independent* of his office. Truman was almost unknown apart from it. Personality alone cannot account for variations in each man's prestige, but as between them it left Truman far more vulnerable to the shock of private hopes belied by public happenings. Yet even Eisenhower, hero though he was, turned out to lack immunity. *His* lack, if anyone's, should serve to make the point. The moving factor in prestige is what men outside Washington see happening to *themselves*.

A President concerned to guard prestige must keep his eye on hopes and on what happens to those hopes in "life" as lived outside the Washington community. He need beware lest the outsiders look to him for pleasures he cannot provide, or lack preparedness for the pains he cannot stop. Either way, what threatens his prestige is popular frustration. "We will merchandise the hell out of the Eisenhower program," C. D. Jackson is supposed to have remarked in 1953. But "merchandising" only has its uses while events remain incalculable. Salesmanship cannot compete with "life." Merchandising is no match for history. A President who values power naturally will want his history productive of a "good" response to him; he naturally will want to minimize the "bad" reactions. But wanting these results, what can *he* do about them? How, if at all, can *he* affect the hopes and happenings that generate frustration?

III

If a President were free to control happenings, to turn them on or off at his discretion, this would be the ideal way to safeguard his prestige. But he has no such freedom. The illustrations in preceding chapters make that plain. Outside the Federal government, events in which he plays no part set off what his constituents will see and feel as happenings. Inside the government courts, congressmen, executive officials act in ways that will contribute to or symbolize such happenings. They often act without recourse to him. The President is no mere spectator. His action also will contribute to and may become the highlight of what happens. What happened in Korea? Truman intervened. What happened when the war dragged on? He sent MacArthur home. But action of this sort is a far cry from control. No President can make most of what happens in his time occur or stop to suit his popularity. Had Truman held the option, Korea never would have been a happening at all.

Because he cannot control happenings, a President must do his best with hopes. His prestige is secure while men outside of Washington accept the hard conditions in their lives, or anyway do not blame him. If he can make them think the hardship necessary, and can make them want to bear it with good grace, his prestige may not suffer when they feel it. Had Truman's public thought interminable warfare-within-limits a necessity his prestige would have risen, not declined, in 1951. A President concerned for leeway inside government must try to shape the thoughts

of men outside. If he would be effective as a guardian of public
standing, he must be effective as a teacher to the public. Truman
was an unsuccessful teacher in the midst of the Korean war. Some
of his troubles will be traced in Chapter 6.

What kind of teaching job is this? It is no classroom exercise.
Presidential teaching is instruction of a very different sort. It has
at least four special features. First, it is instruction aimed at
students who, by definition, are habitually inattentive to the
teacher: his constituents *outside* the Washington community.
These students only grow attentive when they notice public
trouble pressing on their lives. Second, as a consequence, he can
expect attention from them only when the things he need interpret
to his benefit are on their minds for reasons independent of his
telling. Third, again in consequence, he teaches less by telling than
by doing (or not doing) in the context that his students have
established in their minds. And fourth, what he has previously
said and done will figure in that context. When the man inside
the White House gains attention outside Washington, he finds two
other teachers at his podium. Events themselves are there; so are
the memories of his past performance. Under these conditions,
presidential teaching is a formidable job. It is not to be confused
with advertising.

The correspondence between popularity and happenings, as
illustrated in "approval" polls, is matched by correspondence between popular attention and events. Let me illustrate this second
correspondence with some radio program ratings in pretelevision
years, when virtually all presidential broadcasts were rated by a
single commercial source.[19]

From October 1945 (with the war over) through March 1948
(with electioneering not begun) there were eight occasions when
Truman pre-empted *all* radio networks at an evening hour to take
policy issues "to the country"; his subjects ranged from price
inflation, welfare programs, strikes, to the Marshall Plan, and the
Czech *coup d'état*. For those performances his Hooper ratings—
estimating actual against potential auditors in homes—were successively 43.8, 49.4, 34.4, 31.8, 57.6, 30.7, 34.3, and 31.0 per cent.[20]
Whether accurate or not, the basis for these estimates remained

the same in every case; this sequence is internally consistent. The shifts in size of audience on these occasions are due, in part, to time of year and choice of date or hour; listening habits, like more recent viewing habits, change with seasons, days, and times.[21] But factors of this sort are insufficient to explain the sharp peak in the middle of the sequence, the 57.6 per cent that breaks the trend. And what was the occasion for that peak in Truman's audience? His subject was surrender on the price control of meat. He was announcing decontrol in the beef-hungry autumn of 1946, amidst the political campaign that terminated three weeks later in election of the 80th Congress.[22] Only once in his first term did Truman have a higher Hooper rating: 64.1 per cent when he proclaimed V-E Day, shortly after his accession. Only six times during F.D.R.'s third term was *his* rating higher for a comparable evening address; all six came in a seventeen-month period, from May of 1941 to November, 1942.[23] As an audience attraction, meat in 1946 ranks next to the Second World War.

When a President goes on the air the number of his listeners is obviously influenced by what Americans have on *their* minds. It also may be influenced by their sense of his relevance. When Truman vetoed the Taft-Hartley Act in 1947, his explanatory radio address received a rating of only 30.7 per cent. It may be that the issue—union "power," labor "slavery"—mattered to fewer people than had "meat" the year before. Or, possibly, as many people cared, but fewer thought *his* explanation mattered. Decontrolling prices had been taken as a pledge of more supplies and he had the authority to decontrol. But vetoing Taft-Hartley offered no relief from strikes and Congress had the votes to override. At any rate the context of his address and its relevance to their concerns, as understood by radio-owning publics, presumably accounts for a great part of his lost listeners on that occasion— and of those gained on others.

In the early 1950's, the shift from radio to television "listening" casts doubt upon the meaning, in these terms, of ratings for both media. Not until 1956 did "television homes" start to compare in number and in distribution with their radio equivalents a decade earlier. As yet one cannot draw from Eisenhower's television ratings an internally consistent series on the order of those furnished by the older radio ratings.[24] But there is nothing in the scattered data now obtainable to controvert the Truman illustration just presented.

If a President's ability to gain a hearing voice-to-ear is so conditioned by "what happens," these same conditioners no doubt affect the prospect that his words will penetrate through news reports, opinion leaders, neighbors, and the like, to those who have not seen or heard (or anyway, not listened) for themselves. Without a real-life happening to hoist it into view, a piece of presidential news, much like the man's own voice, is likely to be lost amidst the noises and distractions of the day. Local news aside, most daily news reports in print or on the air are geared to wire service coverage and tempo; White House stories, classed with foreign news, are lumped together into factual and unaccented highlights of the day's events from everywhere, *that* day. The weekly magazines of "news" tend to blend commentary with reporting and summation in a mix so well homogenized that everything is equally accented and its impact uniformly predigested. As for word-of-mouth reports at third hand, or at fourth, the principle appears to be the same: events provide the emphasis required for attention.

A President is not in firm control of most events, but there are some that he can manufacture. He must depend on happenings for popular attention; with skill and luck he sometimes makes a happening. He then can ride it to a widened audience. Toward the close of 1953, six weeks of press build-up fed by meticulously staged White House and Cabinet actions, heralded the Eisenhower legislative program for 1954, his first since taking office.[25] By these means, apparently, his making of a program was established as momentous in the nation's life; his address to the country just before its presentation brought him an enormous television audience.[26] This surely was an instance of a self-made happening, and only one of several during Eisenhower's first term. Unfortunately, Presidents can rarely count for long on press cooperation of the sort available to Eisenhower in his early years. And often they will find what they contrive cast into shadow by outside events. Had the first bout of tension over Quemoy and Matsu come in the fall of 1953, instead of a year later, one doubts that the White House could have focused wide attention on its preparation of a *legislative* program. No matter how cooperative the press, a President needs quiet from competitive events if what he does is to be noticed as a happening.

Not only do outside events compete with self-made happenings, a President is frequently in competition with himself. That master of the art of mass communication, Franklin Roosevelt, once wrote an old associate:

> I know . . . you will be sympathetic to the point of view that the public psychology and, for that matter, individual psychology, cannot, because of human weakness, be attuned for long periods of time to a constant repetition of the highest note in the scale . . . . Whereas in this country there is a free and sensational press, people tire of seeing the same name, day after day, in the important head-lines of the papers, and the same voice, night after night, over the radio . . . . if I had tried [in 1935] to keep up the pace of 1933 and 1934, the inevitable histrionics of the new actors, Long and Coughlin and Johnson, would have turned the eyes of the audience away from the main drama itself . . . .[27]

However, in most years since the Second World War, there has been no "main" drama like recovery-with-Roosevelt. Instead there have been half a dozen shows on stage at once, all running simultaneously and interminably and repetitively, act after act, with Presidents assigned a leading role in each, and everything relentlessly translated into headlines. Under mid-century conditions, prospects for the self-made happening secure from competition are not good.

Events determine audience attention for a President; they also make his actions more important than his words. When constituents grow conscious of his relevance to them they are already learning—from events. By then his telling will convey no lessons independent of the things he seems to do within the context of events. When Truman told of decontrolling meat, the act conveyed a meaning that the words, the look, the tone of voice could but embroider, not obliterate. Of course, the very telling is an action, and the words that linger in men's minds can have enormous educative influence. "We have nothing to fear but fear itself," said F.D.R. on March 4, 1933; the teaching he began with those eight words was as extraordinary as his chance, that day, to dwarf all other actors on the nation's stage. Still, what he said then conjured up a prospect not a meaning. It became a lesson learned when what he did thereafter and what happened in men's lives appeared to vindicate the confidence he had expressed. Had there not been the Hundred Days, and work relief, and a degree of real recovery, the lesson of those words would have been bitter for the country and his phrase would be remembered now with mockery not cheers.

What Roosevelt taught in 1933 was governed only by the future. He had no presidential past, nor had the nation a remembered precedent for the dark time when he took office. But for Presidents in other circumstances, talk and action may take meaning from "last time" as well as next, and teaching thus is placed in double jeopardy.

Let me illustrate the jeopardy of Presidents as teachers with an instance drawn from the domestic side of the Korean War. At the start of the Second World War civilian shortages had appeared just as buying power rose, but price inflation was suppressed for the duration by direct controls. When sharp price rises came after the war one antidote proposed by the White House was authority to reimpose controls. In 1947 and in 1948 Truman lost no opportunity to urge that course on an unwilling Congress. Yet when Korea came, and when he went to Congress for the funds and taxes to finance rearmament, he asked for war controls over production but *not* for price controls. By that act of omission Truman tried to stress what made the present different from the past. Economists had told him that rearmament need not cut deep into civilian output. The Speaker of the House informed him (wrongly) that without the old, divisive price issue his other control measures would pass Congress in a week. And Truman was concerned, as well, lest friends or enemies abroad take a request for powers over prices as his forecast of an all-out war. He tried, therefore, by what he did, and by his statements as he did it, to convey the lesson that he was *not* playing politics; that this was *not* the start of the Third World War, that fighting did *not* promise short supplies and price controls.[28]

What followed? Through July and August, 1950, prices rose precipitously in response to panic buying spurred by memories of 1942 and by the wide belief that government had no real remedy but price controls. Truman had not asked for them, but Congress gave him the discretion (and the onus) to impose them anyway. Only with September's great successes in the war did there come signs that buying publics might believe what Truman meant to teach. MacArthur's triumph, not surprisingly, was much the better teacher. But when the Chinese intervened—initially in late October, then with crushing force in late November—buying spurted once again and prices rose alarmingly. The Administration, caught unprepared, promised a general price freeze. The freeze, however, was not actually ordered until late January 1951. Thereafter, that year and the next, when Truman tried to rally public sentiment for strong controls he failed of much response.

A President's instruction is affected by his own performance both before and after. What Truman tried to teach in July 1950 was overborne by recollections of things past. What happened next taught an entirely different lesson than the one he had intended to convey. His own words and actions played a part in both these outcomes. His own doings contributed to public education of the sort he did not want. His past and future did not make him any less a teacher; they made him teach the opposite of what he meant to teach. That is the jeopardy of presidential teaching.

The President-as-teacher has a hard and risky job. If he wants to guard his popular approval he must give real-life experience a meaning that will foster tolerance for him. But happenings create his opportunities to teach. He has to ride events to gain attention. Most members of his public grow attentive only as they grow concerned with what may happen in their lives. When they become attentive they will learn from what he does. And whether his own doings teach the lesson he intends depends on what he did before and on what happens next *as understood by them*. These are the terms and conditions of employment for the President who seeks to be a teacher in our time. It is not a scholar's job—or Madison Avenue's.

IV

Half a century ago, with Theodore Roosevelt still in office, Woodrow Wilson wrote that "more and more" the White House would be occupied by "men . . . of the sort of action that makes for enlightenment." [29] His prediction as to men can be debated; his description of their task cannot. At least, if his successors are concerned for their own power and would guard its every source, his formula describes what they must do. The enemy of their prestige is unreality: the groundless hopes, the unexpected happenings, the unaccepted outcomes that members of their public feel in daily life and relate, somehow, anyhow, to That Man in the White House. From such an enemy there can be no defense save better understanding on the public's part. And for the reasons I have now set forth, such light as Presidents can shed consists of meanings they convey by what they do. "Action making for enlightenment" is but effective teaching. Only as they teach effectively will they ward off the threats to their prestige. I have asked how men in office can protect that valuable commodity from lasting harm. The answer will be found in Wilson's formula.

The formula is sound enough; it ought to be engraved over the White House door. Yet there is no enlightenment in meanings given to the day's events that arouse hopes tomorrow cannot meet, or yesterday belies. And Presidents, no more than other men, can gauge the future with exactitude; far less than most can they expunge their past. Illuminating action is their only sure escape from the backlash of public inability to grasp or to accept what happens next. In the circumstances of mid-century, however, few things can be harder to accomplish. Truman's difficulties over price control were but one aspect of his greater difficulty in imparting a "good" meaning, from his point of view, to the Korean War. This was as hard a task as ever faced a President and one to which we will return in the next chapter. Nine years earlier Roosevelt's urgent educative problem was resolved to his entire satisfaction by the Japanese attack upon Pearl Harbor. His own sense of relief, that Sunday afternoon, is testimony both to the dimensions of the problem and to limits on what he himself could do.[30] In 1941 and 1950 there was no sustained crisis consensus in this country. There has been none since 1945. Without consensus everything conspires to complicate action and to dim illumination. So Wilson himself found in that year foreshadowing mid-century, 1919.

Although the outlook for enlightenment is cloudy, the means are clear. Our question has been how a President, himself, protects prospective leeway inside government by guarding his own prospects for approval outside Washington. The answer brings us to his choices once again. His prestige turns on what the members of his public think they want and think they get. He affects their thoughts by what he does. His choices of what he will do and when and how—his choices, also, of whom he will tell and in what way and words—are *his* means to protect this source of influence, just as they are his means to guard those other power sources: bargaining relationships and professional reputation. No more than in the instance of those others is a President at liberty to make prestige his sole criterion for choice. No more than in the case of the Washington community is what *he* does the sole determinant of public sentiment. But whether his choice-making actually is usable and whether it proves useful or does not, the fact remains that for the human being in the White House choices are the only means in his own hands by which to shield his sources of real power, prestige no less than the rest.

Beyond the reach of his self-executing orders, then, a President's own prospects for effective influence are regulated (in so far as he controls them) by his choices of objectives, and of timing, and of instruments, and by his choice of choices to avoid. Thus we now reach the question: what helps him guard his power stakes in his own acts of choice? Granting that his choices are his means to protect power, granting that these are imperfect means, how can he make the most of them? For the length of two chapters this question has been dangling in mid-air. Now we can deal with it.

Two Matters of Choice . 6

In January 1957 the Secretary of the Treasury, George M. Humphrey, warned of a "depression that will curl your hair" and called for cuts in Eisenhower's budget on the very day the budget went to Congress. The repercussions of this outburst are described in Chapter 4. The net result, as we have seen, was harm to Eisenhower's reputation and relationships in Washington. But colorful remarks were not the only cause of harm; Humphrey's status did more damage than his bluntness. His warning and his hope were voiced to members of the press immediately after he had read a formal statement on the budget. He then appeared to be a spokesman for the President. As Eisenhower told his own press conference a week later:

> Now, in the first place, you will recall there was a memorandum that was the basis of that [Humphrey's] discussion, a written memorandum, and that written memorandum I not only went over every word of it, I edited it and it expresses my convictions very thoroughly.[1]

Not only had the President approved the Treasury statement, he had authorized its presentation to the press on Budget Day. That statement on that day would have harmed Eisenhower even if there had been no harsh comments off-the-cuff. For the statement implied what the comments dramatized: that the President's spokesman had qualms about the President's budget. Eisenhower chose to put his Secretary of the Treasury before the press with such a statement on such a day; in choosing so he jeopardized his influence. The question now before us is how any President protects his stakes of influence when he makes choices. Eisenhower's failure to protect himself in Humphrey's case illuminates the question. A study of this instance starts us toward an answer.

To understand why Eisenhower made the choice he did, it is useful to begin by noting how he did it. Early in January 1957 the President engaged in a last, long discussion of the budget with his Cabinet. This was a post mortem, in effect, since dollar figures had been set and the document had gone to press. The narrow Cabinet room beside the Rose Garden was packed, on this occasion, as almost always during Eisenhower's time. (His Cabinet meetings customarily contained more White House and staff-agency officials than department heads.) By all accounts, the crowd was rather glum. Whatever was thought privately of items in particular, no one who spoke, the President included, showed any pleasure over budget totals. When Humphrey read a statement voicing his concern about tax implications of the spending trends in budgeted programs, no one demurred. When he suggested that he issue such a statement to the press, nobody disagreed; discussion turned, instead, to the best means for doing so. Initially, the Secretary had proposed that he should write a public letter to the President. Eisenhower, among others, thought a press conference preferable and approved that procedure on the spot, agreeing at the same time to review a final text.[2] Budget Director Brundage is said to have remarked that Humphrey need be careful lest the press insert a wedge between him and the President. Humphrey, reportedly, was vigorous in his assent that nothing of the sort should be allowed to happen. Other heads were nodded, the President's among them; on that amicable note discussion closed.

Considering what happened when the Secretary met the press, it may seem strange that nothing more was made of Brundage's remark. Treasury views about the budget were no secret in the Cabinet room. When Humphrey told the press "there are a lot of places in this budget that can be cut," he said no more in public than he often had said privately. Humphrey, reportedly, had fought both loud and long against a budget of the size submitted by the President. For two months past his opposition had been "bitter," "scathing," "vehement," "intense" (the terms in which it was described to me by various participants). This man was primed for an explosion and Eisenhower knew that when he chose him as a spokesman. But Eisenhower also knew, or thought, that Humphrey would restrain himself. As one White House advisor told me:

> Charlie Wilson would have been another story, but George had an *excellent* record of conducting himself with discretion, staying within bounds. He always had been brilliantly effective on the Hill. He never had got into trouble testifying there or talking to the press . . . and since he never had, nobody thought he would.

This may not have been the sole cause of seeming unconcern around the Cabinet table. Many inhibitions work on men in crowded gatherings of peers (and super-peers) and palace guards. Brundage, for one, was poorly placed to press his point of view in open meeting, no matter what he might have thought of Humphrey. But regardless of the reasoning of others, the President himself appears to have been satisfied by Humphrey's reputation for discretion.

Although Eisenhower was unworried lest his Secretary's private anger show itself in cautioning the public, his assurance on this point leaves unexplained why he should have assisted *anyone* to speak for him on Budget Day in terms that called his budget into question. Humphrey's "memorandum" was free of nasty words, but it amounted to a warning that our economic progress called for tax relief and tax relief depended on new standards of restraint in federal spending. As the *New York Times* reported:

> In a prepared statement Mr. Humphrey set the following conditions for a future tax cut:
> Restraint by Congress in appropriating funds beyond budget requests; efforts at savings by every Federal department and agency; planning for further reductions in government employment and spending . . . .
> He emphasized his hope that spending in the next fiscal year would be less, through government economy efforts, than the estimated total of $71.8 billion dollars. In each of the last two years, however, spending had surpassed the original estimates.[3]

Contrast this with the emphasis of Eisenhower's Budget Message:

> . . . the Budget must also reflect the general responsibilities of a Government which will be serving 172 million people . . . . In the face of continuing threats to world peace, our collective security must be strengthened . . . . Progress toward greater equality of opportunity for all of our people as well as toward a balanced development and conservation of our natural resources must go forward. . . .
>
> It is my firm belief that tax rates are still too high . . . . However, the reduction in tax rates must give way, under present circumstances, to the cost of meeting our urgent national responsibilities.[4]

If tax reductions "must give way," why have Humphrey apologize? If "urgent national responsibilities" were now at stake, why have him emphasize how much they hurt? If Eisenhower was preparing to accentuate the positive, why send Humphrey to do the opposite? Or, putting it the other way, if Humphrey on the President's behalf urged "planning for further reductions," why have budget estimates include new programs, new commitments, sure to swell expenditure in future years?

Eisenhower's Message struck a different note than Humphrey's text; a look at budget items makes the difference seem the greater. The President was asking more funds for the Pentagon, and for atomic energy, for housing, and for public health, and public works. He was projecting an increase in foreign economic aid. His current school-aid scheme involved a whole new category of expenditure, and he was urging half a dozen other new commitments in domestic welfare spheres. On information programs overseas, where Cohn and Schine once romped, he was proposing to bestow both larger sums and Arthur Larsen. Yet having raised this monument to "Modern Republicanism," Eisenhower chose that Humphrey should preside at its unveiling. The Treasury press conference took place at the hour that the Budget Message formally reached Congress, in time to share most headlines with the budget itself. And not only was Humphrey's text at hand, his timing seems to have been understood when Eisenhower told him to proceed. Why, then, tell him to do so? Above all else, why have both statements made at the same time on the same day?

No matter how discreet the Secretary might have been, this curious procedure risked the power of the President. What was Eisenhower's risk in Humphrey's statement? Let me digress to answer that before I turn to why the risk was run. A budget presentation is among the cardinal services the President-as-clerk performs for Congressmen and bureaucrats and lobbyists, alike. Without it they would be hard put to do their jobs. Its money estimates and legislative program are the nearest things available to an agenda for their struggle over scope and shape of government. By fixing the position of a chief participant, it gives the rest a reference point in judging their own interests, risks, and tactics. As a device for organizing struggle and for giving strugglers something to respond to or react against, this agenda is perhaps the biggest labor-saver known to Washington. In the degree to which it saves their labor, those who use it are dependent on the President who makes it. In the degree to which his own endorsement helps or hurts their causes, they depend upon his choice of what to ask. In the degree that they may gain protection or publicity by helping (or opposing) him, they depend on his asking. As always, *their* dependence means some leverage for *him*. His clerkship may be onerous, but services like these yield bargaining advantages to him. However, the advantage in this instance turns upon one working premise: that the presidential budget is the President's; that what he says he wants will be supported, within reason, by his "powers" and his influence so long as it is asked. Unless this premise works in practice nobody is served, there is no labor saved, dependence vanishes, the leverage is lost. And Humphrey's statement as approved and timed was bound to call this premise into question.

To cast doubt on this premise would be risky for a President in any year, but never more so than in 1957. For Eisenhower then was at the outset of a four-year term with Congress in the opposition from the start, for the first time since 1849. He was certain not to run again, thanks to the Twenty-second Amendment. His party, patently, was not in shape to substitute for his own popularity. The outcome of the 1956 election guaranteed that politicians of both parties, interest groups of all descriptions, members of the press corps would be specially alert for signs of Eisenhower's response to his "lame duck" status and his party's plight. Here was a novel, central challenge to his influence, a challenge highly advertised in Washington. How did he mean to meet it? Naturally, his postelection budget would be searched for clues. The risks of Humphrey's statement rose accordingly. That statement preached what Eisenhower's budget failed to practice. To sponsor such a statement would make Eisenhower seem a man who had turned heat upon himself. Inevitably, Washingtonians would wonder why. He might be thought the victim of an inadvertence, or naiveté, or ignorance, or sabotage, or clumsy execution of some devious design. He even might be thought the man he was, a man in doubt about his own direction. Eisenhower's choice was bound to put such thoughts into the minds of agency officials fresh from "firm" agreements with the Budget Bureau, and of congressmen awaiting "firm" proposals to react to, and of commentators seeking portents for the second term. Some damage to his reputation and his trading stock in Washington was almost certain from the moment he said "go ahead" to Humphrey.

The prospect, naturally, was for less damage, more easily repaired, than actually became the case when Humphrey failed to show restraint. But there was never likelihood that Eisenhower could escape scot-free if Humphrey's press conference received publicity commensurate with White House sanction and its timing. Inattention would have spared the President embarrassment, but headlines were encouraged by the course he chose. The folkways of Washington assured him trouble in proportion to attention gained. How much attention, how much trouble, Humphrey and the press corps would decide. Eisenhower left it up to them. Among the risks he ran, his delegation, in effect, of that decision was the greatest. Humphrey had *carte blanche* to magnify the rest.

Given the risks why make the choice? Why choose to put the Secretary of the Treasury before the press with such a text on Budget Day? This is the question to which I would now return. Abstractly, one might suppose the answer lay in judging these risks less than risks of other sorts, on conscious calculation of all aspects of the case. Actually, the answer seems to be that power in these personal terms was not assessed at all; not anyway by Eisenhower as he made his choice. He certainly had many things in mind—among them power factors of some sorts—but safeguarding his personal position seems not to have been one of them. He was preoccupied, reportedly, by matters of a rather different order. The key to his behavior is the glumness in the Cabinet Room. When he heard Humphrey's statement read, the President was deep in second-thoughts about his budget. Most of what he heard from others added to his doubts. He "bought" that statement, basically, because he was in doubt. His doubts obscured his risks.

Eisenhower's doubts revolved around the budget's size and trend. Its spending total bothered him. Program commitments mortgaging the future bothered him still more. In 1956 he had sent down a 69 billion-dollar budget; now the total would be nearly 72 billion dollars. Brundage's projections showed that even without price rises and even though there were no further growth of public services, the cost of Federal programs *now* established or approved might outrun 80 billion dollars before Eisenhower left the White House. (New weapons systems, among other things, made that a likely prospect.) Prices, moreover, had been rising for months past; their rate of climb appeared to be accelerating; the current boom was taking an inflationary turn. And Congress, still controlled by Democrats, could not be counted on to keep commitments down to size as specified in Republican budgets. Brundage's projections looked conservative.

Seen thus, in terms of totals and of trend, the pending budget seemed to belie almost everything that Eisenhower personally believed in and was told concerning the requirements of proper fiscal policy. On economic grounds not only orthodox Republicans but the more "modern" men around him (with differences regarding "what" and "when") were anxious to see Federal spending stabilize on some plateau so that tax revenues enlarging with the growth of the economy could furnish surpluses to check inflation, cut the public debt, and bring nearer the day of tax reduction. On grounds of party politics the President did not

lack for advisers who thought this a very practical necessity; pro-
long the combination of high taxes with inflation and the party in
the White House would be punished at the polls. The reasoning,
both economic and political, was scarcely a Republican invention;
seven years earlier, in pre-Korean days, Truman had held military
spending down for roughly comparable reasons.[5] But numbers
of Republicans saw an ideological corollary which had not troubled
Truman. Appealing for economy and tax relief some thirty years
before, a President of the United States had stated:

> We are testing out the success of self-government . . . . We re-
> quire no property qualifications for voters . . . it has too often
> been found that democratic institutions tend to confiscate property
> to such an extent that economic progress becomes impossible. . . .
> This is the test which America must meet and meet constantly and
> unless it is met successfully, the strength, progress and prosperity
> of our country will cease.[6]

So Calvin Coolidge put it, and his words, I gather, would have
evoked warm response from Eisenhower's Secretary of the Treasury.

On any of these grounds, or on them all, the logical response to
Brundage's projections was an effort to check spending at its
source, the statutory mandates which invoked it. As Eisenhower
was to tell the press, quite rightly, in March 1957: "If you are
going to save . . . money you have got to look at programs . . .
think of what programs you want to eliminate."[7] Without cuts
in the program base, mere budgeting could have but marginal effect
in cutting budgets. Curb spending at its source, however, and if
not this budget then the next, or the one after, might show major
savings in the cost of present programs and make room for new
necessities (like military hardware) without overall increases in
expenditures. Here ran the path to a plateau. This was the reasoning, implicitly, of Humphrey's formal statement to the press, and
quite explicitly of his explosive comments off-the-cuff. This was
the course that he had urged upon the budget-makers. Ironically,
it was the course the President himself would espouse just a year
later, and the year after that. But in January 1957 it was not the
course—or rationale—of Eisenhower's budget. The whole "mod-

ern" Republican appearance of that budget was a consequence of choices which inclined the other way. There lay the difficulty, and the doubts.

The President had acted in good faith when he approved the items that enlarged his budget. Individually, all these were things he then thought proper for the country and in keeping with the tenor of his fall campaign. Each item had its share of departmental advocates, its grounds of public policy, its political claims for his support. In sanctioning more spending and new programs, case by case, he had not lacked for signs of Treasury displeasure. Nor had he lacked for data on the trend of his approvals. All through budget season, from late August 1956, the Budget Bureau's "target" for expenditures had been near 71 billion dollars, a figure corresponding to the current rate of spending plus 2 billion dollars for defense. Because increases for other programs pushed above that target, trial balances had gone to Eisenhower with each major estimate for his approval. Although it grew plain, before December, that he would exceed the target by a billion, this was not a great departure, overall, from prior plans. The budget would be balanced still; some surplus would remain; the total rise in spending would be less than increased revenues from economic growth; compared to the economy, expenditures still would be lower than they had been when he first took office. From the start of budget planning, little more had been expected by the planners or, so far as they knew, by the President. With reassurances like these his Budget Message, as they drafted it, and as he sent it, was to minimize the consequences of more spending.

But this had been a budget planned in *1956*. Those "targets" had been set in a convention summer full of promise—and of promises —when prices, it was hoped, would level off and Congress, it was thought, would go Republican. Those estimates had come before the President while he campaigned for re-election or presided over conferences on Hungary and Suez. Whatever Eisenhower may have felt about the budget in September, or October, or November, it is clear that when he looked at final totals in December he did not like what he saw. And neither did assorted White House aides who only then became sharply aware of what impended; their concern heightened his own. Humphrey's warnings now were voiced in chorus.

As always happens in election years, a number of the President's associates who normally would play an active part in budget season had been concerned with other things before December. Budget totals came to them as something of a shock, suggestive of a Budget Bureau fumble while their backs were turned. Reportedly, the President, himself, was not immune to those sensations when he turned from his campaigning and from crises overseas to face the final choices on his budget. However that may be, some members of his circle were decidedly affected by the sense that Budget bureaucrats had let them down.

There remained men around the President whose ideology and preferences were echoed by the Budget Message, not by Humphrey. But with inflation threatening and Congress Democratic, few of them, reportedly, were ready to defend the tactics of so high a budget total. The whole Administration now would be aligned with every congressman and lobbyist who wanted more from government; how could they be held to 72 billion? With spenders on the march, where were the troops to counter them? The President would be in the parade. "We have to create countervailing power," a White House aide would tell me later, rationalizing February's budget-cutting drive, "the military thing will go right through the roof unless there's enough public heat on Congress for economy." But while Eisenhower's theme was confident expansion, how could his Administration rouse and guide that "countervailing power?" These were the sorts of questions that hung, unanswered, in the Cabinet Room at the turn of the year. Even the men who liked the budget as it was were willing to concede a general problem. Even its major beneficiaries confined themselves, for the most part, to guarding their own bailiwicks. The views of the more "orthodox" among them squared with Humphrey's on all points except particulars. Even the most "modern" of department heads were disinclined to argue abstract principles with him. (Their reticence, reportedly, bore some relation to the fact that at preceding meetings there had been no more articulate defender of the budget than the man whose kiss was death in this Administration, Harold Stassen.[8])

As for Eisenhower, personally, let me quote the private recollections of a man much in his confidence who was not at the Cabinet meeting but saw him before and after:

> Pressure to freeze the budget [in time] for [deadlines set by] the Government Printing Office meant that ideological differences and programmatic ones were dangling *unresolved* and the President was left feeling "one more week, one more day to work this over could have made it better, tighter, smaller." That was the frame of mind he carried into Cabinet meeting . . . .

There, in this context, the Secretary of the Treasury advanced his proposition and the President accepted it, forthwith.

II

When Eisenhower made that choice, not even witnesses agree which of the arguments and circumstances sketched above affected him the most. Precisely what he hoped to gain remains uncertain. At the very least, presumably, he meant to ease his conscience, to conciliate a faction, and to please a trusted counselor; at the most, perhaps, he meant to take a step toward "countervailing power." By all accounts, however, something else is plain enough: so far as words and manner show, he made his choice without a thought of what he stood to lose. How could he have done otherwise? A President can only think about the things he is aware of. His awareness can come only from the face the issue turns to him, or from the words of others, or from promptings in his mind. On this occasion, all three sources evidently failed him.

The issue wore a face which featured 72 billion dollars, upward trend, inflationary pressure, Democratic Congress, Republican discomfiture—and Humphrey's reputation for discretion. The latter's proposition showed no flaws upon its surface; neither substantively nor procedurally did its terms proclaim what Eisenhower risked by its endorsement.

The words of others told him no more than the issue did. Few means of consultation were less likely to point up his risks than Cabinet meetings of the Eisenhower sort, especially a meeting timed as this one was and in the given context.[9] Quite apart from inhibitions native to such gatherings, it is an open question whether those who might have argued were aware, themselves, of reasons for resisting Humphrey's course. At most, no one but Eisenhower would look foolish; disproportions between departmental risks and his were great. Except perhaps for Brundage it does not appear that any Cabinet member saw much trouble for himself in carefully phrased cautions from the Treasury (and some, no doubt, saw positive advantage). Without qualms on their own account it is by no means certain that they thought to fear for Eisenhower or, at any rate, to voice concern to him while he showed none. As for Brundage, it suffices to record that after Humphrey's unforeseen explosion his advice was tendered to the President through White House aides; this was no man to urge, unasked, that Humphrey should be stopped before he started.

Which left it up to Eisenhower, and his state of mind was calculated to obscure, not clarify, the risks he ran as President. For these were risks in personal terms, risks to his personal power, risks to his reputation and relationships in Washington's community. But Eisenhower was not thinking in these terms. He saw himself, apparently, as one man in a group with a collective reputation, conscious of a common problem, trying to resolve it, trapped by time. In this perspective Humphrey was his friend and annual budgeting the cause of his entrapment. That Secretaries of Departments *also* are "a President's natural enemies," that "clerical" endeavors like the budget *also* are a source of White House influence, Eisenhower's outlook evidently blurred beyond recognition. In power terms the one thing he most needed to remember was that budgeting brings Presidents advantage. In his circumstances, understandably enough, this seems to have been one thing he forgot. The clarifying question in those terms was, "how may Humphrey's presentation make mine (and me) look when I have endorsed both?" That question Eisenhower had to ask himself since no one else was asking. I find no indication it occured to him. Why should it have? He viewed *his* presentation with distaste, and trusted Humphrey.

This does not mean that power was no object when the President approved a press show at the Treasury, but merely that he laid hold of the wrong end of the stick. Some of his aides were to discourse on "countervailing power"; something of the sort was very likely in his mind. Yet in the circumstances, this would not be power he could wield or could control himself. His Secretary's move might boost the bargaining position of respectable Republicans in Congress and the country, but not Eisenhower's own; not when it would seem aimed, with his connivance, at "his" program. Unquestionably power did flow from that press conference as it turned out in practice; accidently (or on purpose?) Humphrey gained a lot, but not for Eisenhower. And the relative gains and losses would have been the same, though probably far smaller in amount, had Humphrey bit his tongue and stuck to text.

The distinction between one man's power and another's may be fine, but it is crucial. Eisenhower missed it and because he did, his own choice worked against, not for, his influence. I began by asking why make such a choice; here lies the answer, and the answer points a moral: *Influence adheres to those who sense what it is made of.*

If choices are a President's own means to guard his power, he is likelier to hurt than to help himself unless he knows what power is and sees its shape in what he does. Before power can be served, it must be seen. That certainly ranks high among the lessons of this case. Had Eisenhower realized he was courting real embarrassment, presumably he would have answered "no" or "wait" when Humphrey urged a statement to the press. What makes this case so useful as an illustration is precisely the simplicity and ease of such an option. Nothing but lack of realization barred the way to a "stop-order" of a self-executing sort. (The President's approval, after all, was what enlarged his risk.)

It does not follow that because a risk is seen, a President can choose in its terms only. Almost always there will be competing risks in other terms of power, or of policy. When problems stem from substance, personalities, outside events, the choices they impose upon a President have numerous dimensions, each involving risks of different sort. If Eisenhower saw a need in policy and politics for "countervailing power" against spenders, he was duty-bound to further it by every means he could. Saying "no" to Humphrey hardly satisfies. But had Eisenhower thought to answer so, the very sense behind that thought would have alerted him to some alternatives. Humphrey's press show certainly was not the only way to approach "countervaillance" in this situation. To quote again the informant last quoted:

> Sure, there was a need for the President to appear decisive, knowing about everything, knowing all the answers, defending every penny of his budget—it's ridiculous, but that's the way government works . . . . And then he could have turned around and amended it equally forcefully!

So he could. He also could have picked a fight with Congress on some "raid upon the Treasury" that overran his budget. Many variations are conceivable. It was not written in the book of fate that he must burn himself in order to light fires for economy.

Issues may arise, and do, where none of the alternatives appears less risky than the course at hand. But even so, to see the risk one takes is to be cautioned for the future. In the circumstances of the case it can be argued, for example, that once Humphrey had exploded, Eisenhower risked more by a show of irritation than by speaking softly, as he did. But full awareness of the risks he ran in doing so should have sufficed to warn him away from a subsequent, gratuitous display of indecisiveness in public. The whole handling of February's budget-cutting drive showed precious little feel for what I have called "pattern-setting." Had Eisenhower grasped his danger at the start that feel would have been stronger, and among his later choices several, certainly, allowed him scope to use it. There may be arguments, in power terms, for softness toward one's Secretary of the Treasury gone wrong, but none for equal softness toward a taunting resolution by the House of Representatives which asked, with tongue in cheek, where it should cut the budget.[10]

If not as the determinant "right now" then as the means of opening alternatives and posting caution signs "next time," a President's perception of his power stakes (and sources) in each act of choice conditions every chance to make his saying and his doing serve his influence. What choices are to power, these perceptions are to choice: the means in his own hands. To ask how he can guard his power stakes in acts of choice is thus to ask how clearly he perceives. To ask how he can help himself to power is to ask how he can sharpen his perceptions. The question now becomes what helps him see?

The Humphrey story would suggest that nobody and nothing helps a President to see save as he helps himself; that neither issues nor advisers as they reach him are a substitute for sensitivity to power on his part. It follows that in answering this question one must look to his resources for self-help. To ask what helps him see is really to inquire what he can do for himself. That follows from this case, but does it always follow? My own response is "Yes." An incident like Eisenhower's "go ahead" to Humphrey is distinctly *not* unique in this regard. What it suggests applies to every case of which I am aware.[11] The indication of them all is that no man who sits where Eisenhower sat can count on reading his own risks upon the face of issues brought before him; none is safe in counting on subordinates to remedy the lack. Outcomes may be happier by far than in this case; the likelihoods are not.

To demonstrate the point, and test it, let me turn from Humphrey's statement to some choices of a very different sort, involving different policies and personalities, a different order of importance and a different set of risks. These are the choices underlying alteration of American objectives in the third month of the Korean War and leading to the end-the-war offensive that was turned into a rout by Chinese intervention two months later. This new example shifts the scene from 1957 to 1950, from Eisenhower to Truman, from quasi-peace to limited war, from fiscal policy to foreign policy and military tactics. It returns us to the cast of characters encountered in MacArthur's firing (which followed five months after); it affords a context as unlike the Humphrey case as I can find—the better to distinguish common ground.

On its surface, this new case is far more complex than the last, involving choices made not at one moment but by stages. That is why the Humphrey story was put first. Because of its complexity this second story must be told in rather more detail. But I would hope the editorial difference leads no one to believe that I see Truman's problem of self-help as differing *essentially* from Eisenhower's just discussed. Essentially, they seem to me the same.

III

On October 7, 1950 the General Assembly of the United Nations, "recalling that the essential objective was the establishment of a unified independent and democratic Korea," recommended that "all appropriate steps be taken to assure stability" throughout the country, North as well as South. That same day the first non-Korean units of MacArthur's forces crossed the thirty-eighth parallel in pursuit of the enemy so nearly (but not quite) entrapped by the end-run of Inchon three weeks earlier.[12] The General Assembly's words sanctioned this military move, of course, but they did more; they set the "war aim" of the member governments whose troops were under MacArthur's command: a unified, noncommunist Korea. This aim had long been a secondary objective of American foreign policy, pursued by peaceful means. It now became the policy objective of the war. Thus "victory" was now defined for the armed forces and the public of the United States, which never yet—as every school child knew—had failed to "win" a "War."

Three months before, when North Korean armies had invaded South Korea, a less ambitious aim had been envisaged by the authors of American intervention.[13] As Truman, in his *Memoirs*, paraphrases National Security Council minutes of June 29, 1950:

> I stated categorically that . . . I wanted to take every step necessary to push the North Koreans back behind the 38th parallel. But I wanted to be sure that we did not become so deeply committed in Korea that we could not take care of such other situations as might develop.
> . . . I wanted it clearly understood that our operations were designed to restore peace there and to restore the border.[14]

The United Nations Resolution of June 27, which both justified and authorized those operations, was drafted in the American State Department. It recommended "such assistance to the Republic of Korea as may be necessary to repel the armed attack and to restore international peace and security in the area." The last phrase was ambiguous, but its inclusion in the draft cannot be said to have reflected any conscious purpose at top departmental levels different from that stated by the President. And in the early weeks of fighting, as our forces were committed and pushed back to the Pusan perimeter, nothing he or Cabinet members said in public contravened the emphasis of his remarks just quoted.

The United Nations resolution of October 7 thus embodied and expressed a real shift in the foreign policy objective of hostilities, a shift made possible by transformation of the military situation in the last half of September, after Inchon. The new policy objective was no less a war aim of Americans for being an expression of the General Assembly. The United States was in the war as UN agent. In form, not Washington but UN Headquarters at Lake Success was properly the source of such objectives. In fact, the General Assembly's words on this occasion were of Washington's selection. Reportedly, the Secretary of State, Dean Acheson, chose most of them himself. At any rate, the State Department's draft of what became the UN resolution had his personal approval, and the President's. Truman knew its terms before it was proposed at Lake Success. Despite its UN form, the resolution was American in roughly the degree that UN aid to South Korea was American, that is to say in all essentials. Many other governments concurred, of course, the British chief among them. Despite a popular impression to the contrary, this shift of policy objectives was no Washington *diktat*. But the decision was a Washington decision; in that he assented, it was Truman's. Thereby he took a personal risk of such proportions as to make Eisenhower's risk in Humphrey's instance trifling by comparison.

What was Truman's risk? Let me begin by mentioning what it was not. In and of itself, announcement of the new war aim did not *create* a military risk. To be sure, military risks were run by the troop movements that accompanied the announcement (other risks were avoided by abandoning that very poor defense line, the thirty-eighth parallel). But the decision to attempt destruction of the North Korean forces on home grounds preceded the decision on what war aim to announce. The same thing can be said of diplomatic risks. No allies were estranged *by the announcement* of a new war aim. As for potential enemies, it is improbable that their intentions were affected one way or the other. To judge from what the Chinese said, and later did, Peking's concern was with MacArthur's military progress, never mind its foreign policy objective. Chinese concern was not confined to anything so simple as a buffer zone along the border; an entity called North Korea, not the border, was the stake (perhaps in roughly the same sense that South Korea, under reverse circumstances, was for Washington). Even had the UN promised restoration of an independent North once all resistance ceased—which, naturally, no one proposed—I know of nothing to suggest that Peking would have withheld intervention. The communist world does not take kindly, it appears, to the dismantling of a member state's facilities for governance: the party and the army. MacArthur's military progress threatened both, no matter what came after. In short, the military risks and diplomatic dangers usually associated with MacArthur's march across the parallel existed independent of the words used in the UN resolution. MacArthur's march was authorized before the words were seen, much less approved, at Lake Success.

Truman's risk when the UN anounced its new war aim was of another sort. The risk was to his own prospective influence in every facet of his work as President. His risk was not the same as Eisenhower's in the Humphrey case. It did not bear directly on his Washington relationships or reputation. What he endangered, rather, was that other power source, his prestige with his public outside Washington. In the terms of Chapter 5, what Truman risked was leeway. He gambled with his own ability to get done many things far more important to him than the unification of Korea. His risk was that worst risk for Presidents in public: the teaching of a lesson that rebounds against himself, the rousing of expectancies in conflict with his policies, the risk of action making for confusion not enlightenment. "Korea," as a series of events, was bound to be a foremost "happening" in public consciousness, arousing hopes and fears which could not but affect the look of Truman and his policies. In the degree he needed leeway to accomplish what he wanted, he depended on the lessons that this happening would teach. In the degree he needed national attention, he depended on the focus it provided. Only as Korea could be made to point *his* moral could he foster acquiescence in his regime and his aims. Only by his actions could he influence its teaching. Yet that UN resolution risked imparting to "what happened" the least fortunate of meanings from his point of view: the meaning his opponents compressed into two words, "Truman's War," the bloodletting "he" started, would not "win," and could not stop.

Had the unification of Korea been Truman's dearest object, its announcement as a war aim would have been another matter. But it was among the least of the objectives on his mind. In July and August 1950, in December after Chinese intervention, in his struggles with MacArthur, and thereafter through his last two years of office, his behavior leaves no doubt about the many things he wanted more than that. He wanted to affirm that the UN was not a League of Nations, that aggression would be met with counter-force, that "police actions" were well worth their cost, that the "lesson of the 1930's" had been learned. He wanted to avoid "the wrong war, in the wrong place, at the wrong time," as General Bradley put it—and any "War," if possible. He wanted NATO strengthened fast, both militarily and psychologically. He wanted the United States rearmed without inflation, and prepared, thereafter, to sustain a level of expenditure for military forces and for foreign aid far higher than had seemed achievable before Korea. He also wanted to get on with the Fair Deal, keep Democrats in office, strengthen his congressional support from North and West, and calm the waters stirred by men like Senator McCarthy.

None of these aims *required* unification of Korea (however helpful at sufficiently low cost), and all of them took precedence with Truman. One need but read the "minutes" from Wake Island, where he met MacArthur on October 15, to sense Truman's relative disinterest in Korea save as a symbol of UN success and as a source of seasoned troops for Europe. One need but read between the lines of his address at San Francisco, two days later, to recall that war or no war he retained the hopes for November's congressional election which had brought him "whistle-stopping" West in May, before the war began.[15]

Indeed, Korean unity was so low in Truman's order of priorities that it was off his list within three months of its adoption. It went off London's list on first sight of the Chinese in Korea; Truman was somewhat slower, to his cost. But once the Chinese demonstrated that a widespread war in Asia and a risk of World War III would be the lowest price for unification, he showed firm unwillingness to pay it. By December 1950, as the enemy poured south, his object became merely to hang on. By February 1951, with the lines stabilized and an advance in prospect, he reverted to his aim at the beginning of the war: a restoration of the border and cessation of hostilities. By March, he was preparing to dismiss MacArthur. By June, with the Chinese in full retreat (and with NATO Commander Eisenhower in full cry for troops), Truman was prepared to make a truce on the first strong defense line north of the thirty-eighth parallel, and to dismiss as "real estate"—not his term but the Pentagon's—the territory stretching to the next line north of that, the "waist" of the peninsula where London unsuccessfully had urged a halt some seven months before.

If Truman thus retreated from the war aim of October 1950, rather than pay cash for it in coin of other policies, he did so with the full support of Washington advisers, military, diplomatic, and political alike. And their retreat in chorus was a decorous performance next to the stampede at the UN. Within eight weeks the resolution of October 7 had not only dropped from sight but out of mind and, save for twinges of regret and of embarrassment, seems to have figured further in the thoughts of few, indeed, at Lake Success.

Unfortunately, the new war aim was not so easily expunged from public consciousness in the United States, or from the mind of the commander in the field, General MacArthur. What for Washington and Lake Success was but a passing fancy, taken and abandoned as the war news changed, MacArthur seems to have regarded as the only proper outcome of hostilities, at least of those in which *he* was engaged (scarcely an unreasonable notion for the man who had accepted the surrender of Japan). He had not forced this war aim on his government, but very willingly became its instrument with no sign of the mental reservations hedging its choice by his superiors. When they abandoned it, the consequences of that difference grew severe indeed, and I have dealt with some of them in Chapter 2. But even in the weeks before the great Chinese attack, while Truman and MacArthur proclaimed a common aim, the difference in intensity of feeling for that aim contributed to the impending tactical disaster.

Long after the event I once asked Mr. Truman if he had not grown concerned while UN troops, dividing as they went, moved toward their fatal "end-the-war" offensive. His answer, though a retrospective one, reflects, I think, the essence of his viewpoint at the time:

> What we should have done is stop at the neck of Korea right here [pointing to a globe] . . . . That's what the British wanted . . . . We knew the Chinese had close to a million men on the border and all that. . . . But [MacArthur] was commander in the field. You pick your man, you've got to back him up. That's the only way a military organization can work. I got the best advice I could and the man on the spot said this was the thing to do. . . . So I agreed. That was my decision—no matter what hindsight shows.

This raises a nice question about how to get advice and whose to take—a question I will leave for the next chapter—but what requires emphasis just now is that a "man on the spot" no more committed to the terms of "victory" than Truman proved to be would have been much less likely to take military risks of such proportions as MacArthur did. The Pentagon's discomfort as his isolated columns moved to north and east is most suggestive on the point.

Thus by choosing unification as a war aim the President not only tied Korea's meaning and his prestige to an easy occupation of the North, but he also added something to the likelihood that he would have no benefits to show by way of substitute. The halting of MacArthur short of "victory" might have been troublesome enough, once victory had been defined as unification. Instead, because that was its definition, Truman let MacArthur risk and lose the tangible advantages of ground and of diplomacy gained from five months of fighting. The lessons that Korea taught might not have been as pleasant with a stalemate at the "waist" as with a victory. The actual outcome made those lessons sad, indeed, for Truman and his causes—the sadder since his war aim meant so little in his scheme of things.

These are the terms in which to measure Truman's power risk when he endorsed his State Department's words for the UN. The many things he wanted more than North Korea's conquest called for leeway from his public. To foster public tolerance of him and his aims he needed object lessons that would demonstrate the worth of what he wanted. To make Korea's teaching turn on unification was to risk the opposite result. Korea was the teacher at the center of the stage. To reach and teach his public any President must ride events; he teaches by his doing in the context of events; he teaches as his actions attach meaning to "what happens." The publicizing of a new war aim invited Truman's "students" to attach "wrong" meaning in precisely the degree it should turn costly of accomplishment. Truman gave MacArthur, of all people, the initiative in calculating costs. MacArthur is the Humphrey of this case. The greatest risk that Truman ran lay in MacArthur's capability to magnify all other risks.

However, these were not the terms in which the issue came to Truman. The clarifying questions would have been: What should the outcome of this war convey to men outside the Washington community? How may this war aim color what they came to see and feel? Few Presidents, presumably, much less their State Departments, would formulate such questions so precisely; to do so puts an instinct into words. The formulation, though, is not in point. What matters is that nothing of the sort, however stated or implied, seems to have reached the President. Instead, the issue of a new war aim wore the disguise of military choices; the risks that showed themselves were military risks. The danger in the issue was political, but this was not apparent on its face or in the words of Truman's chief advisers.

How did Truman come to choose a new war aim? The question

can be answered only by a chronological account. The story starts in August 1950. In early August after some hesitation, not without some doubts, the President and the Joint Chiefs of Staff approved MacArthur's daring plan to crush the North Koreans: a landing at Inchon, behind them, simultaneous with an offensive at their front on the Pusan perimeter. The date then set (and met) was September 15; as it approached, MacArthur was supremely confident; the White House and the Pentagon were not. But it was clear to Washington that if MacArthur should succeed, even in part, the war would be transformed and he would need some new directives. "What next?" was put to the Departments of State and Defense, and their response eventually became a National Security Council paper, initialled by Truman on September 11. His paraphrase of its conclusion will suggest the hopes and fears—and the uncertainties—involved in the discussions that preceded his approval:

> General MacArthur was to conduct . . . military operations either to force the North Koreans behind the 38th parallel or to destroy their forces [south of it]. If there was no *indication or threat of entry of Soviet or Chinese Communist elements in force* . . . [he] was to extend his operations north of the parallel and to make plans for the occupation of North Korea . . . . no ground operations were to take place north of the parallel in the event of Soviet or Chinese Communist entry. [Italics added.] [16]

The first part of the foregoing was turned into a directive for quick dispatch to MacArthur; the balance was left to await allied consultations and the outcome of Inchon.

MacArthur's purpose, as reported to the Pentagon in August, was destruction of the North Korean forces before they could get behind their border. This he did not manage, as the National Security Council discussions had foreseen he might not do. With this exception (a momentous one), his Inchon operation was a triumph, transforming not the war alone but the emotions felt in Washington and Lake Success. Appetites rose as the troops went forward. On September 26 the UN army from the south made contact with the units from Inchon. On September 28 Seoul was finally liberated. On October 1 some South Korean units crossed the parallel without much opposition.

The North Koreans, though, had crossed ahead of them. The communist troops were battered, disorganized, but still a force in being. And from no quarter did there come the faintest sign that they were ready to surrender or even to negotiate. On September 21, Senator Knowland of California, gave it as his opinion that to leave them in that state behind the parallel would be "appeasement." For once his views were shared by the Administration and by friendly governments. The border, at the parallel, had proved its insufficiency as a defense line. To break off when it was reached was to invite a new attack across it, when and as the North Koreans chose. Short of pursuing and destroying their field forces, there seemed no effective way to meet that threat. No one around the President proposed to live with it.

Within a week of Inchon all Truman's advisers were agreed upon pursuit, if nothing else turned up to simplify (or complicate) the problem militarily. In consequence, and after some amount of inter-allied consultation, the Defense and State Departments urged and he approved a second missive to MacArthur; approval seems to have been given on or about September 24; the directive was dispatched September 27. To quote from Truman's *Memoirs:*

> . . . [MacArthur] was told that his military objective was "the destruction of the North Korean Armed Forces." In attaining this objective he was authorized to conduct military operations north of the 38th parallel . . . provided that at the time of such operation there had been no entry into North Korea by major Soviet or Chinese Communist forces, no announcement of an intended entry, *and no threat by Russian or Chinese Communists to counter our operations militarily . . . .* [Italics added.] [17]

Had Truman (and his Chiefs of Staff) been fully confident of Inchon from the first, or had a measure of success not come so fast thereafter, forethought might have counseled hedging the military objective for MacArthur even further than was done in this second directive. (Within two days of its dispatch he had submitted and gained approval for a plan committing him to moves beyond the waist of the peninsula.) But flat refusal to attempt *some* military exploitation of his sudden, great advantage was not to be expected, in the circumstances, from governments with troops engaged; from Washington and London and the rest it certainly was not forthcoming. There is no evidence that any of the governments with forces under his command were in the least reluctant to pursue the North Koreans.[18]

Strictly speaking, the decision to pursue the North Koreans did not call for UN action; strictly speaking, its approval was already on the books. Destruction of the enemy's armed forces, whether on home grounds or not, was well within the terms of that vague, early-summer phrase: "the restoration of peace and security in the area." But in practice Truman's chief advisers, and the President himself, seem to have taken as a matter of course the need for something more from Lake Success, once it had been decided that MacArthur should go north. In theory Washington might have authority, but the fine print of prior resolutions had been little publicized. Before Inchon, repelling the aggression had meant getting North Koreans out of South Korea in the emphasis of news dispatches generally. Although the Administration might conceive "what next" in terms of how to liquidate the enemy, the press and congressmen and certain UN delegates now posed the issue publicly in terms of the thirty-eighth parallel. To cross or not to cross might seem irrelevant inside the Pentagon and State, but most insiders were aware that on the outside it was being called *the* question.

From the President on down, responsible officials wanted to avoid a look of "going it alone," or putting something over, or relying on fine print, especially when such a look was undeserved. In the circumstances some specific UN sanction seemed to follow logically from the dispatch of new orders to MacArthur. "That is a matter for the UN to decide," said Truman on September 21, when queried at press conference about crossing the parallel; thereafter, UN action was not only logical, it had to happen.[19]

Besides, no one in Washington was now disposed to doubt MacArthur's power to make daring pay. Once he was ordered north it was assumed that he would go there in a hurry. So he did—by October 10 the east coast was in his hands up to Wonsan, just below the waist of the peninsula; on the west, Pyongyang, the North Korean capital, was taken October 19; before the month was out he would control the whole peninsula, and with it the great bulk of North Korea's population ("mainland" Korea to the north and east was mostly barren ground). Foreseeing this in late September both State and Pentagon thought UN guidelines indispensable for occupation of a territory that did not belong to Syngman Rhee. The South Koreans claimed their government, by rights, embraced the North. This belied the UN's declaration of intent, dating from 1947, that a united government should stem from free elections. The issue had been academic for three years; now it would be joined within three weeks, and with it other issues, reconstruction and the like, which went beyond American authority as UN military agent. Psychology aside, these seemed reason enough for something new from Lake Success.

What that something should be does not seem to have taken a great deal of time or long attention from the President's advisers, to say nothing of the President. The desired General Assembly resolution was formally presented by eight UN delegations, *not* including the United States, on the last day of September.[20] Initial drafting must have been completed well before the Joint Chiefs of Staff dispatched their new directive to MacArthur. In line with the instructions given him, what Washington proposed through friends at Lake Success contained no mention of the parallel—Assembly action, in itself, would settle that—and phrased policy objectives briefly and obliquely (quoted on p. 123). The cautions to MacArthur about Russians and Chinese might not embody likelihoods; it was not thought they did. But just in case, there were to be no highly charged, unbreakably committing words upon the record. Instead, the resolution was devoted, mainly, to machinery or intentions for political and economic reconstruction of the country. What I have called a new war aim was conveyed less by the specific words than by the clear assumption underlying all the words: that military action would produce a unified, noncommunist Korea.[21]

Except from UN delegates in Moscow's sphere there was little disposition at Lake Success to argue against prompt endorsement of what Washington proposed. Only the Indians strongly urged delay. Their suggestion was put forward in the interest of a further search for some way to negotiate (which they themselves were not sure how to find). Only the Yugoslavs distinguished sharply between military tactics and policy objectives, while decrying shifts in both. But Tito's delegation, which had chosen to abstain three months before, could not claim much attention from the friends of South Korea. At any rate, the partners in the fighting were agreed, most other delegations willing, votes available, and Washington committed to its own proposal. On October 4 the resolution passed the Political Committee; three days later it went through the General Assembly by a vote of 47 to 5 with 7 abstentions.[22]

It will be clear from this account what face that outcome and its preparations showed to Truman: a tying up of loose ends in his choice of a new target for the troops, a choice which merely set their prior target on new ground. It also will be clear what sort of word he had from his advisers in the circle of the National Security Council and on the day he saw the drafted UN resolution. If other words were heard from other sources, as of course they may have been, they left no traces I can find. In all events, with Acheson and the Joint Chiefs agreed, it is unlikely that he would have listened very hard. Of course, he read five newspapers; no doubt he saw expression of concern about the UN's move. But what the press conveyed were pros and cons couched mostly in the language of a crossing of the parallel. That emphasis, itself, had a significance and held a warning for him. But the language was so academic, from where Truman sat, as to dilute his interest and divert attention. I have no doubt it did. From where he sat the crossing of the parallel had already "occurred," and for good reason, on the day *he* chose to send MacArthur north, two weeks (or more) before the vote at Lake Success.

One difficulty with the press as an adviser to a President is that he has enough to crowd his calendar and mind without attending closely to debate on prospects which for him are past (unless, of course, a trial balloon is up; this was no trial balloon). Not even readers of the *New York Times*—not even its columnists—move in precisely the same time-dimension as the man who sits where Truman did in the days after Inchon.

Had something tangible occurred during those days to emphasize the diplomatic risks of moving north, one can assume that Truman's advisers would have changed their tune, the State Department, Pentagon, and press alike. But unless one took as tangible the casual word of Chinese generals or the phrasing of a Peking speech—which no one in authority inclined to do—nothing of the sort developed in the interval between Inchon and the last stages of UN proceedings.[23] Not until the first week of October did there come the sort of threat presumably envisaged in September's two directives to MacArthur. Then it came from such a source, in such a way, as to invite discounting by Americans.

On October 3 the Indian ambassador to mainland China, K. M. Panikkar, advised his government—which passed the word abroad —that Chou En-lai, the Chinese Foreign Minister, had told him:

> . . . if the United Nations forces crossed the 38th parallel China would send in troops to help the North Koreans. However, this action would not be taken if only South Koreans crossed the 38th parallel.

I quote the paraphrase in Truman's *Memoirs*, where he also sets forth, faithfully, the gist of the appraisal he received from his advisers:

> . . . the problem . . . was that Mr. Panikkar had in the past played the game of the Chinese Communists . . . . It might . . . be no more than a relay of Communist propaganda. There was also then pending in . . . the General Assembly . . . a clear authorization for the United Nations commander to operate in North Korea. The key vote on the resolution was due the following day, and it appeared quite likely that Chou En-lai's "message" was a bald attempt to blackmail the United Nations . . . .[24]

Besides, since the directives to MacArthur, Moscow not Peking had been the Pentagon's great worry. Now that the UN was on the march, an intervention by Chinese, alone, seemed relatively easy to withstand and *therefore* most unlikely to occur (an interesting exercise in logic). "They have no air," as Truman was to be told, wrongly, at Wake Island; further comfort was derived from the reflection that their ground attack had not come when it could have been decisive, near Pusan. In Washington no less than at MacArthur's headquarters there was some lack of readiness "to take seriously a country which up until this time had been notorious for its political and military weakness." [25]

Even had Peking appeared more formidable, more in earnest, less a mere blackmailer; even had the British, say, not Panikkar, been chosen to transmit Chou's threat, it is improbable that Truman's chief advisers would have counseled abandoning MacArthur's broad advance or putting off the General Assembly action. It is equally improbable that Truman would have accepted such advice if offered. A threat of intervention *in Korea* could but stress the military need for rapid movement north; only there would troops find strong defense lines. And by that late date, October 3, the UN's pending action had become identified in press accounts as the "clear authorization" Truman later called it. By that time, to proceed without it would have caused immense embarrassment both at home and abroad. Not to proceed at all would have meant overturning every tactical consideration and diplomatic assumption on which policy had rested for three weeks with no more reason than a verbal warning, given second-hand, and such evaluation as could be obtained in one or two days after its receipt. Before Chou's warning, Truman's power risk was called to his attention neither by the terms of what he was deciding nor by what he learned from his associates. When the warning came, he scarcely could have chosen *not* to take the risk, no matter how aware he might have been.

This chronological account explains why Truman acted as he did in making unification the aim of the Korean War. He chose his aim because it seemed to follow from the military movement at virtually no diplomatic risk. With the military opportunity before them and with diplomatic dangers out of sight, the men he leaned on for advice saw little risk of any sort. There is nothing in the record to suggest that he saw more than they did. In June it had been clear to him that restoration of the border was worth fighting for. In August when he sanctioned plans for Inchon he evidently saw no need to take an early stand on what should happen if the enemy escaped destruction south of the border. When the contingency arose, he met it in the way that then appeared most opportune. Chou's warning challenged the perspective of the moment, but the warning was too suspect and arrived too late to affect choices taken ten days earlier. The President incurred his power risk without seeing it, or at least without assessing it, when he made the choices put to him in August and September.

Having incurred the risk before Chou's warning came, why make it worse thereafter? The question arises because Truman spent October adding to his power risk with every choice he made. The new war aim had been announced by the UN in cautious words; Truman promptly and repeatedly restated it himself without equivocation. MacArthur's northward march had been approved with qualifications; Truman promptly waived the major qualification. The President's own course throughout October heightened every danger of "wrong" meaning for Korea if there should be some substance in Chou's warning. And it cannot be said that an alternative approach was urged on Truman by his circle of advisers. Unhappily for him he chose as they advised.

The President's own choices in October consisted of words addressed to MacArthur and of other words addressed to public audiences. On October 8, the second day of general advance past the parallel, Truman approved new instructions to MacArthur in the words proposed by the Joint Chiefs of Staff and endorsed by General Marshall, now the Secretary of Defense, with Acheson's concurrence:[26]

In light of the possible intervention of Chinese Communist forces in North Korea the following amplification of our directive [of September 25] is forwarded for your guidance:

"Hereafter in the event of open or covert employment anywhere in Korea of major Chinese Communist units, without prior announcement, you should *continue the action as long as, in your judgment, action by forces now under your control offers a reasonable chance of success.*" [Italics added.][27]

"Success" as thus unqualified could not now be expected to mean anything but enemy destruction for the sake of unification. "Reasonable" now was delegated to the judgment of MacArthur with no other qualifier than a limit on his forces. In the weeks to come he would misjudge with tragic consequences, but it cannot be charged that he exceeded his instructions. Nothing said by anybody at Wake Island on October 15 qualified this delegation to MacArthur; indeed, it was confirmed by the prevailing atmosphere of confidence in him. Nothing said in public on the President's return diluted the commitment to a unified Korea. Rather the Wake Island communique, the San Francisco speech, a presidential address to the UN (at its birthday celebration on October 24), all added weight and definiteness to the war aim, publicized it further, promised its achievement cheap, and made it Truman's own. The discretion given to MacArthur in October contributed directly to disaster in November. When disaster came, the White House bore the brunt of popular frustration with the consequences of MacArthur's judgment. Truman's public statements of October contributed to this result.

Why was the President so optimistic in October? His optimism was the product, mainly, of MacArthur's confident assurance at Wake Island. The General had told Truman flatly (as the latter recollects their private conversation), "that if any Chinese were to enter Korea they would face certain disaster, but he did not expect them to try anything that foolish." [28] The President had this to match against Washington estimates that Peking *could* mount an effective intervention but probably *would* do no more than covertly assist the North Koreans. Intervention of the sort suggested by Chou's warning was discounted on all grounds of logic (Washington's) as buttressed by some diplomatic inquiries in other capitals (including Taipei, naturally, but not, of course, Peking). These estimates were scarcely worrisome; they were made less so by the General's reassurance. For Truman and his speech writers MacArthur's word sufficed—and so it seems to have done for the others at Wake Island, the Chairman of the Joint Chiefs of Staff, the State Department's Ambassador-at-Large, the Secretary of the Army, and assorted lesser lights.

Chou's warning of October 3 thus faded out of sight, and everything looked as it had before: a military victory assuring in its train a gratifying policy objective. Perhaps it is more accurate to say that the look of things by mid-October was not as it had been, it was more so. Victory was closer, the war aim was embraced in public by the President, and privately in government Korean unification grew weightier each day. In White House memoranda and in papers for the National Security Council, in intelligence evaluations, and the like, repeated use of such terms as "the UN objective," "the decision of the UN," "the UN's purpose to unify," soon dulled awareness that the new war aim was nothing but a target of opportunity chosen rather casually (and at first provisionally) by the very men who read these words. The tendency of bureaucratic language to create in private the same images presented to the public never should be underrated. By the middle of October, I would say, in their minds no less than in public, Truman and the rest were thinking of the UN aim not as a mere convenience but as a cause.

When Truman spoke at San Francisco and at Lake Success he had no inkling that the Chinese had begun a massive, hidden move across the Yalu. Two weeks after Wake Island some five Chinese armies were established in the mountainous terrain directly north of the peninsula. Reinforced, by stealth, for four weeks more, that striking force was almost to destroy MacArthur. Even before November 1 it made a mockery of his existing orders. We know that now, but Truman did not know it then. The location of the Chinese striking force remained unknown to the Americans until it struck, November 28.

Truman did learn early in November that the war would not end on the pleasant note his government had sounded. Two weeks after his address at the UN he knew the outcome could not be successful in the way he had defined success. By late October Chinese presence in Korea was confirmed from contacts on the battlefield. In the first week of November MacArthur insisted upon bombing Yalu bridges because troops "pouring" south threatened "ultimate destruction of the [UN] forces . . . ." [29] Before November 10, Truman's advisers had informed him, in

effect, that military action limited to present forces, confined
to Korea, could not achieve the military target set September 27:
destruction of the enemy's armed forces. Everyone agreed that
no more troops could be spared for MacArthur and that he should
not enlarge the boundaries of the war. But he now faced a new
enemy with airpower and troops massed north of the Yalu and
with several tens of thousand men already south of it. So Washington believed when UN aircraft were employed against the Yalu
bridges. Washington was wrong about proportions north and
south, but it was no secret that the river probably would be a
bridge of ice before MacArthur could complete his occupation
of North Korea. At the least, negotiation would be necessary to
that occupation; necessary to its maintenance and probably to its
achievement. At the most, if Peking meant the worst, unification
would no longer be a viable objective; Chinese *capabilities* were
not in doubt.

Thus within a month of MacArthur's march past the thirty-
eighth parallel, it became plain that the policy objective, the war
aim, once supposed to follow from the military action, now could
only follow from a diplomatic deal with the unrecognized, avowedly hostile claimants to Formosa—or be given up entirely. That
these were the alternatives of policy, and that there were no others
short of risking general war, was clear from the intelligence available to Washington in the first week of November. As Truman's
Memoirs show, the policy dilemma was implicitly *accepted* by
all parties to a National Security Council discussion on November 9. The President was not among the parties on that day.
He got a briefing afterwards, however, and acceded to the views
he heard expressed. Truman has recorded Acheson's summation
of those views:

> . . . [Acheson] pointed out that it was agreed that General Mac-
> Arthur's directive should not now be changed and *he should be free
> to do what he could in a military way*, but without bombing Man-
> churia. At the same time, the State Department would seek ways to
> find out whether negotiations with the Chinese Communists were
> possible, although one problem was that we lacked any direct con-
> tacts with the Peiping regime . . . . [Italics added.] [30]

In other words, MacArthur's opportunity, once the *occasion* for a new war aim, now was reduced to "doing what he could" in aid of diplomatic efforts no less dubious than those urged by the Indians six weeks earlier. So far as this had the discussion wandered from assumptions—and from preconditions—voiced in mid-September.

With Washington's assumptions changed, why were MacArthur's orders left unaltered? Why was he still to pursue the objective of September 27 with the discretion of October 8? Why was the man whom Truman had considered firing in August now left the discretion to attempt what Washington no longer thought he could achieve? The National Security Council discussion of November 9 suggests an answer. To quote again from Truman's *Memoirs:*

> General Bradley stated that . . . [if] the Chinese desired only to set up a buffer area . . . negotiations might be fruitful . . . [but if not] . . . *we should be able to hold in the general area of our present positions* . . . [with] . . . increasing question of how much pressure we could stand without attacking Manchurian bases.
> . . . Marshall pointed out . . . that our eastern front in Korea was widely dispersed and thinly spread and that this represented an added risk. . . . Bradley replied that of course General MacArthur had done this in order *to carry out his directive that he was to occupy the whole country and hold elections.*
> . . . Acheson asked . . . if there was any line that was better from a military point of view than the *present* one, and Bradley replied that . . . the farther *back* . . . the easier it would be to maintain . . . . however, he realized that *any backward movement* . . . *might lose us the South Koreans' will to fight.* [Italics added.] [31]

In terms of foreign policy, to halt MacArthur or to pull him back would not have clarified Chinese intentions; neither would it aid the diplomatic bargaining. In military terms to call a halt seemed overcautious, given *policy* objectives and the chance these could be salvaged by diplomacy. In fact there was no chance, but Truman's National Security Council advisers did not know that. Instead, they knew, or rather thought, that Peking very likely wanted only a buffer zone. They reasoned, it appears, that mainland China was dependent on the Russians and that more ambitious wants would mean *Russia* was courting war. As Bradley put it to the National Security Council, Peking's alternative intentions might be either "to force us into a war of attrition . . . where we might be in danger of losing if the Soviets decided to start a global war," or "to drive us completely off the Korean peninsula . . . [which] would mean World War III because [the Chinese] would be unable to do it alone, and Soviet entry would inevitably extend the fighting . . . ." But Moscow, it was thought, did not want general war; the Chinese, then, would have to show restraint.

Why these Americans, who had proclaimed *their own* aversion to world war, should have thought Stalin would assume that *he* risked general war if Peking acted, I will not endeavor to explain. It is enough to see that this is how they reasoned; thereby they discounted what they knew on November 9. Besides, there was the thing they did not know: that Peking's striking force was on the *south* side of the Yalu.

With Chinese aims misunderstood, with Moscow's risks misread, with this one fact unknown, Truman's advisers focused on the diplomatic prospects as intently as they once had done on military opportunities. While they sought to assess the chances for diplomacy, MacArthur should "do what he could." This was the course they urged upon the President after their meeting of November 9. This was the course he followed. The issue as it reached him wore a diplomatic face which fatally obscured the military risk, a reversal, in effect, of late September's situation. But this time, in contrast with the other, the issue's look cannot be said to have obscured the risk to his own influence. On the contrary, its diplomatic features bore a strong family resemblance to those of his prestige. By then United States prestige, UN prestige, were quite as much committed in the world as his at home. By then his problem in relation to his public had become how best to back away from his October promises without harming the many things that made retreat worthwhile. His problem had become how best to make some outcome short of "victory" teach tolerance for him and for his aims. His problem had become how best to *act* in order to *enlighten*. And with but a change of pronoun this conveys his country's problem in relation to its enemies and its allies.

There is no reason to believe that Truman's chief advisers, or the President, himself, considered his prestige apart from issues of diplomacy. Had they done so in these circumstances it is probable that their course would have been much the same. In essence the considerations were alike on either score. Both counseled a postponement of decision. While it was thought that Peking might negotiate, why halt MacArthur before bargaining began? If the Chinese intended otherwise, there was all the more reason for allowing them to demonstrate, so everyone could see, that their aggression, not timidity in Washington, had thwarted the UN and stopped MacArthur. Besides, he had done better at Inchon than his superiors expected; conceivably he might do so again. Thus ran the logic, it appears, beneath the surface of discussion in the National Security Council, a logic quite as good in prestige terms as in those of diplomacy.

This was good logic if Peking's forces were where they were thought to be and if MacArthur's generalship was as infallible as Inchon had suggested. In the fifteen days between November 9 and MacArthur's march into an enemy trap, Washington learned little more of Chinese dispositions. Indeed, their forward elements now broke off contact, which encouraged the opinion that their purpose was defensive and their show of force intended but to emphasize the border. Meanwhile MacArthur, seeming confident again after his scare about the Yalu bridges, hurried preparations for a victory march with scattered forces fanning out to occupy the country. His troops began to move November 25; within three days the Chinese struck, not from beyond the Yalu but from mountains to the south of it, between MacArthur's columns and behind them. What then occurred, in military terms, was "one of the major decisive battles of the present century, followed by the longest retreat in American history." [32] The Chinese did not demonstrate mere power to deny the UN victory; they demonstrated power to deprive MacArthur of his whole success since Inchon—a power his deployment placed into their hands.

It was one thing to leave MacArthur's orders unchanged on

November 9; it was quite another to leave them unchanged day by day thereafter while he prepared and began his victory march. On November 9 the National Security Council had agreed that directives to MacArthur should be "kept under review," pending "clarification" of Peking's intent. In accepting this agreement Truman had postponed a change of orders; he had not intended to decide the issue for all time. Yet this postponement of decision proved to be one of the most decisive actions Truman ever took. So far as I can ascertain his National Security Council advisers did not raise with him, nor he with them, the question of concluding that postponement. In the two-week interval before MacArthur's march the General, not the President, became the judge and arbiter of White House risks. Action in October had heightened Truman's personal risk; inaction in November heightened every danger, military, diplomatic, and personal alike. Why, then, did Truman passively await the outcome of MacArthur's plans for victory? I have explained why orders to the General went unchanged in the second week of November. But why were they not altered in the third week or the fourth?

Poor intelligence, or poor evaluation, may account for Mac-Arthur's conduct, but it does not suffice to explain Washington's behavior in the days before his victory march. Although no one there *knew* where the Chinese were, the Pentagon, at least, included men who could read maps and knew where they *might* be. By mid-November some of these men felt virtually certain of the real Chinese location and were becoming worried lest MacArthur fail to concentrate his forces. Before those forces marched, the worry had touched Truman's chief advisers. In the last days, reportedly, it was intense in Bradley's mind and Marshall's and in Acheson's. The British, whose diplomatic fears had outrun Washington's kept urging that the troops be stopped and forward columns pulled back to the "waist." The American Joint Chiefs of Staff were not prepared to sacrifice MacArthur's plans on London's say-so, but Pentagon unhappiness about those separate columns grew apace, and he was practically implored to show more caution. When he demurred, as under his instructions he had every right to do, the Chiefs of Staff lacked courage (lacking certainty) to seek their alteration from the President. Despite the worry, no one went to Truman—and that outcome turns on matters more complex than poor intelligence.

No one went to Truman because everyone thought someone else should go. Before November 25 the men who had concluded two weeks earlier that Truman should not change MacArthur's orders were agreed, it seems, in wishing that he would. The diplomatic emphasis of earlier discussion ceased to obscure military risks; when those grew sharp enough, it reinforced them. The logic of November 9 led to an opposite conclusion some days later, in the light of what these men had come to fear. On November 9 the Chairman of the Joint Chiefs, Bradley, had waived military risks in deference to foreign policy; his words appear on p. 141. But policy had not envisaged tactical disaster; policy suggested its avoidance at all costs. When worry grew, the military chiefs deferred to State; let Acheson, as guardian of "policy," ask Truman to reverse MacArthur. But Acheson, already under fire from the Capitol, was treading warily between the Pentagon and that inveterate idealist about generals, Harry Truman. In immediate terms the risk was "military"; if it justified reversing the commander in the field, then the Joint Chiefs must make the judgment and tell Truman. So Acheson is said to have insisted, understandably enough, and there the matter rested.[33] On a "military" issue the Chiefs of Staff were loath to balk the victor of Inchon, whose tactics might be better than they seemed 8000 miles away. As for the Secretary of Defense, he had preceded Acheson in State and had been Army Chief of Staff when Bradley was a subordinate commander. Since his return to government Marshall had leaned over backwards not to meddle with the work of his successors in *their* jobs. He also had leaned over backwards not to revive the old Army feud between him and MacArthur. What Acheson and Bradley were not ready to initiate, Marshall evidently felt he could not take upon himself.

For Cabinet members and for military chiefs, a decision to go to the President is something like a government's decision to go to war; it is not something done each day on every issue. When the issue is reversal of established plans on grounds of sheer conjecture, men of prudence and responsibility may pause, and no wonder. In this instance, moreover, the plans were MacArthur's, and Truman was a man who liked to deal in the concrete.

The President, meanwhile, had little thought of overriding, on his own, the tactical decisions of a qualified commander. That seems to be the face the issue wore for Truman, personally, just before the win-the-war offensive: "You pick your man, you've got to back him up. That's the only way a military organization can work." If he perceived the policy and power risks beneath this surface, these were outweighed by fidelity to military doctrine. That weighting his advisers did not urge him to reverse. Instead, they all kept up the search for clarification. They still were seeking it on November 28.[34]

IV

By hindsight it is tragic that MacArthur did not halt along a line on which he might have blunted or withstood attack—tragic in human terms as well as in the worldly terms of policy and politics. But the elements of tragedy were not produced from nowhere in November; they were seeded before Inchon and matured at Wake Island. By November only the precise amount of loss remained in question. By then the answer rested with a government that Washington knew least of any in the world, and with a general Truman had considered firing in August. The essence of the tragedy, though not its outside shape, is that a President should have walked into such a corner facing front; he was not pushed, he chose. September's choices, and October's, took him there.

Truman walked in step with his advisers; on numbers of occasions he could hardly have done otherwise; now and then, however, he might have changed the pace or the direction. In August 1950, when he approved plans for Inchon, Truman might have nailed down publicly his aim of June: a restoration of the South Korean border. If he had done so then, success at Inchon would have achieved "victory" and Truman could have called on the UN to guard the border. In September 1950, after he approved a crossing of the parallel, he might have justified MacArthur's northward march on other grounds than unification. Eight months later, as UN troops were marching north again, their target came to be the first good natural defense line past the border. In October 1950 it might have been the "better" line above the waist of the peninsula. This line was north of the most populous, productive part of North Korea. More realism and less appetite in Washington might have suggested this as victory enough. But Truman did as his advisers urged and tied himself to unification. He tied himself tighter by his statements in October; MacArthur's confidence erased Chou's threat. This is quite understandable but scarcely seems inevitable. And early in November when Washington deferred a change of orders to MacArthur, Truman might have taken steps to let the General know that his directives now meant something rather different than they had been thought to mean when they were issued. In mid-November, a few Pentagon officials talked among themselves about a Marshall visit to Mac-Arthur. Nothing came of this. Something like it—or a new directive—might have cut the costs of Chinese intervention. Truman could have taken the initiative; he did not take it. These might-have-dones are not presented as suggestions of what should have been. Truman, after all, proceeded without benefit of hindsight. These speculations have no other purpose than to demonstrate that he had *some* control of his direction.

This story of choice-making was preceded by another, where a different President in other circumstances also strode face-forward to a corner. By comparison, that Eisenhower instance may appear a "simple" matter, almost comic in its momentary setting and results. But with a longer view it takes on a complexity, even a tragic quality, to match this example from the Korean War. For Humphrey's press explosion was the first of many episodes in a domestic war of interests and of policies foreshadowing the future of our politics. What caused the doubts in Eisenhower's mind were durable dilemmas we shall carry with us through the 1960's. By letting Humphrey speak for him in different words than his, Eisenhower merely publicized the fact that he was forced to seek opposed objectives which had torn the patchwork holding them together through his earlier years: stability *and* growth, defense *and* welfare, funds for public services *and* funds in private hands. At the moment he was re-elected Eisenhower faced the job of reconciling these anew, or of opening the way toward reconciliation by a successor of his choosing. This proved to be a harder job than he was prepared for. Within a year he virtually abandoned it and jettisoned his tentative approach to reconciliation, "Modern Republicanism." Taken alone, his approval of the Humphrey press conference is a minor incident. Perspective dignifies it as a sign of things to come.

Despite their surface differences, my two examples are alike in what they have to show: how *not* to extract power out of choice. The Presidents in both these cases failed to make their choices serve their influence. They failed because they left out of account the stakes for them, in person. They did not reckon their own risks because they saw the issues through the eyes of their advisers. And personal stakes were not the terms in which they got advice. What Eisenhower saw around his Cabinet table in January 1957 was gloom upon the faces of the men he most respected in the spheres of economics and finance and *party* politics. The choice before him featured fiscal policy; accordingly he took those spheres of expertise as relevant, and worried as he watched the experts worrying. What Truman heard in late September and the first weeks of October 1950 was a confident discounting of the military-diplomatic dangers in Korea. The choices then before him wore the guise of military orders backed by diplomatic action; expertise in those two spheres he took to be controlling, and he acted as his experts recommended.

In both these instances the net result was a neglect of the one sphere of expertise where "experts" were laymen: the sphere of personal power for the President himself. It can be said of Truman's instance that the experts went astray on their home grounds; in Eisenhower's case their views diverged. But error or division is to be expected among experts. Amidst the revolutions of our time expert misjudgments are the norm, and experts regularly differ with each other. It also can be said of both these cases that the President, as layman, would not challenge his own experts on *their* grounds. But this should be expected from most Presidents, the more so as the issues grow remote from their experience. In democratic systems—and in modern life—a Winston Churchill is a rarity. The lesson of these cases does not come down to the fact that experts often will be wrong, or to the further fact that Presidents may balk at second-guessing them. Those facts but underscore the perils of neglecting personal power.

The lesson of these cases is that when it comes to power, nobody is expert but the President; if he, too, acts as layman, it goes hard with him.

Expertise in power terms is not a substitute for expertise in policy; it offers some protection, though, from errors and from bafflements in policy appraisal. From those a President needs all the guarding he can get, as the examples of this chapter have made plain. And he, himself, the layman in most areas of policy, has no better protector than concern for his own power. A sense of Truman's power stakes could not have clarified Peking's intent, but what it could have done was shift the weight assigned Chou's threat. A small risk militarily or diplomatically was a big risk in terms of Truman's influence, considering his order of priorities. Once Panikkar's report was seen, if not before, a firm appreciation of the *presidential* risk would have suggested caution, militarily, and moves to qualify, not boost, the new war aim. Similarly, a sense of Eisenhower's personal stakes could not have eased his policy dilemmas, but it could have changed the weight assigned to Humphrey's sense of urgency. The latter might be trustworthy, but why entrust to anyone the blurring of the President's own budget presentation? The moment Humphrey's text was read at Cabinet meeting, sensitivity to Washington reactions would have prompted doubts about a Treasury press conference on Budget Day. To compensate for deficiencies in other sorts of counsel, expertness on power has some obvious advantages.

It may be, in a given situation, that counsels both of power and of policy point in the same direction. I have suggested that this could have been the case when Truman, in November 1950, agreed to a postponement of decision on changed orders for MacArthur.

Even so, a consciousness of power stakes apart from policy affords a President protection toward the future. I think it highly likely that had Truman been more mindful of his personal risk when he postponed decision on a change of orders, he would have been insistent, day by day thereafter, that his chief advisers justify renewed postponement. Had he pushed them hard they scarcely could have done so.

In other situations it may be that an event or policy leaves no room for maneuver, regardless of the risk in personal terms. I have suggested that this might have been the case with Eisenhower in the days just after Humphrey's press conference. It certainly appears the case with Truman in the days just following Chou's statement to the Indian Ambassador. Yet here again the service of a power sense in posting *caution* signs could have helped both these Presidents to side-step later pitfalls in the paths laid out for them by their advisers.

No doubt there can be quite as much uncertainty, as much misjudgment, in the expert use of power as in a specialty expertise of any other sort. *A sensitivity to power's stakes and sources is no cure-all.* Oversensitivity to any one aspect at any time might wreck the very things a President most wanted and leave him beneath the ruins. To speculate, it appears possible that in the spring of 1951 a full-scale war with China would have heightened, momentarily, the response of home publics to the man then in the White House. But its net effect on Washington, on publics overseas, and on his own priority objectives could have been disastrous. Ultimately, one supposes, so would have been popular reaction in this country. Truman never put that sort of stock in popularity; it was as well for him that he did not.

Appearances can be no less deceptive in the sphere of personal power than in spheres of diplomacy, or military tactics, or economics, or party politics, or any other. The sources of a President's own influence are various; his stakes in any act of choice are multiple and changeable. At given times he may misread the face of power no less than of policy. At some times he may be unable to affect his situation even though he reads them both aright. My point is *not* that he can guarantee against those fates, but merely that his chance to ward them off improves as he impresses on his choices expertise from *every* sphere of relevance, his own sphere with the rest: the sphere of personal power.

But if he is to bring his own sphere into play, *he* has to do it. If he is to do it, he must overcome the difficulty that his personal stakes may not show on the surface of the issues put before him or be stressed in the advice of his advisers. The likelihoods, indeed, are that those stakes will be obscured. This chapter's two examples merely indicate the likelihoods. What occurred in these cases is what always tends to happen. While experts in all spheres except his own advised the President from where they sat, their judgments hid from him the need for personal perspective. They did not take his own look for him (how could they?), but neither did their presentations prompt him to start looking. Presumably, there was in this no "sabotage," no bad intent. In neither instance is there much indication that advisers acted "irresponsibly." Each seems to have performed his duty as he saw it; none sat where the President did. Truman's choices were more serious and his own risks less obvious than Eisenhower's. But both men were the victims of reliance upon issues and advisers to do more than any President can count on them to do—to clarify his stakes of personal power.

I prefaced the account of Truman's war aim for Korea with assertions drawn from Eisenhower's "go ahead" to Humphrey: if choices are the means by which a President builds power, it is only as he sees his power stakes in what he does that choices become building blocks *for him*. To see may or may not be to decide, but at the least it is to be forewarned. *Yet nobody and nothing helps a President to see, save as he helps himself.* Those are the words my second story was to test. The question still remains, how can he help himself?

Men in Office . 7

""The President needs help," wrote the Brownlow Committee of 1936 in its famous report on administrative management.[1] Since then "help" has been heaped upon his *office* in the form of staff facilities of every sort.[2] The visibility of this development has been so high that scholars have a name for it: the "institutionalized Presidency." Some of its advantages have been so obvious that competent observers are unstinting in their praise. "It converts the Presidency," writes Clinton Rossiter, "into an instrument of twentieth century government; it gives the incumbent a sporting chance to stand the strain and fulfill his constitutional mandate . . . ."[3]

As Rossiter suggests, the Presidency's clerkship could no longer be performed without the staff support provided now to Presidents. In that sense the great growth of staff since 1936 is an undoubted help to White House occupants who seek effective power for themselves. Shorn of the possibility of actual performance, formal powers would confer few practical advantages and Washington relationships would cease to be a source of influence for Presidents in person.

However, only in that sense can it be said that modern staffing has helped Presidents hold power. A "sporting chance" to do the chores of office will not automatically turn doing into influence. Helping a President perform his chores is a far cry from helping him see personal stakes in his own acts of choice. The question now before us is how help in this second sense can be obtained. By way of answer, it is not sufficient to gesture toward the "institutionalized Presidency." A Budget Bureau and a Cabinet secretariat were little help to Eisenhower in the Humphrey case. The absence of a National Security Council did not harm Truman's handling of the Marshall Plan. Its presence did not help him in Korea.

A President is helped by what he gets into *his* mind. His first essential need is information. No doubt he needs the data that advisers can provide. He also needs to know the little things they fail to mention. To illustrate, it is reliably reported that by mid-December 1956 the Secretary of the Treasury was declining to take phone calls from the Director of the Budget. In effect, Humphrey had broken off diplomatic relations with Brundage. This is a little thing and an affair of "personalities"; a thing of just the sort that Eisenhower seemingly disliked to hear and his associates disliked to tell him. But what could be more useful for a President to know while those two personalities conversed at Cabinet table? If nothing else aroused his sense of danger to himself, this knowledge might have done it. In January 1957, immediately after Humphrey's press explosion, Brundage was prepared to argue strongly for the rightness of the Eisenhower budget as it stood, and for the practical necessity of rallying to its defense in public. Brundage went so far as to prepare a White House press release for issuance that very afternoon. But he got no encouragement from White House staff officials, and he did not feel he could appeal over their heads. Within a week he had lost heart and changed his tune. Eisenhower, it appears, was spared the knowledge that his Budget Director once had thought it right as well as politic for him to disassociate himself from Humphrey's stand. Yet few things could have helped as much as this to give the President a sense that *he* was playing in a hard game for high stakes. No matter what he might have done with Brundage's advice, the very force of Brundage's reaction was a warning sign.

It is not information of a general sort that helps a President see personal stakes; not summaries, not surveys, not the bland amalgams. Rather, as these illustrations will suggest, it is the odds and ends of tangible detail that pieced together in his mind illuminate the underside of issues put before him. To help himself he must reach out as widely as he can for every scrap of fact, opinion, gossip, bearing on his interests and relationships as President. He must become his own director of his own central intelligence. For that directorship two rules of conduct can be drawn from the case studies in this book. On the one hand, he never can assume that anyone or any system will supply the bits and pieces he needs most; on the other hand, he must assume that much of what he needs will not be volunteered by his official advisers.

To fill one's mind with odds and ends is only the beginning. What helps is not the information, merely, but its meaning. Not only need a President know tangible details, he also needs to have a frame of reference. The information that a Brundage wanted White House disavowal of a Humphrey might mean no more than "parochialism" to a President unless he grasped the workings of the budget process well enough to sense that every agency and scores of congressmen were treasuring commitments which they took to be from *him*. Yet sensitivity to processes, to who does what and how, is hard to gain except by joining in the doing. The same thing can be said of sensitivity to substance; one gains by joining in the argument. Presidents are always being told that they should leave details to others. It is dubious advice. Exposure to details of operation and of policy provides the frame of reference for details of information. To be effective as his own director of intelligence, a President need be his own executive assistant.[4] He need be both, that is to say, *if he would help himself*.

This is the help that starts a man along the road to power. Information in his mind and rightly understood alerts him to his personal stakes when choices come before him. By taking his own stakes into account he does what he can do to make a choice contribute to his influence. By choosing he builds power in the only way he can. If power is his object, to inform himself is help indeed. By the same token, though, it is not help enough.

A President in search of power cannot rest content to be informed. Along with data in his mind he needs the choices in his hands. But power-laden choices may not reach him; others may pre-empt them or foreclose them. Or they may reach him so late that personal perspective has no bearing on his options. Situations of both sorts will be familiar to the readers of case studies in this book. In theory, any President, informed enough and sensitive enough to what he knew, could make such situations go away, at will, by reaching out and down for just the choices that he wanted. In practice, though, he rarely has the time. However much he knows, however sharp his senses, his time remains the prisoner of first-things-first. And almost always something else comes first.

A President's own use of time, his allocation of his personal attention, is governed by the things he *has* to do from day to day: the speech he has agreed to make, the fixed appointment he cannot put off, the paper no one else can sign, the rest and exercise his doctors order. These doings may be far removed from academic images of White House concentration on high policy, grand strategy. There is no help for that. A President's priorities are set not by the relative importance of a task, but by the relative necessity for him to do it. He deals first with the things that are required of *him* next. Deadlines rule his personal agenda. In most days of his working week, most seasons of his year, he meets deadlines enough to drain his energy and crowd his time regardless of all else. The net result may be a far cry from the order of priorities that would appeal to scholars or to columnists—or to the President himself.

What makes a deadline? The answer, very simply, is a date or an event or both combined. The date set by MacArthur for a landing at Inchon, or the date set by statute for submission of the budget, or the date set by the White House for a press conference, these and others like them force decisions on a President, pre-empt his time. And statements by MacArthur, or a Humphrey press explosion, or a House appropriations cut, or sputniks overhead, may generate such pressure inside government or out as to affect him in precisely the same way. Dates make deadlines in proportion to their certainty; events make deadlines in proportion to their heat. Singly or combined, approaching dates and rising heat start fires burning underneath the White House. Trying to stop fires is what Presidents do first. It takes most of their time.

The rule of first things first is a decided drag upon a President who seeks to make his choices serve his power. The choices lacking dates or heat may end in others' hands or be precluded by events; the choices he takes first may be distorted by their urgency. And even though he knows an issue he should reach for, even though he senses one escaping from his hands, the knowledge will not help him if the rule of first things first gets in his way. To sense what he should do if he had time is not enough. The most informed and most alert of Presidents needs something more: he needs the means to make himself take time. He needs means of putting pressure on himself, of imposing new deadlines on himself, to come to grips with those things he would want to make his own if he were free to interfere and pick and choose at will. Deadlines self-imposed are no less helpful to a President than tangible details. The one informs his mind, the other arms his hand. Together they contribute what he needs when he seeks power.

No President has been more conscious of those needs or more adroit in meeting them than Franklin Roosevelt. Roosevelt can be criticized on many grounds, but least of all for failure to protect his personal power stakes in his own acts of choice. As Arthur Schlesinger reports:

> The first task of an executive, as he evidently saw it, was to guarantee himself an effective flow of information and ideas. . . . Roosevelt's persistent effort therefore was to check and balance information acquired through official channels by information acquired through a myriad of private, informal, and unorthodox channels and espionage networks. At times he seemed almost to pit his personal sources against his public sources.[5]

His personal sources were the product of a sociability and curiosity that reached back to the other Roosevelt's time. He had an enormous acquaintance in various phases of national life and at various levels of government; he also had his wife and her variety of contacts. He extended his acquaintanceships abroad; in the war years Winston Churchill, among others, became a "personal source." Roosevelt quite deliberately exploited these relationships and mixed them up to widen his own range of information. He changed his sources as his interests changed, but no one who had ever interested him was quite forgotten or immune to sudden use. Roosevelt's search for information was an extraordinary, virtuoso performance. Besides, it was effective. Through his long tenure F.D.R. had more grasp of the details that can help a man build power than most Presidents before or either President since.

The essence of Roosevelt's technique for information-gathering was competition. "He would call you in," one of his aides once told me, "and he'd ask you to get the story on some complicated business, and you'd come back after a couple of days of hard labor and present the juicy morsel you'd uncovered under a stone somewhere, and *then* you'd find out he knew all about it, along with something else you *didn't* know. Where he got his information from he wouldn't mention, usually, but after he had done this to you once or twice you got damn careful about *your* information."

Roosevelt was as much a master of the self-created deadline as of self-directed networks of intelligence. Here, too, his method centered on the fostering of competition. To quote Schlesinger again:

> His favorite technique was to keep grants of authority incomplete, jurisdictions uncertain, charters overlapping. The result of this competitive theory of administration was often confusion and exasperation on the operating level; but no other method could so reliably insure that in a large bureaucracy filled with ambitious men eager for power the decisions, and the power to make them, would remain with the President.[6]

Not only did he keep his organizations overlapping and divide authority among them, but he also tended to put men of clashing temperaments, outlooks, ideas, in charge of them. Competitive personalities mixed with competing jurisdictions was Roosevelt's formula for putting pressure on himself, for making his subordinates push up to him the choices they could not take for themselves. It also made them advertise their punches; their quarrels provided him not only heat but information. Administrative competition gave him two rewards. He got the choices and due notice, both.

As a result he also got that treasure for a President, time to defer decision. By and large, his built-in competitions forced the choices to him early, or at least made him aware that they were coming. He, not others, then disposed of time to seek and to apply his own perspective. Schlesinger provides a sharp, insightful sketch of F.D.R.'s approach to a decision:

> He evidently felt that clear-cut administrative decisions would work only if they expressed equally clear-cut realities of administrative competence and vigor. If they did not, if the balance of administrative power would not sustain the decision, then decision would only compound confusion and discredit government. And the actualities of administrative power were to be discovered, not by writing—or by reading—Executive orders, but by apprehending through intuition a vast constellation of political forces. His complex administrative sensibility, infinitely subtle and sensitive, was forever weighing questions of personal force, of political timing, of congressional concern, of partisan benefit, of public interest. Situations had to be permitted to develop, to crystallize, to clarify; the competing forces had to vindicate themselves in the actual pull and tug of conflict; public opinion had to face the question, consider it, pronounce upon it—only then, at the long, frazzled end, would the President's intuitions consolidate and precipitate a result.[7]

But this approach was only possible if he held the decision in *his* hands. It may seem paradoxical, but deadlines self-imposed helped him employ the technique of postponement. Delay then helped him see and weigh his stakes of personal power. Sometimes he miscalculated, but he rarely failed to make the calculation and he rarely lacked for time.[8]

These Rooseveltian devices are almost literally the opposite of those employed in Eisenhower's Presidency. Eisenhower often was reported in the press to have transformed the White House into an Army Headquarters. That he did not do—nobody could —but he did manage to impart more superficial symmetry and order to his flow of information and of choices than was ever done before. Thereby, he became typically the last man in his office to know tangible details and the last to come to grips with acts of choice. His one-time chief assistant in the White House, Sherman Adams, is reported to have told a close associate: "I count the day lost when I have not found some new way of lightening the President's load." This but suggests the spirit of the "staff system," so called, in Eisenhower's time. The aims of that system were of the best. Within its limits it was reasonably well-designed and rather more than reasonably effective. In Eisenhower's instance there is no disputing that it may have been essential to his health and peace of mind. But its workings often were disastrous for his hold on personal power.

What was pernicious about all the staffs and inter-agency committees and the paper-flows around this President was not their mere existence. Many of them had been there before; others no doubt will go on long after. The difficulty, rather, was that they became almost his only source of information and of issues to decide. This was the case particularly, and quite understandably, after his heart attack in 1955. Thereafter for at least three years the "staff system" came to be, in fact, almost as much in charge of Eisenhower's business as it always was in theory. The only great exception seems to have been foreign relations; there, at least while Dulles was alive, the Secretary of State in person took the "system's" place.[9]

The Humphrey case in Chapter 6 and many of the incidents described in Chapter 4 attest to details or to choices spared the President, until too late, by staff work aimed at lightening his load. And there is reason to believe that his dependence on such staff work grew the greater as it served him so. In the words of one official close to White House operations and decidedly in sympathy with Eisenhower:

> The process has been cumulative since the heart attack. Then there were massive delegations which simply followed the existing lines to Adams and on down. Those delegations were administered by men who told each other (and themselves), "don't bother the boss," "can't do this to him now." But the less he was bothered, the less he knew, and the less he knew, the less confidence he felt in his own judgment. He let himself grow stale. . . . That made the delegations irreversible. It made him cling the tighter to the judg-

ments of the people already around him. The less he trusted himself, the more he *had* to trust them. And they thought the way to help him was to "spare" him. A lot of this was very well intentioned.[10]

The process of cumulative delegation seems to have been reversed by Sherman Adams's resignation in the fall of 1958 and by the loss of Dulles some months later. Reportedly, more issues and more detail reached the President in 1959 than at any time since 1955. Apparently, however, these still reached him through his "system." The change lay not in his methods but in partial relaxation of the system's vast protectiveness upon departure of the prime protectors. Even so, the relaxation helped him. Within the White House, Adams was replaced not by one man but a group of former subordinates who now gained equal access to the President. Most members of this group were more experienced in government than Adams had been. The "new" Eisenhower of 1959 is attributable partly to this new arrangement. The irony is that Eisenhower had been loath to let Adams resign.

An Eisenhower fully fit, much less a cardiac case, could not have been expected to assist himself in quite the Roosevelt way. The government he headed in the Fifties was far bigger, more impersonal, than Roosevelt's in the Thirties. No President can spread himself across the whole of *post*-Rooseveltian government. Roosevelt, for his own part, took the first steps toward the "institutionalized Presidency." But Roosevelt rarely let himself become its prisoner. Few persons or procedures ever got exclusive license to secure his information or to time his choices for him. None held such a license very long. That is the essential difference. Eisenhower did not merely alter Roosevelt's methods; Eisenhower's methods often left him helpless. The contrast goes considerably deeper than the presence or the absence of a "staff system." The crucial thing is that effective competitions were not built into the system.

Eisenhower had no need to foster competition by confusing jurisdictions. Cold war and welfare programs automatically confused them; policies and operations cut across the boundaries marked on organization charts. Yet Eisenhower evidently made no conscious effort to turn these confusions to his own account by mixing in competitive personalities. To be sure there were men of different temperaments and views around him. But a Stassen does not guarantee much competition for a Humphrey if the one is merely a Disarmament Assistant while the other holds that massive post of institutional authority, the Treasury Department. And even though their institutional positions seem to match, a Budget Director scarcely offers competition to the chief White House assistant when the one man is a Brundage and the other an Adams. Eisenhower's use of men tended to smother, not enhance, the competition roused by overlapping jurisdictions. Apparently this was intentional; the Roosevelt formula was not misused, it was rejected. Eisenhower, seemingly, preferred to let subordinates proceed upon the lowest common denominators of agreement than to have their quarrels—and issues and details— pushed up to him.

The contrast between Roosevelt's way and Eisenhower's way suggests a further question: why does one man give himself the help he needs; why does the other man deny it to himself? I have outlined what a President can do to help himself. But what brings him to do it?

II

Roosevelt's methods were the product of his insights, his incentives, and his confidence. No President in this century has had a sharper sense of personal power, a sense of what it is and where it comes from; none has had more hunger for it, few have had more use for it, and only one or two could match his faith in his own competence to use it. Perception and desire and self-confidence, combined, produced their own reward. No modern President has been more nearly master in the White House.

Roosevelt had a love affair with power in that place. It was an early romance and it lasted all his life. Behind his sensitivity there lay a long and relevant experience: seven years of bureaucratic free-wheeling as *the* Assistant Secretary of the Navy, four years as the Governor of New York State, a quarter-century in party politics, and with it all, an "Uncle Ted." Experience informed a temperament precisely suited to absorb what it could teach about the nature and the uses of real power in high office. For Roosevelt, this was fun. Experience also informed a fixed *intention* to possess the power of the highest office. Roosevelt always wanted the Presidency and mastery was what he wanted from it.

He wanted power for its own sake; he also wanted what it could achieve. The challenge and the fun of power lay not just in having, but in doing. His private satisfactions were enriched by public purposes and these grew more compelling as more power came his way. Political experience and private life created in him not an ideology but a decided feeling for what government should be and where its policies should lead. In terms of fixed commitments to particular solutions he was neither a "New Dealer" nor an "internationalist." But he shared with men in both of these camps a feeling of direction. And happily for him, his own sense of direction coincided, in the main, with the course of contemporary history. His purposes ran with and not against the grain of what was going to happen in his time. His sense of power thus was reinforced by his sense of direction. Unlike a Herbert Hoover he was not caught in the trap of fighting history. But neither was he caught asleep and left behind.

Roosevelt had another ground for wanting to be President: it seemed to him so fitting. The White House was for him almost a family seat and like the other Roosevelt he regarded the whole country almost as a family property. Once he became the President of the United States that sense of fitness gave him an extraordinary confidence. Roosevelt, almost alone among our Presidents, had no conception of the office to live up to; he was it. His image of the office was himself-in-office. The memoirs left by his associates agree on this if nothing else: he saw the job of being President as being F.D.R. He wanted mastery, projected that desire on the office and fulfilled it there with every sign of feeling he had come into his own. Self-confidence so based was bound to reinforce his sense of purpose and to guarantee reliance on his sense of power. His methods of self-help in seeking power were precisely what one would expect from such a combination of interior resources.

Where Roosevelt let his channels and advisers become orderly he acted out of character.

With Eisenhower, seemingly, the case is quite the opposite. Apparently he had a sense of power and a source of confidence as unlike Roosevelt's as were the two men's methods. For Eisenhower the promotion of disorder was distinctly out of character. When he could not work through a set procedure, or when channels failed him, or when his associates quarreled openly, he grew either disheartened or enraged. As Robert Donovan attests, reactions of both sorts were characteristic of this President from his first days in office.[11] All indications are that they remained in character throughout the following years. If Eisenhower's "system" did not help him see his power stakes, the reason, basically, is that this help was not the sort he wanted. His sensitivities did not prompt him to want it and his confidence was highest when he could assure himself that *personal* advantage had no place among his aims. So, at least, it seems.

One cannot assess Eisenhower's motives with the same assurance one can bring to F.D.R.'s. Roosevelt had an entourage of diarists and note-takers; most of them have published what they wrote. Members of his family circle write and speak with candor. He, himself, was a prodigious correspondent and a most revealing talker to the press. And he has fascinated the historians. In a few years when Frank Friedel and Arthur Schlesinger are done with him, he will have had more serious attention than has been accorded yet to four-fifths of his predecessors. Eisenhower, on the other hand is only to be known, as yet, by what he has said publicly and by what men around him will say privately. Appraisal on the basis of such sources calls for caution. It may turn out that he was not the man they make him seem. But at the present everything suggests that with his motivations as with methods, Eisenhower has been a sort of Roosevelt in reverse.

Through Eisenhower's first six years his power sense was blunt in almost the degree that F.D.R's was sharp. As late as 1958 he had not quite got over "shocked surprise" that orders did not carry themselves out. Apparently he could not quite absorb the notion that effective power had to be extracted out of other men's self-interest; neither did he quite absorb the notion that nobody else's interest could be wholly like his own. And he seems to have been unaware of all his natural advantages in turning different interests toward his own. By 1959 he certainly had learned to use the veto as a vantage point, but other points less obviously "constitutional" appear to have eluded him; the Humphrey case and its long aftermath bear witness.

This relative insensitivity can be explained, at least in part, by Eisenhower's background. He lacked Roosevelt's experience. Instead he had behind him the irrelevancy of an army record compiled for the most part outside Washington. As a member of his entourage once told me:

> In the Army—at least in the old Army, Eisenhower's Army—everybody knew everybody, and knew what kind of job the other fellow had, and how he was supposed to do it. . . . Responsibility was a two way flow, with the lower echelons acting in terms of what the boss wanted as laid down in his master plan—and with the boss out in the field making inspections. Here [in civil government] there's no master plan, no two way flow, and no inspections. Besides, nobody fathoms the boss's job and he's never done theirs. And they haven't been together since West Point. They don't expect to stay together, either. The Army was full of politics, sure, but it was personality politics; everybody knew the game and knew who he was playing with and for what—and it was all inside the *family.* Here, there's no family.

Coming to the White House from that background, Eisenhower also lacked Roosevelt's enjoyment. At least until his seventh year the politics of power in the Presidency never was his sport; not recreation for him; certainly not fun. Like most politically inexperienced Americans, he seems to have thought party politics a "dirty" business (which may explain why his campaigning sometimes was so disingenuous). And the politics of self-aggrandizement as Roosevelt practiced it affronted Eisenhower's sense of personal propriety. Besides, the General seems to have had mental reservations about politicians as a class, mistrusting not alone their business but their characters. To quote the private comment of another of his aides:

It really surprises me how mad he gets and the things that upset him . . . . He won't say anything personal against a member of Congress in public, but in private he can get much madder than any "pro" would. . . . And it isn't just the Democrats; deep down I think he feels the same way about Republicans.

Robert Donovan supplies us Eisenhower's answer when it was suggested to him a few weeks before his heart attack that Congress might be called back for a special session in the fall of 1955:

He slowly twisted his head around to [Arthur] Burns and told him painfully that the cost of a special session might be the sanity and possibly the life of one Dwight D. Eisenhower.[12]

Such comments simply strengthen the suggestion of the Humphrey case that this man neither liked the game he was engaged in nor had gained much understanding of its rules.

Yet Eisenhower was not dragged protesting to the White House and he was not kept there against his will. In 1952 he actively sought nomination; in 1956 he actively sought re-election. By the time of his first campaign his candidacy had been debated publicly and privately for some five years.[13] By the time of his second campaign he had been President for almost a full term. By then he was no longer "inexperienced." His fingertips, however, remained blunt. Every Eisenhower illustration in this book is taken from his *second* term.

What kept experience from sharpening his sense of power and his taste for it? The answer, seemingly, turns on a single point: Eisenhower wanted to be President, but what he wanted from it was a far cry from what F.D.R. had wanted. Roosevelt was a politician seeking personal power; Eisenhower was a hero seeking national unity. He came to crown a reputation not to make one. He wanted to be arbiter, not master. His love was not for power but for duty—and for status. Naturally, the thing he did not seek he did not often find.

The most inhibiting effect of Eisenhower's past career lay not in its irrelevance for presidential politics but its influence upon his image of himself as President. He genuinely thought himself the hero others thought him. In Marquis Childs's chilling words, "his view of himself was the official view of the Eisenhower personality, the view seen through channels." [14] And he genuinely thought the Presidency was, or ought to be, the source of unifying, moderating influence above the struggle, on the model of George Washington —the Washington, that is to say, of legend, not of life. As Eisenhower told the press in 1955:

> . . . in the general derogatory sense you can say that, of course, I do not like politics.
> Now on the other hand, any man who finds himself in a position of authority where he has a very great influence in the efforts of people to work toward a peaceful—a peaceful world—toward international relationships that will eliminate or minimize the chances of war, all that sort of thing, of course, it is a fascinating business. . . .
> There are in this office thousands of unique opportunities to meet especially interesting people, . . . leaders in culure, in health, in governmental action, and from all over the world.
> There are many things about the office and the work, the work with your associates, that are, well, let's say, at least intriguing, even if at times they are very fatiguing. But they are—it is a wonderful experience.
> But the word "politics" as you use it, I think the answer to that one, would be, no. I have no great liking for that.[15]

What drew him to the Presidency and held him there, it seems, was a conception of the good man above politics, emulating the Father of his Country.

With this image before him his self-confidence was high when he took office; higher still, perhaps, when he acceded to a second term. With this to guide him he could not dispute the arguments of all his friends that his "place in the world was unique," that he had "a God-given ability for reconciling differences among . . . nations," and for "healing divisions among the American people" —and, inferentially, that he fulfilled the Presidency just by being there.[16] But the reverse side of the coin was a diminished confidence when he dealt with the hard, divisive issues forced upon a President by dates and by events. His heightened confidence in 1956, after three years of office, suggests no change of image but a trick of history. When he decided on a second term the signs abounded that to be there was enough: "peace" in Korea, prosperity at home, the "spirit of Geneva," the censure of McCarthy, all these signs and others made beneficence appear its own reward. But precisely at the moment of his re-election, history caught up with him in giant jumps: Hungary, and Suez, and George Humphrey. Others followed after.

So long as he could play the statesman and the moderator, Eisenhower's sense of fitness for his job seems to have been no less than F.D.R.'s. His confidence, like Roosevelt's, was rooted in a sense of being naturally equipped to match his image of the office. But quite unlike the Roosevelt image, Eisenhower's, seemingly, did not delineate the politician and initiator in that lonely place where no one else's interests are one's own and no one else's expertise is expert. Thus the source of his self confidence was frequently *an enemy of his power sense* and not, as with Roosevelt, a constant ally. Only in Eisenhower's seventh year, with his last congressional campaign behind him and his re-election barred by Constitutional Amendment, did his image of himself enhance his sensitivity to power in one sphere, the sphere of congressional relations. By then he could assure himself—reportedly he did—that "politics" played no part in his reach for personal influence.

Had Eisenhower been more purposeful as President his own sense of direction might have come to the rescue of his power sense. Occasionally this seems to have occurred, but not often. His purposes were not well suited to the task. His public statements, taken altogether, show he very much desired peace-with-honor both at home and abroad. He was more or less committed to the aims of foreign policy he had inherited, and more or less committed to maintain the welfare heritage from the New Deal. He was committed, also, to his party as the safest source of leadership for the United States; he hoped to see Republicans in office after he was gone. Taken on their face, such goals as these might have sufficed a man with a keen sense of power. Eisenhower's purposes seem tangible enough to have kept such a man in motion without being so precise as to impel him down blind alleys or to turn him against history. Their very imprecision, though, made them unsuitable to sharpen a dull power sense. If anything, they dulled it more. Eisenhower often seemed to mistake generalities for concrete undertakings; when he did pursue a concrete aim he often seemed to lose sight of his broad objectives.

Throughout Eisenhower's years of office there can be no doubt that peace, in the sense of a fundamental easing of the threat of war, was the broad objective he had most in mind, the one that stirred and interested him most, the one for which he felt himself particularly fitted. The thought that he, uniquely, could contribute to the cause of peace may have decided him upon a second term. As Robert Donovan reports in tracing that decision, "Constantly Eisenhower heard this appeal repeated, sometimes expressed in terms of duty to which he seemed peculiarly responsive. 'It was this advice,' an intimate said later, 'that he took to bed with him when he was making up his mind.' " [17] Yet both before and after 1956, this personal commitment seemed to guide him only on the mountaintop of general goals; down in the valley of specific applications he often appeared lost. In 1955 he personally was at great pains to create and to gain credit for the "spirit of Geneva." But in the weeks between the summit conference and his heart attack he gave no sign of knowing what he meant to do with either the creation or the credit. In 1957, during the London disarmament talks, Eisenhower backed Dulles over Stassen on approaches to the Russians without disallowing Stassen's premises. At the same time Eisenhower moved toward a Treasury view on defense budgeting which did not square at all with Dulles's premises. That year—among others—foreign policy disputes in his Administration found the President committed and uncertain on both sides, a situation reminiscent of the Humphrey case. Results were somewhat similar. Even in the sphere of peace which mattered to him most, Eisenhower's purposes were frequently too general to provide a guide line for him on specific undertakings.

It is no wonder that in other spheres of policy and politics which meant far less to Eisenhower than did peace, there should have been still greater gaps between his advocacy of a general goal and his sense of direction on particulars. When broad objectives were inapplicable or in conflict—as broad objectives usually are—he was inclined to throw the issue to the experts and to follow where the men he thought most expert chose to lead. He had enormous respect for successful businessmen, the more so as their manner matched the layman's expectations; if he did not equally admire politicians, he accorded them a layman's deference in what he took to be *their* line of work. When Eisenhower dealt with the particulars of home affairs and party politics, these were the experts he inclined to follow. They took him rather far, sometimes, from his avowed objectives.

It would be a distortion of the Eisenhower record to suggest that he invariably acted in this fashion. Intermittently, specifics came to interest him, even the political specifics. Sometimes his energies and personal enthusiasm fastened upon very concrete aims. Particularly in the months before his heart attack and, again, after the Democratic landslide of 1958, one senses that his own assertiveness about specific aims was definitely on the rise. His aides report that when and as this happened he was frequently quite capable of being his own guide, of taking his direction on particulars from his own sense of where and how to go. But it appears that these excursions to the realm of the specific often disengaged his mind from general aims. The classic instance seems to be his concentration on the budget in the seventh year of his Administration.

In part, perhaps, because his time was running out; in part, perhaps, because the Democratic victories of 1958 roused his combative instincts, Eisenhower turned his mind to budget-balancing with the enthusiasm once reserved for peace alone. By 1959 he was as purposeful about his budget aim as Humphrey had been two years earlier. What Humphrey then had advocated, Eisenhower made his own: an effort to keep *future* budgets balanced by resisting new commitments and reducing those on hand; in long-run terms an effort to keep spending down so that the rising revenues from economic growth could be applied to debt and tax reduction without adding to inflationary pressures. As we have seen in Chapter 4, the President pursued this negative objective with a fervor—and a skill in utilizing vantage points—which made him seem a "changed man" from the hesitant performer of 1957. By the same token, though, the positive objectives that had caused his hesitations in the first year of his second term seem almost to have vanished from his mind.

Eisenhower did not change the labels on his broader aims. In

1959 he still avowed the goals of 1956: peace, prosperity, and Modern Republicanism. But the meaning of those goals was altered rather markedly when each became identified with holding down the budget. Whether he was conscious of that alteration is an open question. And whether the new meanings were compatible with Soviet containment, with American advance, and with Republican advantage is decidedly in doubt. The answer will be given in the 1960's. Meanwhile, an affirmation of compatibility is only credible on the assumption that the Eisenhower program at the outset of his second term was based on faulty premises in almost every sphere—and that the reports of the Rockefeller Brothers Fund are fantasy. To assume otherwise is to conclude that Eisenhower's campaign for a balanced budget, with its pressure wholly on the spending side, involved a risk not only to his other goals of policy but also to the power prospects *after* 1960 of the Republican he hoped would follow him into the White House. For if Eisenhower's budgeting promoted expectations which the future could not meet, his political legacy was likely to be popular frustration in the time of the next President. Reportedly, the moral was not lost on either Rockefeller or Nixon. But there are no reports that Eisenhower saw the risk he ran, if not for himself then for them, in anything like these terms. On the contrary, by 1959 he seems to have been satisfied that Humphrey's aim was not merely good policy but quite sufficient as a base for White House power politics.

Conceivably, the "new" Eisenhower of 1959 bespeaks a change of outlook more profound than the foregoing analysis suggests. Conceivably, this President in his last years came to perceive his office and his power very differently than he had done before. It is conceivable but unlikely. A sympathetic member of his Administration told me:

> This is the Eisenhower of North Africa and Normandy, motivated by the same belief: that the only battle that counts is the last battle. After 1958 he knew the war was nearly over and the time was now or never for the final fight.

But in political warfare, the outcome for a President depends as much or more on the *first* battles. These are the battles that decide his public image and create a pattern for his Washington reputation. A President who makes himself a "new" man in his *seventh* year must be presumed a stranger, still, to politics and power.

With Eisenhower as with F.D.R., performance on the job reflected qualities inside the man which shaped his whole approach to personal power. In Roosevelt's case a striking sensitivity to power was heightened by vast confidence in using it, and by his sense of what to use it for. In Eisenhower's case a relative *in*sensitivity was reinforced by a self-confidence that wavered least when "politics" was farthest off, and by a set of purposes that either raised his eyes too high or cast them down too low to see the middle ground where strategy and tactics meet. It is no wonder that an F.D.R. on most occasions seemed acutely conscious of his power risks, whereas an Eisenhower frequently seemed unaware of them. Nor is it any wonder that the one man's methods helped him see his stakes of power, while the other man worked in a manner likely to obscure them. Roosevelt always knew what power was and always wanted it.

III

In his reach for personal power Harry Truman differed both from Roosevelt and from Eisenhower. Truman's methods of self-help were different. So were his insights, his incentives, and his image of himself as President. In these respects he neither forecast his successor nor proceded like his predecessor. However, Truman's own behavior will confirm what theirs suggests: that there exists the closest of connections between self-help in the Presidency and three aspects of a President's interior resources: his power sense, his confidence—which turns on his self image—and his sense of direction.

Truman's methods in the White House followed forms somewhat like Eisenhower's to results somewhat like Roosevelt's. In theory Truman was as much committed as was Eisenhower to straight lines and tidy boxes on the organization chart, and to "completed staff work." But in practice Truman had more feel for personalities than jurisdictions, and his instinct was to improvise arrangements around problems rather than to work through fixed procedures. In dealing with his staff he set no precise lines of demarcation or of hierarchy; those he did establish he was likely to ignore. As best he could he saw whoever wished to see him, whether congressmen or private persons or department heads or staff assistants, and he listened to their talk and read their documents. Truman theorized like a reserve officer impressed with Army doctrine; he acted like a Senator. His office was decked out with many of the trappings of what later became known as a staff system, but he, himself, remained incurably informal and accessible. Besides, in Truman's practice there was one ingredient which cannot be described as senatorial: he loved to make decisions. Unlike Eisenhower he was not disposed to keep away from them and unlike Roosevelt he had little inclination to defer them once he got them. On the contrary, his own initial impulse when an issue came before him was to make a firm decision then and there; his staff and State Department were forever clinging to his coattails. Although Truman rather frowned on Roosevelt's methods and would not have dreamed of fostering disorder for its own sake, his accessibility and personal decisiveness combined to furnish him —under the table, so to speak—with information in his mind and choices in his hands on a scale more like Roosevelt's than like Eisenhower's.

However where Roosevelt was instinctively an intelligence operative, Truman was instinctively a judge. Details reached him, ordinarily, as a by-product of his listening and reading, case by case. He did not seek as avidly as F.D.R. had done for bits of information unrelated to the day's affairs. Although he relished gossip when he got it, Truman did not often try to fit the pieces into patterns, or to speculate about their implications, or to make connections between something learned in one context and something done in another. Characteristically, he concentrated on the "here" and "now" in terms befitting a decision-machine, looking for what was to be decided, looking at what bore directly on the case, and tending to dismiss all else as interesting but irrelevant. Moreover, while he dealt with the decision next in line, the ones already processed and the ones that might come after were not often on his mind. No more than in the case of tangible details was Truman prone to fit his choices into patterns or to visualize the one at hand outside of its own context. And just as in the case of information, Truman usually let other men's initiatives time his decisions for him. The issues that existed were the issues on his desk. Because his door was open and he listened and he read, details piled in upon him; because he was so willing to decide, decisions piled in, too. But Roosevelt had pursued these things with power as an object; Truman rather welcomed them in line of duty. The difference is significant. Information in his mind and choices in his hands were not the help to Truman they had been to F.D.R.

Truman's sensitivity to power was no match for his predecessor's. Truman's past experience had been less relevant and he lacked Roosevelt's instinct for the uses of *Executive* position. Truman's instincts ran another way. He had been ten years a Senator, beginning at a time when Roosevelt's emissaries were both blunt and curt with new men at the Capitol. Truman never did like White House meddling in legislative *tactics;* indeed he entered office with his mind set on restoring "proper" balance between President and Congress. Moreover, Truman shared with many senators a sense of the Executive as "they," conceiving it much more an entity and much more an extension of the Chief Executive than it looks from within. Roosevelt seemed to him a poor administrator—as Roosevelt seemed, of course, to many others—and Truman entered office with his mind set on administering by and through the Cabinet. As the first volume of his *Memoirs* shows (a volume based in part on notes written in 1945), Truman carried to the White House certain of the preconceptions commonly identified with Eisenhower.[18] The experience of senators like that of generals can be far removed, it seems, from life as lived at 1600 Pennsylvania Avenue. And Truman had not only been a Senator, he had been the Kansas City organization's candidate and office holder for a quarter century. He reached the Presidency possessed of that great virtue in an organization politician, loyalty up and loyalty down. Truman had remained a Roosevelt Democrat, loyal to his party's leader in the White House, even after F.D.R. tried to unseat him from the Senate in the primary campaign of 1940. When Truman took the leader's place, when *he* became the boss, he gave an equal loyalty to his followers. He sensed—indeed he could not help but know—that Roosevelt had been loyal above all else to F.D.R. In this respect as in some others Truman entered office with his mind set on revising the procedure of his predecessor.

Truman learned by doing; to a marked degree he rid himself of his illusions about government administration, notably with regard to the Cabinet, and in practice if not theory he changed many of his views about congressional relations. The unpublished diary of his holdover Budget Director, Harold Smith, does much to trace the education—on the job and by it—of a very educable man.[19] Truman often learned a great deal more than he articulated and his *Memoirs* scarcely show the sweep of his self-education; but in fact, if not in memory, it was vast. Yet never having been an agency official, Truman never did acquire Roosevelt's intimate awareness of just how the work got done (or stopped) around him and beneath him in the bureaucratic world. And never having let ambition for the White House shape his code of loyalty, Truman, once he got there, had no motive to reshape the code by which he had been living all his political life. Throughout his Presidency, Truman's lack of bureaucratic "feel," in combination with his loyalty down, left him decidedly less sensitive than F.D.R. to stakes of personal power. The way these two men chose and dealt with appointees is most instructive on the point.

Truman, it must be remembered, had not aimed at the Presidency; his own aims reached no farther than a lifetime in the Senate. Before his unsolicited vice-presidential nomination, thoughts of being President had scarcely crossed his mind, and by his own account they scarcely crossed it afterward, until the day that Roosevelt died. Until then Truman had been hungry neither for the Presidency's power nor its status. Nothing in his life had been planned around visions of himself as boss; Roosevelt was the boss, and after Roosevelt there would be another. In 1948 Truman fought to get himself *elected* President; he did so for the record's sake, for vindication, for his pride's sake, as a man who made good on his own and always faced a fight. But even then he had no notion of himself as fit above all others to be President. As late as 1952 he was quite capable of saying, and believing, "There are a great many people, I expect a million in the country, who could have done the job better than I could, but I had the job and I had to do it." [20] In that remark one finds the essence of his image of himself in office.

Truman's image of the Presidency and of himself as President kept job and man distinct to a degree unknown in Roosevelt's case or Eisenhower's. Truman built his image of the office out of his perceptions as a politician, as a Democrat, as a young worshipper of Woodrow Wilson, as a mature follower of F.D.R. and as a constant reader of political biography, who found a lot to like in Jackson, Polk, and Johnson. Truman saw the Presidency as the place "where the buck stopped"; he saw the President as man-in-charge of government, as maker of a record for his party, and as voice for the whole body of Americans. The job he had to do, as Truman saw it, was to make decisions and to take initiatives; those were the duties of the boss-and-spokesman; so his perceptions told him. Mixed into those perceptions, perhaps guiding them, were Truman's private values; decisiveness was high upon his list. But never in his tenure does he seem to have conceived that he fulfilled the Presidency by being Harry Truman. He saw himself not as a man for whom the job was made, but as a man who had the job to do. He drew his confidence from seeing himself do it.

The source of Truman's confidence was his ability, in his own mind, to live up to that image of the President as man-in-charge. His confidence was highest when he saw himself deciding and initiating. Rarely was he calmer or more certain of himself than when he had to act amidst a crisis. Few things made him more uncomfortable than mulling over "ifs" and "buts" with nothing to decide. But Truman's confidence required more than sheer decision-making. It required that he see himself deciding in terms worthy of a *President*. His image of his office made it seem to him the focal point of governmental policy, of national politics, and of American history. He could not feel that he had done his job if he let personal proclivities or personal self-interest out-

weigh what he took to be a presidential duty. His own sense of
the separateness of man and office made him more self-conscious
than most Presidents about each shift of role among the six or eight
or ten into which modern writers split the Presidency. He played
"Chief of State" like a gracious host, "Chief of Party" like an organization politician, "Chief of Foreign Policy" like a career official
anxious to obey his own injunction that "politics stops at the
water's edge." When he was not playing one role or another he
saw nothing inappropriate in being Harry Truman, but he rarely
thought that Truman's likes or dislikes had a warrant to determine
what he did in any role.

Truman's kind of confidence was capable of offsetting the weakness in his power sense, but it was also capable of rendering the
weakness all the worse. Everything depended on the given situation. As Chapter 3 records, he was enormously successfully in his
handling of the Marshall Plan. As Chapter 6 records, he got into
deep trouble with his handling of Korean war aims. And these
two results were products of the same approach. In both these
instances the President remained intensely loyal to his subordinates
and did his personal best to smooth *their* way as they conducted
their share of Administration policy. In both instances he shunned
ideas and interventions which might lay him open, *in his own
mind*, to the charge that he "played politics with national security."
In both cases he deferred to the counsel of the men he least sus-
pected—as a rule—of partisan motivation, generals above all. (His
lay regard for their career line more or less matched Eisenhower's
faith in businessmen.) And in both instances he made decisions
willingly and fast, whenever his advisers brought him some to
make. The political adroitness and the look of calculation in the
case of the Marshall Plan can give a false impression. Truman was
not being subtle; he was simply doing what he thought a President
should do from day to day. As Jack Redding has written in another
connection:

> What so many people failed to understand was that the President
> [Truman] rarely used circumlocution to gain his ends. He meant
> what he said. That is why so many pundits failed in trying to

analyze the President's actions. They were always looking behind what he said and did, looking for an explanation other than the obvious.[21]

Truman's sense of personal direction was cut from the same cloth as his self-confidence and had a like effect upon his power sense, sharpening it or dulling it in different situations. He came to office very conscious of his heritage from F.D.R. In policy terms he saw himself as heir to the New Deal and internationalism; in political terms he saw himself as heir to Roosevelt's coalition of the Democratic South and the Progressive West with Northern ethnic and religious minorities. Truman was not only mindful of this heritage, but also he felt obliged to guard it and refurbish it and pass it on. In combination with his image of his office that feeling quite sufficed to give him all the purposes a man can carry while he tries to cope with an eight-year supply of modern history. Indeed the combination spurred this man toward fixed positions of a sort not easily abandoned in the face of changed events, and made him, very often, most reluctant to retreat. Where Roosevelt had shunned fixed positions, Truman staked them out. As Roosevelt characteristically kept fire-exits open, Truman characteristically slammed doors. When Eisenhower went "all out" to hold down Federal spending, his stance, if not his object, reminded one of Truman.

"The President's got to set the sights," was Truman's comment in a conversation after leaving office. To him the task included dotting "i's" and crossing "t's." Advocacy in specific terms was his conception of appropriate initiative. If the specifics were ignored, or if they later rose to haunt him, he would still have done his duty as a President. In his words: "What the country needed in every field . . . was up to me to say . . . and if Congress wouldn't respond, well, I'd have done all I could in a straightforward way." Sometimes this approach directed him toward power as it certainly did in 1948. But sometimes his specifics left him small room for maneuver when events produced a shift in his priorities or altered public expectations of his office. In 1943 a Roosevelt could drop "Dr. New Deal" for "Dr. Win-the-War," and seem in character and make a point. The indications are that Truman could have managed no such thing in 1950–1951. Besides, he would have thought it wrong to try.[22]

The help that Truman gave himself in calculating power stakes was help of an uneven sort; his power sense was equally uneven. His methods in the Presidency brought him into contact with details and with decisions more consistently than Eisenhower, but the timing of those contacts was not on a par with Roosevelt's from the standpoint of protecting personal power. As in his predecessor's case and his successor's also, Truman's methods bear an obvious relationship to his own "feel" for power and its purposes and to his source of confidence. His methods were the methods of a man who loved the Presidency less for what he could get out of it, by way of personal power or of status, than for what he saw in it as an embodiment of government and party and of history apart from him. Truman loved his image of the institution. When stakes of power for the office—in his image of it—coincided with his stakes of personal influence, his sensitivities were quick to be aroused. But when there was no obvious coincidence he could be quite insensitive to personal stakes, or even deprecate them, if he saw them, as beneath a President's dignity. His dealings with MacArthur provide classic illustrations on both scores.

Truman's distaste for the "merely" personal was not much less than his successor's. Eisenhower also deprecated personal advantage as a guide in presidential choice-making. But Truman's image of the office made him sensitive to anything that challenged his position as decider and proposer. His feeling for the Presidency's clerkship was so strong that often he was led to self-protection in the process of protecting what he took to be his duties. Eisenhower's image offered no such compensation. Eisenhower's sensitivities were reserved, in the main, for what he took to be his place above the struggle. Paradoxically, his instinct for the Presidency's honorific element often made his own reactions seem intensely personal. But rarely did they seem "political." In Eisenhower's image, "politics" defined the merely personal. In Truman's image "politics" was duty.

In Roosevelt's image, unlike both of these, "politics" and all else was a vehicle for *him*. Roosevelt, of the three, was much the most effective in protecting personal power.

IV

These observations on our recent Presidents conclude a line of argument begun in Chapter 2. Let me restate it briefly. Governmental power, in reality not form, is influence of an effective sort on the behavior of men actually involved in making public policy and carrying it out. Effective influence for the man in the White House stems from three related sources: first are the bargaining advantages inherent in his job with which to persuade other men that what he wants of them is what their own responsibilities require them to do. Second are the expectations of those other men regarding his ability and will to use the various advantages they think he has. Third are those men's estimates of how his public views him and of how their publics may view them if they do what he wants. In short, his power is the product of his vantage points in government, together with his reputation in the Washington community and his prestige outside.

A President, himself, affects the flow of power from these sources, though whether they flow freely or run dry he never will decide alone. He makes his personal impact by the things he says and does. Accordingly, his choices of what he should say and do, and how and when, are his means to conserve and tap the sources of his power. Alternatively, choices are the means by which he dissipates his power. The outcome, case by case, will often turn on whether he perceives his risk in power terms and takes account of what he sees before he makes his choice. A President is so uniquely situated and his power so bound up with the uniqueness of his place, that he can count on no one else to be perceptive for him. Yet he can scarcely see and weigh his power stakes himself unless he is alerted by significant details and deals with his decisions in good time. Useful information, timely choices may not reach him; he must do the reaching. To do so is to help himself enhance his personal influence. This is the sort of help he needs the most. But he will neither feel that need nor fill it if his image of his office keeps him faced away from power.

It is natural that Franklin Roosevelt, hungry for the Presidency's power as his birthright, should exemplify the man who helps himself. It is ironic that a Truman, who felt no such hunger and laid claim to no such birthright, still created from his background, and his heroes, and his reading, an image of the office that impelled him toward self-help. It is an equal irony that Eisenhower, hailed by commentators and by voters (and by many intellectuals) as quite uniquely qualified for power in the Presidency, was turned away from self-help by his very qualifications. Only an extraordinary politician could have managed to exploit the opportunities for influence created by the presence of a hero in the White House. But had Eisenhower been a man of politics he never would have come there as the hero that he was. And being what he was, he looked upon his presence there through the eyes of an *anti*-politician. There can be little doubt that he exchanged his hero's welcome for much less than its full value in the currency of power. But how could Eisenhower have done otherwise? His image of himself in office dictated the terms of that exchange.

One never can be sure that when a man becomes the President of the United States his sense of power and of purpose and his own source of self-confidence will show him how to help himself enhance his personal influence. But there is every reason to believe that he will be shown nothing of the sort if he has made the White House his first venture into politics. The Presidency is no place for amateurs.

CHAPTER

The Sixties Come Next . 8

To make the most of power for himself a President must know what it is made of. This book has treated power in the sense of personal influence and influence in the sense of effectiveness *prospectively*, looking toward tomorrow from today. That look conveys the essence of the task before a man who seeks to maximize his power. If he wants it for the future, he must guard it in the present. He mounts guard, as best *he* can, when he appraises the effects of present action on the sources of his influence. In making that appraisal he has no one to depend on but himself; his power and its sources are a sphere of expertise reserved to him. But the issues that present themselves for action day by day rarely show his personal risks upon their surface. His expertise must first help him to see beneath the surface if it is to help him weigh what may be there. The President as expert does himself a double service. Without the expertise he cannot do it.

The Presidency, to repeat, is not a place for amateurs. That sort of expertise can hardly be acquired without deep experience in political office. The Presidency is a place for men of politics. But by no means is it a place for every politician.

There is no reason to suppose that politicians, on the average, have the wherewithal to help themselves build *presidential* power. The men of politics who specialize in organization work and party office scarcely qualify at all; governmental office is the relevant experience. For present purposes we can regard as politicians only those who build careers in public office. Yet skillful use of presidential power does not follow automatically from such experience. No post in government at any level necessarily equips a man to recognize the Presidency's peculiar sources of influence. Those sources have as many parts as a President has constituencies, foreign and domestic; the posts that furnish insights into one part often obscure others. Besides, past officeholding is no guarantee that any man brings with him to the White House the degree and kind of feeling for direction that can help him once he gets there. Former Commerce Secretary Hoover had a sense of purpose so precise as to be stultifying. Former Senator Harding seems to have had none at all. And mere experience, however relevant, is no assurance that a President will find the confidence he needs just when he needs it most. Such confidence requires that his image of himself in office justify an unremitting search for personal power. But it requires, also, that his image of himself allow for failures and frustration in the search.

F.D.R. is said to have remarked that Lincoln "was a sad man because he couldn't get it all at once. And nobody can." [1] If a President is to assist himself through the vicissitudes of four long years or eight, *his source of confidence must make him capable of bearing Lincoln's sadness with good grace*. The power-seeker whose self-confidence requires quick returns and sure success might make a mess of everything including his own power. Grace calls for humor and perspective. Political experience does not assure those qualities. Indeed, it may diminish them in the degree it brings a taste for power. The officeholder who combines them with an insight into presidential influence and hunger for it is no average politician.

Expertise in presidential power seems to be the province not of politicians as a class but of extraordinary politicians. What sets such men apart? Mr. Justice Holmes once characterized Franklin Roosevelt as a "second-rate intellect but a first-rate temperament." Perhaps this is a necessary combination. The politics of well-established government has rarely been attractive to and rarely has dealt kindly with the men whom intellectuals regard as first-rate intellects. Temperament, at any rate, is the great separator. Experience will leave its mark on expertise; so will a man's ambitions for himself and his constituents. But something like that "first-rate" temperament is what turns know-how and desire to his personal account. The necessary confidence is nourished by that temperament. It is a human resource not discovered every day among American politicians.

II

If skill in maximizing power for himself served purposes no larger than the man's own pride or pleasure, there would be no reason for the rest of us to care whether he were skillful or not. More precisely, there would be no reason except sentiment and partisanship. But a President's success in that endeavor serves objectives far beyond his own and far beyond his party's. For reasons I will come to in a moment, an expert search for presidential influence contributes to the energy of government and to the viability of public policy. Government is energized by a productive tension among its working parts. Policy is kept alive by a sustained transformation of intent into result. Energetic government and viable public policy are at a premium as we begin the seventh decade of the twentieth century. Expertise in presidential power adds to both. A President's constituents, regardless of their party (or their country for that matter), have a great stake in his search for personal influence.

In the American political system the President sits in a unique seat and works within a unique frame of reference. The things he personally has to do are no respecters of the lines between "civil" and "military," or "foreign" and "domestic," or "legislative" and "executive," or "administrative" and "political." At his desk—and there alone—distinctions of these sorts lose their last shred of meaning. The expectations centered in his person converge upon no other individual; nobody else feels pressure from all five of *his* constituencies; no one else takes pressure in the consciousness that *he* has been elected "by the Nation." Besides, nobody but the President lives day by day with *his* responsibility in an atomic age amidst cold war. And he alone can claim unquestionable right to everybody's information on the mysteries of that age and that war. His place and frame of reference are unique. By the same token, though, his power is mercurial. Since no one shares his place, nobody is committed to uphold what he may do there. The consequences are described by every illustration in this book.

The things a President must think about if he would build his influence are not unlike those bearing on the viability of public policy. The correspondence may be inexact, but it is close. The man who thinks about the one can hardly help contributing to the other. A President who senses what his influence is made of and who means to guard his future will approach his present actions with an eye to the reactions of constituents in Washington and out. The very breadth and sweep of his constituencies and of their calls upon him, along with the uncertainty of their response, will make him keen to see and weigh what Arthur Schlesinger has called "the balance of administrative power." [2] This is a balance of political, managerial, psychological, and personal feasibilities. And because the President's own frame of reference is at once so all-encompassing and so political, what he sees as a balance for himself is likely to be close to what is viable in terms of public policy.

What he sees in terms of power *gives him clues in terms of policy* to help him search beneath the surfaces of issues.

Viability in policy has three ingredients. First is a purpose that moves with the grain of history, a direction consonant with coming needs. Second is an operation that proves manageable to the men who must administer it, acceptable to those who must support it, tolerable to those who must put up with it, in Washington and out. Timing can be crucial for support and acquiescence; proper timing is the third ingredient. The President who sees his power stakes sees something very much like the ingredients that make for viability in policy.

Our system affords nobody a better source of clues. Presidential expertise thus serves effective policy. Deciding what is viable has grown more critical and more complex with almost every turn of world events (and of home politics) since the

Second World War. Substantive considerations have become so specialized that experts in one sphere lose touch with expertise in any other. Substantive appraisals have become so tricky that the specialists in every sphere dispute among themselves. In consequence the viability of policy may be the only ground on which a substantive decision can be reached. When that ground is itself inordinately complicated by the tendency of policies to interlock, and overlap, and to leap national boundaries, it becomes a sphere of expertness as specialized as others. In the sphere of viability our system can supply no better expert than a President intent on husbanding his influence—provided that he understands what influence is made of.

The more determinedly a President seeks power, the more he will be likely to bring vigor to his clerkship. As he does so he contributes to the energy of government. In Congress and the agencies and in the national parties, energy is generated by support or opposition. But first there must be something to support or to oppose. Most Washingtonians look to the White House for it. There often is no other place to look. The need of others for a President's initiatives creates dependence on him. Their dependence becomes his advantage. Yet he can only capture the advantage as he meets the need. An energetic clerk will energize all government; the man intent on influence will be that sort of clerk. (So may a man intent on history, provided that he has the heroes of a Harry Truman. But one cannot expect that many men will know their history as well as he, and those who know it may choose other heroes.)

The contributions that a President can make to government are indispensable. Assuming that he knows what power is and wants it, those contributions cannot help but be forthcoming in some measure as by-products of his search for personal influence. In a relative but real sense one can say of a President what Eisenhower's first Secretary of Defense once said of General Motors: what is good for the country is good for the President, and *vice versa*. There is no guarantee, of course, that every President will keep an eye on what is "good" for him; his sense of power and of purpose and the source of his self-confidence may turn his head away. If so, his "contributions" could be lethargy not energy, or policy that moves against, not with, the grain of history. The way he sees his influence and seeks it will affect the rest of us, no matter what becomes of him.

III

There is reason to suppose that in the years immediately ahead the power problems of a President will remain what they have been in the decades just behind us. If so there will be equal need for presidential expertise of the peculiar sort this book has stressed. Indeed, the need is likely to be greater. The President himself and with him the whole government are likely to be more than ever at the mercy of his personal approach.

What may the Sixties do to politics and policy and to the place of Presidents in our political system? The Sixties may destroy them as we know them; that goes without saying. But barring deep depression or unlimited war, a total transformation is the least of likelihoods. Without catastrophes of those dimensions nothing in our past experience suggests that we shall see either consensus of the sort available to F.D.R. in 1933 and 1942, or popular demand for institutional adjustments likely to assist a President. Lacking popular demand, the natural conservatism of established institutions will keep Congress and the party organizations quite resistant to reforms that could give him a clear advantage over them. Four-year terms for congressmen and senators might do it, if the new terms ran with his. What will occasion a demand for that? As for crisis consensus it is probably beyond the reach of the next President. We may have priced ourselves out of the market for "productive" crises on the pattern Roosevelt knew—productive in the sense of strengthening his chances for sustained support *within* the system. Judging from the Fifties, neither limited war nor limited depression is productive in those terms. Anything unlimited will probably break the system.

In the absence of productive crises, and assuming that we manage to avoid destructive ones, nothing now foreseeable suggests that our next President will have assured support from any quarter.

There is no use expecting it from the bureaucracy unless it is displayed on Capitol Hill. Assured support will not be found in Congress unless contemplation of their own electorates keeps a majority of members constantly aligned with him. In the Sixties it is to be doubted—for reasons to be mentioned in a moment—that pressure from electorates will move the same majority of men in either House toward consistent backing for the President. Instead the chances are that he will gain majorities, when and if he does so, by *ad hoc* coalition-building, issue after issue. In that respect the Sixties will be reminiscent of the Fifties; indeed, a closer parallel may well be the late Forties. As for "party discipline" in English terms—the favorite cure-all of political scientists since Woodrow Wilson was a youth—the first preliminary is a party link between the White House and the leadership on both sides of the Capitol. But even this preliminary has been lacking in eight of the fifteen years since the Second World War. If ballot-splitting should continue through the Sixties it will soon be "un-American" for President and Congress to belong to the same party.

Even if the trend were now reversed, there is no short-run prospect that behind each party label we would find assembled a sufficiently like-minded bloc of voters, similarly aligned in states and districts all across the country, to negate the massive barriers our institutions and traditions have erected against "discipline" on anything like the British scale. This does not mean that a reversal of the ballot-splitting trend would be without significance. If the White House and the legislative leadership were linked by party ties again, a real advantage would accrue to both. Their opportunities for mutually productive bargaining would be enhanced. The policy results might surprise critics of our system. Bargaining "within the family" has a rather different quality than bargaining with members of the rival clan. But we would still be a long way from "party government." Bargaining, not "discipline," would still remain the key to congressional action on a President's behalf. The critical distinctions between presidential party and congressional party are not likely to be lost in the term of the next President.

Our parties are unlikely to be revolutionized as instruments of government because they are unlikely to be altered fundamentally as voter coalitions differently aligned for different offices in different places. The long awaited "nationalization" of our parties, breaking the old sectionalism, may be on its way despite the current setback in the South. But even if each party's voting base were nationalized tomorrow, the issues of the next few years hold out no prospect that the partisans in one place will stay put on the same terms as those in every other. In the next years we face a snarly sort of politics with party followings more likely to be brittle and unstable than secure and likely to shift differently in different locations. Nationalization may be coming, but if we find it with us in the Sixties we should not expect to find that it has brought us those clean cleavages so dear to advocates of "party realignment." Our history suggests that only sustained crises, striking deep into the private lives of voters everywhere, will produce *stable* partisan alignments; crises on the order of the Civil War and of the Great Depression. But a comparable crisis in our time would strike so deep that there might well be nothing left of our contemporary party system. Again we probably have priced ourselves out of the market for the useful products of an old-style crisis. Assuming no catastrophe, the Sixties, like the Fifties, probably will be a time of changeability without great change in terms of party preferences. The alterations now foreseeable will not be of the sort to promote unanimity among a party's congressmen.

This is not to argue that our politics will be as tepid in the next decade as in the middle Fifties. The Sixties, it appears, will be a fighting time. Our politics in the next years are likely to revolve around at least four overlapping areas of controversy; these are visible in 1959, others may emerge. One of the four can be identified, though imprecisely, as a shift in capital resources from private use to public purposes; the issues of inflation, and taxation, and of economic growth are bound up with the issue of a larger public "take." How much shift of resources there should be, and whether absolute or relative, and for what ends, and by what means, and at whose cost, need not detain us here. It is enough to note that these will be the subjects of hot argument, politically, throughout the next decade, perhaps long after. No one who looks squarely at "competitive coexistence," or at population trends, or at our cities (and their suburbs), or at subsidy and service needs of private enterprise, and then considers that a ceiling on the public sector has been advertised as *the* cure for inflation and a key to growth, can doubt what the late Fifties are bequeathing to the Sixties by way of heat in politics. The heat will be proportional to a great lack of light.

Debate over the sources, size, and distribution of the public "take" may raise as many issues in the sphere of foreign policy as in domestic spheres. Indeed, this is the likely way in which foreign relations will be linked directly and continuously to domestic politics. Among the pressing claims upon our Treasury will be the claims of those who do not vote in our elections. We face substantial bills for capital development. We are not done with paying bills for military forces. And all these bills will come due while we fight about expansion of domestic public services. The competitions between claims abroad and claims at home will affect every sphere of policy from military deterrence, to arms control, to economic aid, to foreign trade, to political relations in our system of alliances. The pressure of competing claims is certainly not new, but the intensity of pressure may make foreign policy more controversial in our politics than it has been for many years. And while it grows more controversial it will also grow more critical. What happens in the Sixties may decide the long-term outcome of "competitive coexistence."

A second area of controversy can be described in simplest terms as when, and where, and how to squeeze farm subsidies. While agricultural employment shrinks to a small fraction of the American labor force, and rural population drops proportionately, the present scale of subsidies will come under attack by every other claimant known to Washington. But between those rival claimants and the money stands the legislative influence of the farm organizations, buttressed by the rural gerrymander, helped by our inheritance of rural values. Clamorous attack and powerful resistance make for heat in politics; this second area becomes a likely source of it.

If agriculture's place in our society is likely to be challenged in the Sixties, so is the place of organized labor. This is a third area of controversy; conceivably it may produce as much heat as the others, or still more. For there are signs in 1959 of something deeper than a relatively generalized distaste for certain trade unions. There now are signs that we may be approaching a distinct deterioration in industrial relations. During the Fifties, management concern about union prerogatives found principal expression on the front of politics—with limited effect—while economic pressure was suspended rather generally wherever the trade unions were entrenched. The Sixties, though, may bring us warfare on both fronts. A struggle on the economic front will sharpen every struggle on the other; it will also sharpen rank-and-file allegiances in both the warring camps. But Labor's camp is shrinking in proportion to the labor force, and it is far from clear that this would be "class" war. Much depends on management approaches to unorganized or loosely organized industrial and service workers. If we have warfare on the economic front there is no knowing how it will turn out. But clearly, if and as it comes it will add heat to politics.

There will be a fourth area of controversy in the Sixties, and it ranks with all these others put together: the integration of non-white Americans. This is so plainly in our future that to name it is enough. The future features Northern housing quite as much as Southern schools; it also features economic *and political* opportunity. No domestic issues are more likely to bring heat into our politics; none are more inflammable and none may turn more critical in the years just ahead.

These four are merely the most readily foreseeable as areas of controversy in the Nineteen-sixties. A hint of other issues can be found in a variety of present signs. Among them, for example, are the signs that Soviet production and trade policy (and markets) may become a serious factor in the near-term outlook for some major segments of American industry. Other signs suggest that in our legacy of foreign policy and posture from the Fifties are some fixed positions which will have to change but cannot without turning into issues in our politics. As a further source of issues there are dozens of contingencies abroad which might arise at any time to complicate home politics. And finally, there are matters like the spread of nuclear weapons, or radiation hazards, or the race for the moon, matters too arcane to heat our politics consistently but capable of flaring into issues overnight if sparked by a conjunction of events.

The purpose here is not to be exhaustive but indicative; this list should indicate why party politics in the next years can hardly bring us "party government." It does not matter whether the list covers every issue or describes it as it may appear in retrospect. What matters is that in so far as one can see ahead our politics will be made out of *issues with disparate local impacts,* impacts bound to alter rather suddenly depending on the way the issues mix. In combination with the timing of elections and the localism of electorates in party primaries, those disparate impacts almost guarantee that no congressional party will provide assured support, day in and out, to any President, and that no President will be the passive instrument of those who claim his party's name in Congress. Older sectionalisms may be fading (or may not); disparate local impacts are at hand to take their place. Until there is a marriage between presidential and congressional electorates, particularly at the stage of nomination, there will be no marriage between President and Congress. Until then Presidents will have to seek support as best they can from case to case. While this holds true on Capitol Hill, it will hold true along Pennsylvania Avenue. The reverse side of the coin is that a President's position and perspective will remain unique in the American political system.

The issues of the Sixties will be fought out in a system that keeps Presidents uniquely placed and gives them no assurance of sustained support. "Emergencies in policy with politics as usual" was my introductory characterization of the fifteen years just passed. Everything suggests that these mid-century conditions will persist into the new decade. But policy is likely to grow still more difficult, and politics is likely to grow hotter. Conditions will not be just what they were, they may be more so. It follows that our need will be the greater for a presidential expert in the Presidency.

IV

We are confronted by an evident necessity for government more energetic, policies more viable, than we have been enjoying in the Fifties. The areas of controversy, just described, are also fields for governmental action. But every path to action leads through controversy. Effective policy can only be created out of the material our politics provides. It is not very promising material. If policy is to be viable, ways must be found in every field to reconcile all sorts of things now called irreconcilable. This is the special province of the President-as-expert whose concern for power brings him face to face with the ingredients that make for viability in policy.

A President who knows what power is and wants it has to face irreconcilables whenever he considers his own stakes in acts of choice. The sources of his influence are such that one may suffer from whatever serves another. The move that gains him ground on some particular may scar his general Washington reputation. The move that brightens Washington impressions may raise public hopes the future cannot meet. And moves that seem imperative for reasons of high policy may threaten all three sources of his power. The essence of his expertise is an awareness that these are irreconcilable and that they must be reconciled. Viability in policy calls for the same awareness.

A President-as-expert is no cure-all. The illustrations in this book suggest his limitations. Power cannot be his sole criterion for choice, nor will his choices be the only regulators of his influence. They are the only levers in *his* hands, but other hands hold other levers. And his influence, at most, is only one of many factors shaping what eventuates as governmental action; events and men beyond his personal control are much the greater shapers. One cannot look around the world in the late Fifties with any special confidence in men or in events throughout the Sixties. It is not easy, after such a look, to quarrel with those who think that science and technology have pushed our social competence too far. Yet it seems premature to write off the adaptability and the inventiveness of American public policy. Admitting that the future is not wholly in our hands, our policy responses may make a substantial difference. Despairing views could have been voiced —and were—in 1950, or in 1940, or in 1930. At a time and in a world where rates of change accelerate, the Sixties may be the decade that finally proves too much for us. But on the record of the past, the policy responses of our political system give us grounds for hope. (In the whole perspective of this century so far, our recent pause seems relatively brief; besides, it was a pause, not a regression.) We might as well enjoy the hope; there is no present prospect that we soon shall change the system. Nor is there any prospect that a change of system would eliminate our policy dilemmas.

An expert in the White House does not guarantee effective policy, but lacking such an expert every hope is placed in doubt. If past experience is reassuring, its assurances are conveyed with that caveat. The responses of our system remain markedly dependent on the person of the President. "As matters have stood," Edward Corwin writes, ". . . presidential power has been at times dangerously *personalized*," and with unerring instinct for an expertise in influence he distrusts Franklin Roosevelt only less than Abraham Lincoln.[3] But if one wants effective policy from the American system, danger does not lie in our dependence on *a* man; it lies in our capacity to make ourselves depend upon a man who is inexpert. Any human judgment is worth fearing nowadays, but save for this the expert is a boon. His expertise assures a contribution to the system and it naturally commits him to proceed within the system. The system, after all, is what he knows. The danger lies in men who do not know it.

A dangerous dependence on the expertise of the top man— dependence on his "feel" for power in the going system—is not confined to the United States. It seems to be a feature of all democratic governments (presumably of communist regimes as well) though sometimes, as in Britain, it is so disguised that numbers of Americans may not have noticed it. The British cabinet system tends to cover up the weaknesses and to show up the strengths of the top man; ours tends to do the opposite. English politics does not place amateurs on top, while ours has put an amateur in office very recently. But Britain, in this century, has not lacked for inexpert heads of government, albeit quite professional, and British policy has paid a heavy price for them; most recently in Eden's case, to say nothing of Chamberlain's. With the English, as with us, structure and conventions and traditions count for everything *within* the system since the top man's expertise is wedded to them. But the English seem to be no less dependent than Americans upon the contributions of an expert at the top. If we were to import the British system overnight, power at the White House would be personalized still—and the person might turn out to be a Ramsay MacDonald. Some dangers in political society are not escaped by structure.

One of those dangers is the yearning in our national electorate for political leaders "above politics." Eisenhower, to be sure, is *sui generis*. But part of Stevenson's appeal was that he had not been in politics for long and did not seem to be a "politician." Currently, contenders for the 1960 nomination are doing all they can, each in his way, to take the curse off their political careers by assertions of amateur standing. Desire for an amateur is not new in American politics; Wendell Willkie's instance makes that plain. Now we have had Eisenhower. Significantly, to the limited extent that Eisenhower has been criticized in public his detractors, for the most part, deal in arguments *ad hominum*. Much of the criticism is unjust. Little of it makes allowance for the words attributed to Speaker Rayburn in the spring of 1952: "No, won't do. Good man. Wrong profession." But this is the heart of the matter.

The striking thing about our national elections in the Fifties was not Eisenhower's personal popularity; it was the genuine approval of his candidacy by informed Americans whom one might have supposed would know better. A sizeable majority of voters twice elected him. And save for one brief interval, his conduct as a President has always had commensurate approval on the showing of the Gallup Poll. Why not? The popular hero in a genuine sense, the man who is both great and friend, has never been in long supply with us. In the later Forties and throughout the Fifties, Eisenhower was the only one we had. To place him in the White House without losing him as hero seems both reasonable and prudent on the part of average citizens, no matter what their general view of politics or Presidents. The same thing can be said of the Republican professionals who managed Eisenhower's nomination in 1952; their action appears reasonable and prudent in *their* terms. They twice had tried a leading politician as their candidate; this time they wanted most of all to win. But when it comes to journalists, and government officials, and business leaders, and professors, who joined in the parade or urged it on, one deals with a phenomenon decidedly less reasonable. Some of Eisenhower's sharpest critics at the present time were once among his most articulate admirers. What was their understanding then— what is it now—of our political institutions? His virtue was supposed to be that he was above politics, and disenchantment with him rarely seems a disenchantment with this odd criterion. Instead it is all Eisenhower's fault that he is not what temperament and training never equipped him to be. When one finds attitudes of this sort in the circle of articulate observers, one wonders at the meaning for American society.

Before he reached the White House Woodrow Wilson once remarked: "Men of ordinary physique and discretion cannot be Presidents and live, if the strain be not somehow relieved. We shall be obliged always to be picking our chief magistrates from among wise and prudent athletes—a small class." [4] In the perspective of this book his formula needs some revision. The strain is vastly greater now, with no relief in sight. If we want Presidents alive and fully useful, we shall have to pick them from among experienced politicians of extraordinary temperament—an even smaller class.

Afterword: JFK

Eight years have passed since those last paragraphs were printed. The skilled congressional politician who then was Majority Leader of the Senate now is President of the United States. Shortly he will retire with his reputation as a *presidential* politician mortgaged to the war he made his own. Before him, briefly, we had still another President, catapulted into history by an assassin's bullet: John F. Kennedy.

There are many ways to look at the performance of an American President. One way is to assess his operational effectiveness as man in office—a single individual amidst a vast machine. This has been my approach in previous writings on past Presidents. Regarding Kennedy, it is foolhardy to attempt an appraisal in these terms. He died too soon. But, assuming that my readers will indulge the folly, I shall try.[1]

I

In appraising the personal performance of a President it is useful to ask four questions. First, what were his purposes and did these run with or against the grain of history; how relevant were they to what would happen in his time? Second, what was his "feel," his human understanding, for the nature of his power in the circumstances of his time, and how close did he come in this respect to the realities around him (a matter again of relevance)? Third, what was his stance under pressure in office, what sustained him as a person against the frustrations native to the place, and how did his peacemaking with himself affect the style and content of his own decision making? This becomes especially important now that nuclear technology has equipped both Americans and Russians with an intercontinental capability; stresses on the Presidency grow apace. Fourth, what was his legacy? What imprint did he leave on the office, its character, and public standing; where did he leave his party and the other party nationally; what remained by way of public policies adopted or in controversy; what remained as issues in American society, insofar as his own stance may have affected them; and what were the American positions in the world affected by his own diplomacy?

To answer these four questions, the outside observer must look for certain clues.

1. Regarding purpose, clues are found in irreversible commitments to defined courses of action. By "purpose" I mean nothing so particular as an endorsement for, say, "Medicare," or anything so general as a pledge to "peace." (All Presidents desire peace.) By "course of action" I mean something broader than the one but more definable than the other: Harry S Truman's commitment to "containment," so called, or Dwight D. Eisenhower's commitment to what he called "fiscal responsibility." By "commitment" I mean personal involvement, in terms of what the man himself is seen to say and do, so plain and so direct that politics—and history—will not let him turn back: Truman on civil rights, or Eisenhower on the Army budget, or Lyndon B. Johnson, alas, on South Vietnam where turning even slightly has been rendered credible only by his promise to leave office.

2. Regarding feel for office, sensitivity to power, clues are drawn from signs of pattern in the man's own operating style as he encounters concrete cases, cases of decision and of follow-through in every sphere of action, legislative and executive, public and partisan, foreign and domestic—Truman seeking above all to be decisive; Eisenhower reaching for a place above the struggle.

3. Regarding pressure and its consequences, clues are to be drawn again from cases; here one examines crisis situations, seeking signs of

pattern in the man's response—Truman at the time of the Korean outbreak, or of Chinese intervention; Eisenhower at the time of Hungary and Suez, or of Little Rock—times like these compared with others just as tough in terms of stress.

4. With regard to the man's legacy, one seeks clues in the conduct of the *next* Administration. Roosevelt's first New Deal in 1933 tells us a lot about the Hoover Presidency. Truman's troubled turnabout in postwar foreign policy casts shadows on the later Roosevelt Presidency. And Kennedy's complaint at Yale six years ago about the "myths" regarding economic management is testimony to one part of Eisenhower's legacy: the part identified with the redoubtable George Humphrey.

To list these sources of the wherewithal for answers is to indicate the folly of pursuing my four questions when the object of the exercise is Kennedy-in-office. He was President for two years and ten months. If one were to assess Franklin Roosevelt on the basis of performance before January 1936, or Harry Truman on his accomplishments before enactment of the Marshall Plan, or Eisenhower if he had not survived his heart attack, or LBJ before the 1966 Congressional elections—or Lincoln, for that matter, if he had been assassinated six months after Gettysburg—one would be most unlikely to reach judgments about any of these men resembling current judgments drawn from the full record of their terms. We cannot know what Kennedy's full record would have been if he had escaped assassination. Still more important, we can never know precisely how to weigh events in his truncated term.

Truman's seven years and Eisenhower's eight years suggest a certain rhythm in the modern Presidency. The first twelve to eighteen months become a learning time for the new President who has to learn—or unlearn—many things about his job. Regardless of his prior training, nothing he has done will have prepared him for all facets of that job. Some aspects of the learning process will persist beyond the first year and a half. Most Presidents will go on making new discoveries as long as they hold office (until, at last, they learn the bitterness of leaving office). But the intensive learning time comes at the start and dominates the first two years. A President's behavior in those years is an uncertain source of clues to what will follow. It is unreliable in indicating what will be the patterns of performance "on the job" once learning has been done. Yet the fourth year is also unreliable; traditionally it brings a period of pause, dominated by a special test requiring special effort—the test of reelection. The way that test is taken tells us much about a President, but less about his conduct on the job in other years. The seventh year is the beginning of the end—now guaranteed by constitutional amendment—as all eyes turn toward the coming nominations and the *next* Administration.

Thus, in the search for signs of pattern, clues to conduct, the key years are the third, the fifth, and the sixth. Kennedy had only one of these.

Moreover, in this presidential cycle, retrospect is an essential aid for sorting evidence. What a man does in his later years sheds light on the significance of what he did in early years, distinguishing the actions that conform to lasting patterns from the aspects of behavior that were transient. The man's early performance will include a host of clues to what is typical throughout his term of office. But it also will include assorted actions that turn out to be unrepresentative. Looking back from later years these become easy to distinguish. But in the second or third year it is hard indeed to say, "This action, this behavior will be dominant throughout." That is the sort of statement best reserved for retrospect. Kennedy's case leaves no room for retrospect; he was cut off too early in the cycle.

No scholar, therefore, should have the temerity to undertake what follows.

II

Turning to an appraisal of this President in office, I come to my first question, the question of purpose. This is not a matter of initial "ideology," fixed intent; far from it. Franklin Roosevelt did not enter office bent upon becoming "traitor to his class." Truman did not swear the oath with any notion that he was to take this country into the cold war. Lincoln certainly did not assume the presidency to gain the title

of "Great Emancipator." Johnson's massive victory of 1964 surely was
not *intended* as a prelude to the Vietnam war we know today.

   The purposes of Presidents are not to be confused with their intentions at the start; these are a matter, rather, of responses to events. Nor
should these purposes be confused with signs of temperament, with
"passion." Whether Kennedy was "passionate" is scarcely relevant.
Truman certainly deserves to have the cause of civil rights cited among
his purposes, but if he were to be judged in temperamental terms according to the standards of, say, Eastern liberals, he scarcely could be
called a man of passion on the point. And FDR is considered historically as "Labor's friend," although his coolness toward the great show
of that friendship in his time, the Wagner Act, remained until he
sensed that it was sure to be enacted. What counts here is not "passion,"
but the words and acts that lead to irreversible *commitment*.

   In Kennedy's three years of office, what were his commitments?
Never mind his private thoughts at twenty or at forty; never mind his
preferences for one thing or another; never mind his distaste for a
passionate display—taking the real world as he found it, what attracted
his commitment in the sense that he identified himself beyond recall?

   The record will disclose, I think, at least three purposes so understood. First, above all others, most compelling, most intense, was a
commitment to reduce the risk of holocaust by *mutual* miscalculation,
to "get the nuclear genie back in the bottle," to render statecraft manageable by statesmen, tolerable for the rest of us. He did not aim at anything so trite(or unachievable) as "victory" in the cold war. His aim,
apparently, was to outlast it with American society intact and nuclear
risks in check. Nothing, I think, mattered more to Kennedy than
bottling that genie. This, I know, was deeply in his mind. It also was
made manifest in words, among them his address at American University on June 10, 1963. That speech is seal and symbol of this purpose.
But other signs are found in acts, as well, and in more private words
accompanying action: from his Vienna interview with Khrushchev,
through the Berlin crisis during 1961, to the Cuban missile crisis and
thereafter—this commitment evidently deepened with experience as
Kennedy responded to events.

   Another speech in June of 1963 stands for a second purpose: the
speech on civil rights, June 11, and the message to Congress eight days

later which launched Kennedy's campaign for what became the Civil Rights Act of 1964. Thereby he undertook an irreversible commitment to Negro integration in American society, aiming once again to get us through the effort with society intact. He evidently came to see the risks of social alienation as plainly as he saw the risks of nuclear escalation, and he sought to steer a course toward integration that could hold inside our social order both impatient Blacks and reactive whites— as tough a task of politics as any we have known, and one he faced no sooner than he had to. But he faced it. What Vienna, Berlin, and Cuba were to his first purpose, Oxford and then Birmingham were to this second purpose: events that shaped his personal commitment.

A third speech is indicative of still another purpose, a speech less known and a commitment less apparent, though as definite, I think, as both of the others: Kennedy's commencement speech at Yale on June 11, 1962, soon after his short "war" over steel price increases. He spoke of making our complex economy, our somewhat *sui generis* economy, function effectively for meaningful growth, and as the means he urged an end of ideology in problem solving. His speech affirmed the notion that the key problems of economic growth are technical, not ideological, to be met not by passion but by intellect, and that the greatest barriers to growth are the ideas in people's heads— "myths" as he called them—standing in the way of reasoned diagnosis and response. Kennedy, I think, was well aware (indeed, he was made painfully aware) that only on our old-style Left is ideology defunct. Elsewhere it flourishes, clamping a lid on applied intelligence, withholding brainpower from rational engagement in the novel problems of our economic management. He evidently wanted most of all to lift that lid.

Failing a response to his Yale lecture, Kennedy retreated to the easier task of teaching one simple economic lesson, the lesson the tax bill carried through after his death: well-timed budget deficits can lead to balanced budgets. This, evidently, was the most that he thought he could manage in contesting "myths," at least before election. But his ambition, I believe, was to assault a lot more myths than this, when and as he could. That ambition measures his commitment to effective growth in the economy.

Stemming from this third commitment (and the second), one discerns a corollary that perhaps would have become a fourth: what Kennedy's successor named "the war against poverty." During the course of 1963, Kennedy became active in prompting plans for an attack on chronic poverty. His prospective timing no doubt had political utility, but it also had social utility that evidently mattered quite as much. Historically, the "war" is Lyndon Johnson's. All we know of Kennedy is that he meant to make one. Still, for either of these men the effort, if sustained, would lead to irreversible commitment. So it has seemed to be for Johnson, even though he let another such commitment take priority for energy and funds.

Each purpose I have outlined meant commitment to a course of action that engaged the man—his reputation, *amour propre*, and sense of self in history—beyond recall. The question then becomes: how relevant were these, historically? How relevant to Kennedy's own years of actual (and of prospective) office? Here I can only make a judgment (tentative, of course) devoid of long perspective. These purposes seem to me entirely relevant. In short perspective, they seem precisely right as the preeminent concerns for the first half of this decade.

What of Vietnam? The worst thing one can say of Kennedy's decisions in that quarter is that these were offhand, intermittent, and discontinuous—in short, the reverse of "committal." No doubt, there was a frightful lapse in management but not in purpose. By way of purpose, small attention to Vietnam, a low priority, seems *right* for this decade. Consider the results of high priority since Kennedy left the scene!

III

So much for Kennedy as a man of purpose. What about the man of power?

He strikes me as a senator who learned very fast from his confrontation with the Executive establishment, particularly after the abortive Cuban invasion which taught him a great deal. On action-issues of particular concern to him he rapidly evolved an operating style that he maintained consistently (and sharpened at the edges) through his years of office. If one looks at Berlin, or Oxford, Mississippi, or the Cuban missile crisis, or at half a dozen other issues of the sort, one finds a pattern: the personal command post, a deliberate reaching down for the details, hard questioning of the alternatives, a drive to protect options from foreclosure by sheer urgency or by *ex parte* advocacy, and finally a close watch on follow-through. Even on the issues that were second-ary to the President and left, perforce, primarily to others, Kennedy was constantly in search of means and men to assure that those others used this personalized pattern with its stress on open options and on close control. Numbers of outsiders—Hans Morgenthau and Joseph Alsop for two—sometimes viewed the pattern with alarm and saw this man as "indecisive." But that was to consult *their* preferences, not his performance. Kennedy always seemed keen to single out the necessary from the merely possible. He then decided with alacrity.

Not everything was always done effectively, of course, and even the successes produced side effects of bureaucratic bafflement, frustration, and irritation, which were not without their costs. Even so, the pattern testifies to an extraordinary feel for the distinction between President and Presidency, an extraordinary urge to master the machine. This took him quite a way toward mastery in two years and ten months. We shall not know how far he might have gone.

Kennedy's feel for his own executive position carried over into that of fellow rulers everywhere. He evidently had great curiosity and real concern about the politics of rulership wherever he encountered it. His feel for fine distinctions among fellow "kings" was rare; it was com-parable to the feel of Senate-Leader Johnson for the fine distinctions among fellow senators. And, with this, Kennedy apparently absorbed in his short time a lesson Franklin Roosevelt never learned about the Russians (or de Gaulle): that in another country an *effective* politician can have motives very *different* from his own. What an advantageous lesson to have learned in two years time! It would have served him well. Indeed, while he still lived I think it did.

The cardinal test of Kennedy as an executive in his own right and also as a student of executives abroad was certainly the confrontation of October 1962 with Khrushchev: the Cuban missile crisis. For almost the first time in our foreign relations, the President displayed on that occa-sion both concern for the psychology of his opponent and insistence on a limited objective. Contrast the Korean War, where we positively courted Chinese intervention by relying on Douglas MacArthur as psychologist and by enlarging our objective after each success. "There is no substitute for victory," MacArthur wrote, but at that time we virtually had a nuclear monopoly and even then our government hastened to find a substitute. Now, with mutual capability, the whole traditional meaning has been taken out of "victory." In nuclear confrontations there is room for no such thing. Kennedy quite evidently knew it. He also knew, as his performance demonstrates, that risks of escalation lurk in high-level misjudgments *and* in low-level momentum. Washington assuredly was capable of both; so, probably, was Moscow. Accordingly, the President outstripped all previous efforts to guard options and assure control. His operating style was tested then as not before. It got him what he wanted.

Unhappily, another, subtler, seemingly less pressing test came his way a year later with the Buddhist agitation in Vietnam. That test he flunked. Diem's assassination may have made this plain to him three weeks before his own demise.

In confrontations with Congress, quite another world than the Executive, the key to Kennedy's congressional relations lay outside his feel for power, beyond reach of technique; he won the Presidency by a hair, while in the House of Representatives his party lost about twenty of the seats gained two years earlier. The Democrats *retained* a sizeable majority as they had done in earlier years, no thanks to him. With this beginning, Kennedy's own record of accomplishment in Congress looks enormous, indeterminate, or small, depending on one's willingness to give him credit for enactment of the most divisive, innovative bills he espoused: the tax and civil rights bills passed in Johnson's Presidency. Certainly it can be said that Kennedy prepared the way, negotiating a bipartisan approach, and also that he took the heat, stalling his whole program in the process. Equally, it can be said that with his death—or by it—the White House gained advantages that he could not have mustered. Johnson made the most of these. How well would Kennedy have done without them? My own guess is that in the end, with rancor and delay, both bills would have been passed. But it is a moot point. Accordingly, so is the Kennedy record.

Whatever his accomplishment, does it appear the most he could have managed in his years? Granting the limits set by his election, granting the divisiveness injected after Birmingham with his decisive move on civil rights, did he use to the fullest his advantages of office? The answer may well be "not quite." Perhaps a better answer is, "This man could do no more." For Kennedy, it seems, was not a man enamored of the legislative way of life, and legislators knew it. He was wry about it. He had spent fourteen years in Congress and he understood its business, but he never was a "member of the family" on the Hill. "Downtown" had always seemed his native habitat; he was a natural executive. They knew that, too. Besides, he was a young man, very young by Senate standards, and his presence in the White House with still younger men around him was a constant irritant to seniors. Moreover, he was not a "mixer" socially, not, anyway, with most members of Congress and their wives. His manners were impeccable, his charm impelling, but he kept his social life distinct from his official life and congressmen were rarely in his social circle. To know how Congress works but to disdain its joys is an acquired taste for most ex-congressmen downtown, produced by hard experience. Kennedy, however, brought it with him. Many of the difficulties he was to encounter in his day-by-day congressional relations stemmed from that.

But even if he had been a man who dearly loved the Congress, even if that feeling had been reciprocated, nothing could have rendered their relationship sweetness and light in his last year, so long as he persisted with his legislative program. As an innovative President confronting a reluctant Congress, he was heir to Truman, and to Roosevelt after 1936. Kennedy's own manner may have hurt him on the Hill, but these were scratches. Deeper scars had more substantial sources and he knew it.

In confrontations with the larger public outside Washington (again a different world), Kennedy made a brilliant beginning, matched only by the start in different circumstances of his successor. The "public relations" of transition into office were superb. In three months after his election, Kennedy transformed himself from "pushy," "young," "Catholic," into President-of-all-the-people, widening and deepening acceptance of his presidency out of all proportion to the election returns. The Bay of Pigs was a severe check, but his handling of the aftermath displayed again superb feel for the imagery befitting an incumbent of the White House, heir to FDR *and* Eisenhower. That feel he always had. I think it never failed him.

What he also had was a distaste for preaching, really for the preach-iness of politics, backed by genuine mistrust of mass emotion as a tool in politics. These attitudes are rare among American politicians; with Kennedy their roots ran deep into recesses of experience and character where I, as an outsider, cannot follow. But they assuredly were rooted in this man and they had visible effects on his public style. He delighted in the play of minds, not of emotions. He doted on press conferences, not set performances. He feared "overexposure"; he dreaded over-reaction. Obviously he enjoyed responsive crowds, and was responsive to a sea of cheering faces, but I think he rarely looked at their reaction —or his own—without a twing of apprehension. He never seems to have displayed much fondness for the "fireside chat," a form of crowd appeal without the crowd; television talks in evening hours evidently struck him more as duty than as opportunity, and dangerous at that; some words on air-raid shelters in a talk about Berlin could set off mass hysteria—and did. At the moment when he had his largest, most atten-tive audience, on the climactic Sunday of the Cuban missile crisis, he turned it away (and turned attention off) with a two-minute announce-ment, spare and dry.

Yet we know now, after his death, what none of us knew before: that with a minimum of preaching, of emotional appeal, or of self-justifica-tion, even explanation, he had managed to touch millions in their private lives, not only at home but emphatically abroad. Perhaps his very cool-ness helped him do it. Perhaps his very vigor, family, fortune, sense of fun, his manners, taste, and sportsmanship, his evident enjoyment of his life and of the job made him the heart's desire of all sorts of people everywhere, not least among the young. At any rate, we know now that he managed in his years to make enormous impact on a world-wide audience, building an extraordinary base of public interest and affection (interspersed, of course, with doubters and detractors). What he might have made of this or done with it in later years, nobody knows.

IV

So much for power; what about pressure? What sustained this man in his decisions, his frustrations, and with what effect on his approach to being President? For an answer one turns to the evidence of crises, those already mentioned among others, and the *surface* signs are clear. In all such situations it appears that Kennedy was cool, collected, courteous, and terse. This does not mean that he was unemotional. By temperament I think he was a man of mood and passion. But he had schooled his temperament. He kept his emotions under tight control. He did not lose his temper inadvertently, and never lost it for long. He was observer and participant combined; he saw himself as coolly as all others—and with humor. He always was a witty man, dry with a bit of bite and a touch of self-deprecation. He could laugh at himself, and did. Often he used humor to break tension. And in tight places he displayed a keen awareness of the human situation, human limits (his included), but it did not slow his work.

Readers beyond the age of forty may recognize this portrait as "the stance of junior officers in the Second World War"; Elsbeth Rostow coined that phrase and, superficially at least, she is quite right. This was the Kennedy stance, and his self-confidence, his shield against frustration, must have owed a lot to his young manhood in that war.

This tells us a good deal but not nearly enough. At his very first encounter with a crisis in the Presidency, Kennedy's self-confidence seems to have been severely strained. The Bay of Pigs fiasco shook him deeply, shook his confidence in methods and associates. Yet he went on governing without a break, no change in manner, or in temper, or in humor. What sustained him? Surely much that went beyond experience of war.

What else? I cannot answer, I can only conjecture. His family life and rearing have some part to play, no doubt. His political successes also played a part. In 1952 he bucked the Eisenhower tide to reach the Senate; in 1960 he broke barriers of youth and of religion which had always held before; on each occasion the Conventional Wisdom was against him: "can't be done." Beyond these things, this man had been exceptionally close to death, not only in World War II but ten years after. And in his presidential years his back was almost constantly a source of pain; he never talked about it but he lived with it. All this is of a piece with his behavior in a crisis. His control, his objectivity, his humor, and his sense of human limits, these were but expressions of his confidence; its sources must lie somewhere in this ground.

Whatever the sources, the results were rewarding for this President's performance on the job. In the most critical, nerve-straining aspects of the office, coping with its terrible responsibility for use of force, Kennedy's own image of himself impelled him neither to lash out nor to run for cover. Instead, it released him for engagement and decision as a reasonable man. In some of the less awesome aspects of the Presidency his own values restrained him, kept him off the pulpit, trimmed his guest list, and made him shy away from the hyperbole of politics. But as a chief *executive*, confronting action-issues for decision and control, his duty and his confidence in doing it were nicely matched. So the world discovered in October 1962.

V

Now for my last question. What did he leave behind him? What was the legacy of his short years? At the very least he left a myth: the vibrant, youthful leader cut down senselessly before his time. What this may come to signify as the years pass, I cannot tell. He left a glamorous moment, an engaging, youthful time, but how we shall remember it depends on how we shall remember Lyndon Johnson. He left a broken promise, that "the torch has been passed to a new generation," and the youngsters who identified with him felt cheated as the promise, like the glamor, disappeared. What do their feelings matter? We shall have to wait and see (although the evidence is mounting year by year).

May this be all that history is likely to record? Perhaps, but I doubt it. My guess is that when the observers can appraise the work of Kennedy's successors, they will find some things of substance in his legacy. Rashly, let me record what I think these are.

To begin with, our first Catholic President chose and paved the way for our first Southern President since the Civil War. (Woodrow Wilson was no Southerner *politically;* he came to the White House from the State House of New Jersey.) Although Texas may be suspect now in Southern eyes, it certainly is of the South in Northern eyes, as Johnson found so painfully in 1960. Kennedy made him President. How freely he chose Johnson as vice-presidential candidate is subject to some argument. But what appears beyond dispute is that, once chosen, Johnson was so treated by his rival for the White House as to ease his way enormously when he took over there. Johnson may have suffered great frustration as Vice-President, but his public standing and his knowledge of affairs were nurtured in those years. From this he gained a running start. The credit goes in no small part to Kennedy.

Moreover, Kennedy bequeathed to Johnson widened options in the sphere of foreign relations: a military posture far more flexible and usable than he himself inherited; a diplomatic posture more sophisticated in its whole approach to neutralists and Leftists, markedly more mindful of distinctions in the world, even among allies. In European relations and in dealings with the Soviets, LBJ built on this diplomatic legacy. In Vietnam he departed from it, squandering his military legacy. Unhappily it must be recorded that without the military posture Kennedy left behind, the officials whom he also left behind would not have had the wherewithal to offer Johnson the disastrous option of a full-scale intervention in Vietnam.

The most dubious thing Kennedy left Johnson was American involvement with Saigon. Rashly, this had been enlarged in Kennedy's last months of life by acquiescence in the overthrow of Diem, which transferred to that abstract entity, "the Government of South Vietnam," an undertaking hitherto identified with Diem. Involvement might have been conditioned upon Diem's regime and dropped as he departed, or devolved as his associates dealt with the North. The reverse happened. Kennedy's decisions made it so. By hindsight these were mistaken. Johnson took the consequences. Thereupon he made still less fortunate decisions, which produced a war more costly and more futile than Korea.

Would Kennedy have done the same? We cannot know. My guess is that he would have done quite differently. Given his age, experience, and temperament, given the priorities emergent from three years of office, given the advantages in our domestic politics accorded to a man who had faced down Khrushchev—given all these, I think he would have kept his bombers and his combat troops away, leaving the Saigonese of 1965 to fashion such accommodation as they could. "It's their war, they have to win it," he declared two months before he died. Presumably he would have stood so as they lost it. But the point is moot.

On the domestic side, Kennedy left a large inheritance of controversies, opened by a youthful, Catholic urbanite from the Northeast, which his Southwestern, Protestant successor might have had more trouble stirring at the start, but now could ride and maybe even "heal." Vietnam aside, this might have been a productive division of labor. Even if not, Kennedy lived long enough to keep at least one promise. He got the country "moving again."

In American politics, the *sine qua non* of innovative policy is controversy. By 1963 we were engaged in controversy with an openness that would have been unthinkable, or at least "un-American," during the later Eisenhower years. Events, of course, have more to do with stirring controversy than a President. No man can make an issue on his own. But Presidents will help to shape the meaning of events, the terms of discourse, the attention paid, and the noise level. Eisenhower's years were marked by a pervasive fog of self-congratulation, muffling noise. The fog machine was centered in the White House. Perhaps there had been need for this after the divisive Truman years. But by the late 1950's, it fuzzed our chance to innovate in time. Kennedy broke out of it. This gave his successor an initial opportunity.

Finally, JFK set a new standard of performance on the job, suitable to a new state of presidential being, a state he was the first to face throughout his term of office: the state of substantial, deliverable, nuclear capability in other hands than ours. Whatever else historians may make of Kennedy, I think they probably will begin with this. There can be little doubt that his successors have a lighter task because *he* pioneered in handling nuclear confrontations. During the Cuban missile crisis and thereafter, he did something that had not been done before, did it well, and got it publicly accepted. Innovation was on our agenda; technology had put it there. But also, in his reach for information and control, his balancing of firmness with caution, his sense of limits, he displayed and dramatized what Presidents must do to minimize the risk of war through mutual miscalculation. This may well be the cardinal risk confronting his successors. If so, he made a major contribution to the Presidency.

VI

What a President now lives with is the consequence of a nuclear second-strike capability acquired by the Soviet Union as well as the

United States. It is the mutual capability that pushes our choice-making—and theirs, too, of course—into a new dimension of risk. In previous writings I have termed this the risk of "irreversibility," the risk that either bureaucratic momentum in a large-scale undertaking or mutual miscalculation by atomic adversaries, or both combined, may make it infeasible to call back, or play over, or revise an action taken in our foreign relations, at least within the range of the cold war. But the term "irreversibility," standing alone, does not really suffice to convey what is new in this dimension. Bureaucratic momentum and multiple miscalculations made a German Emperor's snap reaction after Saravejo "irreversible" as long ago as July 1914. Therefore, to amend the term: what is new since the Soviets acquired their missiles is the risk of *irreversibility become irreparable*. Unlike the problems facing Kaiser Wilhelm 54 years ago—or those of FDR in World War II, or even those of Truman in Korea—a possible result of present action is that nothing one does later can ward off, reduce, repair, or compensate for costs to one's society.

The Cuban confrontation seems to me a relatively simplified affair, geographically, in the issue raised, in the number of contestants, and in duration. What if there were two or three such issues simultaneously, or stretched over two months instead of two weeks? What if there were a multiplicity of nuclear powers, a multiplicity of possible miscalculators, each capable of setting off irreparable consequences? Consider the next President's risk-taking, let alone Kennedy's or Johnson's. This new dimension deepens year by year.

The consequences for the Presidency are profound.

One consequence is that the sitting President lives daily with the knowledge that at any time he, personally, may have to make a human judgment—or may fail to control someone else's judgment—which puts half the world in jeopardy and cannot be called back. Many of us recognize his burden intellectually; he actually experiences it emotionally. It cannot help but set him and his needs sharply apart from all the rest of us, not least from the officials who have only to advise him. As Kennedy remarked in his year-end television interview for 1962: "The President bears the burden of the responsibility. The advisers may move on to new advice."

A second related consequence is that now, more than ever before, his mind becomes the only source available from which to draw politically legitimated judgments on what, broadly speaking, can be termed the political feasibilities of contemplated action vis-à-vis our world antagonists: judgments on where history is tending, what opponents can stand, what friends will take, what officials will enforce, what "men in the street" will tolerate—judgments on the balance of support, opposition, and indifference, at home and abroad. Our Constitution contemplated that such judgments should emanate from President *and* Congress, from a combination of the men who owed their places to electorates, who had themselves experienced the hazards of nomination and election. *The democratic element in our system consists essentially of reserving these judgments to men with that experience.* But when it comes to action risking war, technology has modified the Constitution: the President, perforce, becomes the only such man in the system capable of exercising judgment under the extraordinary limits now imposed by secrecy, complexity, and time.

Therefore, as a matter not only of securing his own peace of mind but also of preserving the essentials in our democratic order, a President these days is virtually compelled to reach for information and to seek control over details of concrete plans, of actual performance, on "small" operations (to say nothing of large ones), where there often is a fleeting chance—sometimes the only chance—to interject effective judgment. And it is at this level that risks of the gravest sort are often run. "Irreversibility become irreparable" is not to be considered something separate from details of operation. If, as reported, Kennedy kept track of every movement of blockading warships during the Cuban crisis of October 1962, this is but a natural and necessary corollary of the new dimension of risk shadowing us all, but most of all a President.

The net effect is to restrict if not repeal a hallowed aspect of American military doctrine—the autonomy of field commanders—which as recently as Truman's time, as recently as the Korean War, was thought to set sharp limits on White House intervention in details of operation. The conduct of diplomacy is comparably affected. So, I presume, is the conduct of intelligence. Also, we now rediscover that age-old problem for the rulers of States: timely and secure communications. The complications here are mind-stretching.

The only persons qualified to give a full appreciation of the President's needs in such a situation are Eisenhower, keeping his last years in view, and Johnson, who watched Kennedy in 1962 and now sits there himself. Nikita Khruschev might be equipped to to offer some contributory evidence. The situation is so new and so unprecedented that, outside the narrow circle of these men and their immediate associates, one cannot look with confidence for understanding of their prospects or requirements *as these appear to them.*

Thus we encounter, at least for the time being, a new source of differences between the President and most executive officials: the former cannot fail for long to see what he is up against; the latter have not seen enough of men so placed to have much sympathy or a sure sense for how it feels these days, in these conditions, to be President. What they see with assurance is what they in their jobs want of him in his— a very different matter. These differing perceptions of the presidential task are bound to widen differences between the White House, where responsibility is focused, and officialdom, where it is not.

The same phenomenon of differing perceptions seems to play a part in other presidential relationships. No doubt it has some bearing on the current difficulties of relationship between the White House and its counterparts in certain allied capitals where political leaders, in their own capacities, have not experienced the risk to which our President is heir because they lack the power that produced it. Presumably, some of the sore spots in congressional relations have a comparable source. Certainly this is the case with some of the complaints voiced against Eisenhower and Kennedy by private groups intent upon particular action programs.

The lack of common outlook increases the Presidency's isolation and thus reinforces the dictates of common prudence for a man who bears the burden of that office in our time, namely, to stretch his personal control, his human judgment, as wide and deep as he can make them reach.

From now on, everything asserted in this book must be transposed into these terms. The President remains our system's Great Initiator. When what we once called "war" impends, he now becomes our system's Final Arbiter. He is no less a clerk in one capacity than in the other. But in the second instance those he serves are utterly dependent on his judgment—and judgment then becomes the mark of "leadership." Command may have a narrow reach but it encompasses irreparable consequences. Yet persuasion is required to exercise command, to get one's hands upon subordinate decisions. With this so-nearly absolute dependence upon presidential judgment backed by presidential skill, we and our system have no previous experience. Now in the 1960's we begin to explore it.

Hopefully, both citizens and Presidents will do so without fear, or histrionics, or withdrawals from reality, or lurches toward aggression. Regardless of the dangers, presidential power, even in this new dimension, still has to be sought and used; it cannot be escaped. We now are even more dependent than before on the mind and temperament of the man in the White House.

RICHARD E. NEUSTADT

Harvard University
Cambridge, Massachusetts
April, 1968

Notes

CHAPTER 2

¹ Robert J. Donovan, *Eisenhower: The Inside Story*, New York: Harper, 1956, p. 151.

² These and later references to the dismissal of General MacArthur and the background of that action are based on the following sources: "The Military Situation in the Far East," *Hearings*, U.S. Senate Committee on Armed Services and Committee on Foreign Relations, 82d Cong., 1st sess., Washington: 1951, parts 1–5 (referred to hereafter as *MacArthur Hearings*); Memoirs by Harry S. Truman, Vol. 2, *Years of Trial and Hope*, Garden City: Doubleday, 1956, copr. 1956 Time Inc., chaps. 23–28.

There has been some supplementation of these sources by interviews with former President Truman in December 1955, and in February 1958, and by personal notes made at the time. For general background I would refer the reader to Walter Millis, Harvey C. Mansfield, and Harold Stein, *Arms and the State*, New York: Twentieth Century Fund, 1958, chap. 7.

³ As reported in the *New York Times*, March 8, 1951 and reproduced in the *MacArthur Hearings*, part 5, pp. 3540–3541.

⁴ These and succeeding references to the steel seizure and related events are based on the case study by Grant McConnell, *The President Seizes the Steel Mills*, Inter-University Case Program, University, Ala.: University of Alabama Press, 1960, supplemented extensively by personal notes made at the time and by interviews with former President Truman in December 1955.

For an illuminating documentation of public and legal developments before and after seizure, the reader is referred to Alan F. Westin, *The Anatomy of a Constitutional Law Case*, New York: Macmillan, 1958. See also Truman *Memoirs*, Vol 2, chap. 29.

⁵ These and succeeding references to the Little Rock affair are based on the following sources: news reports and texts of documents appearing in *Southern School News* and the *New York Times;* former Congressman

Brooks Hays's personal account *A Southern Moderate Speaks,* Chapel Hill: University of North Carolina Press, 1959; the personal account by the former Superintendent of Schools, Virgil T. Blossom, *It Has Happened Here,* New York: Harper, 1959, especially pp. 120 ff.; Corinne Silverman's case study, *The Little Rock Story,* Inter-University Case Program, no. 41, University, Ala.: University of Alabama Press, 1958. These sources were supplemented by interviews in February and April 1958 with three members of the White House staff.

⁶ Truman *Memoirs,* Vol. 2, p. 442.

⁷ Harry S. Ashmore, *An Epitaph for Dixie,* New York: Norton, 1958, p. 41.

⁸ In the period before this action by the District Court, Sawyer's delay was based, in part, on the advice of Commerce legal staff after consultation with Justice attorneys preparing the government's case. The Justice lawyers feared that action on wages would complicate their argument before the court. The lawyers in the White House were unimpressed by this concern; it is doubtful that the Acting Attorney General shared it, either. But Sawyer was the official in charge of the mills, and these were the attorneys in charge of the case. Their preference buttressed his inclination, and the responsibility was his.

⁹ The emergency-disputes provisions of the Taft-Hartley Act, which Truman so far had refused to invoke in this case, require as their first step appointment of a fact-finding board. Only after its report, if he deems its findings justify such action, is the President authorized to have the Attorney General seek an injunction from the courts forbidding a work stoppage for 80 days. Hence the first step, fact-finding, neither stops a strike in progress nor automatically commits a President to the use of an injunction.

¹⁰ Truman *Memoirs,* Vol. 2, p. 448.

¹¹ As indicated especially in MacArthur's message to the Veterans of Foreign Wars, which was "withdrawn" on presidential order of August 26, 1950. By then, an advance text had already been released to the press and was carried in full in *U.S. News and World Report,* September 1, 1950, Vol. 29, no. 9, pp. 32–34. The text is reproduced in the *MacArthur Hearings,* part 5, p. 3477.

¹² Transcript of presidential press conference, July 17, 1957, in *Public Papers of the Presidents: Dwight D. Eisenhower, 1957,* Washington: The National Archives, 1958, p. 546.

¹³ Henry A. Kissinger, *Nuclear Weapons and Foreign Policy,* New York: Harper, for the Council on Foreign Relations, 1957, pp. 50–51.

Notes

CHAPTER 3

[1] The reader will want to keep in mind the distinction between two senses in which the word *power* is employed. When I have used the word (or its plural) to refer to formal constitutional, statutory, or customary authority, it is either qualified by the adjective "formal" or placed in quotation marks as "power(s)." Where I have used it in the sense of effective influence upon the conduct of others, it appears without quotation marks (and always in the singular). Where clarity and convenience permit, *authority* is substituted for "power" in the first sense and *influence* for power in the second sense.

[2] See, for example, his press conference of July 22, 1959, as reported in the *New York Times* for July 23, 1959.

[3] See Douglass Cater, *The Fourth Branch of Government*, Boston: Houghton-Mifflin, 1959.

[4] With the exception of the Vice-Presidency, of course.

[5] See David B. Truman's illuminating study of party relationships in the 81st Congress, *The Congressional Party*, New York: Wiley, 1959, especially chaps. 4, 6, and 8.

[6] As Secretary of the Interior in 1939, Harold Ickes refused to approve the sale of helium to Germany despite the insistence of the State Department and the urging of President Roosevelt. Without the Secretary's approval, such sales were forbidden by statute. See *The Secret Diaries of Harold L. Ickes*, New York: Simon and Schuster, 1954, Vol. 2, especially pp. 391–393, 396–399. See also Michael J. Reagan, "The Helium Controversy" in the forthcoming case book on civil-military relations prepared for the Twentieth Century Fund under the editorial direction of Harold Stein.

In this instance the statutory authority ran to the Secretary as a matter of *his* discretion. A President is unlikely to fire Cabinet officers for the conscientious exercise of such authority. If the President did so, their successors might well be embarrassed both publicly and at the Capitol were they to reverse decisions previously taken. As for a President's authority to set aside discretionary determinations of this sort, it rests, if it exists at all, on shaky legal ground not likely to be trod save in the gravest of situations.

⁷ Truman's *Memoirs* indicate that having tried and failed to make Stevenson an avowed candidate in the spring of 1952, the President decided to support the candidacy of Vice President Barkley. But Barkley withdrew early in the convention for lack of key northern support. Though Truman is silent on the matter, Barkley's active candidacy nearly was revived during the balloting, but the forces then aligning to revive it were led by opponents of Truman's Fair Deal, principally Southerners. As a practical matter, the President could not have lent his weight to *their* endeavors and could back no one but Stevenson to counter them. The latter's strength could not be shifted, then, to Harriman or Kefauver. Instead the other Northerners had to be withdrawn. Truman helped withdraw them. But he had no other option. See Memoirs by Harry S. Truman, Vol. 2, *Years of Trial and Hope*, Garden City: Doubleday, 1956, copr. 1956 Time Inc., pp. 495–496.

⁸ The reference is to Stassen's public statement of July 23, 1956, calling for Nixon's replacement on the Republican ticket by Governor Herter of Massachusetts, the later Secretary of State. Stassen's statement was issued after a conference with the President. Eisenhower's public statements on the vice-presidential nomination, both before and after Stassen's call, permit of alternative inferences: either that the President would have preferred another candidate, provided this could be arranged without a showing of White House dictation, or that he wanted Nixon on condition that the latter could show popular appeal. In the event, neither result was achieved. Eisenhower's own remarks lent strength to rapid party moves which smothered Stassen's effort. Nixon's nomination thus was guaranteed too quickly to appear the consequence of popular demand. For the public record on this matter see reported statements by Eisenhower, Nixon, Stassen, Herter, and Leonard Hall (the National Republican Chairman) in the *New York Times* for March 1, 8, 15, 16; April 27; July 15, 16, 25–31; August 3, 4, 17, 23, 1956. See also the account from private sources by Earl Mazo in *Richard Nixon: A Personal and Political Portrait*, New York: Harper, 1959, pp. 158–187.

⁹ Stenographic transcript of presidential press conference, October 19, 1950, on file in the Truman Library at Independence, Missouri.

¹⁰ Jonathan Daniels, *Frontier on the Potomac*, New York: Macmillan, 1946, pp. 31–32.

¹¹ Transcript of presidential press conference, June 18, 1958, in *Public Papers of the Presidents: Dwight D. Eisenhower, 1958*, Washington: The National Archives, 1959, p. 479. In the summer of 1958, a congressional investigation into the affairs of a New England textile manufacturer, Bernard Goldfine, revealed that Sherman Adams had accepted various gifts and favors from him (the most notoriety attached to a vicuña coat). Adams also had made inquiries about the status of a Federal Communications Commission proceeding in which Goldfine was involved. In September 1958, Adams was allowed to resign. The episode was highly publicized and much discussed in that year's congressional campaigns.

[12] As reported in Marriner S. Eccles, *Beckoning Frontiers,* New York: Knopf, 1951, p. 336.

[13] In drawing together these observations on the Marshall Plan, I have relied on the record of personal participation by Joseph M. Jones, *The Fifteen Weeks,* New York: Viking, 1955, especially pp. 89–256; on the recent study by Harry Bayard Price, *The Marshall Plan and Its Meaning,* Ithaca: Cornell University Press, 1955, especially pp. 1–86; on the Truman *Memoirs,* Vol. 2, chaps. 7–9; on Arthur H. Vandenberg, Jr., editor, *The Private Papers of Senator Vandenberg,* Boston: Houghton Mifflin, 1952, especially pp. 373 ff.; and on notes of my own made at the time. This is an instance of policy development not covered, to my knowledge, by any of the university programs engaged in the production of case studies.

[14] Secretary Marshall's speech, formally suggesting what became known as the Marshall Plan, was made at Harvard on June 5, 1947. On June 20 the President vetoed the Taft-Hartley Act; his veto was overridden three days later. On June 16 he vetoed the first of two tax reduction bills (HR 1) passed at the first session of the 80th Congress; the second of these (HR 3950), a replacement for the other, he also disapproved on July 18. In both instances his veto was narrowly sustained.

[15] *Private Papers of Senator Vandenberg,* pp. 378–379 and 446.

[16] The initial reluctance of Secretary of the Treasury, John Snyder, to support large-scale spending overseas became a matter of public knowledge on June 25, 1947. At a press conference on that day he interpreted Marshall's Harvard speech as a call on Europeans to help themselves, by themselves. At another press conference the same day, Marshall for his own part had indicated that the U.S. would consider helping programs on which Europeans agreed. The next day Truman held a press conference and was asked the inevitable question. He replied, "General Marshall and I are in complete agreement." When pressed further, Truman remarked sharply, "The Secretary of the Treasury and the Secretary of State and the President are in complete agreement." Thus the President cut Snyder off, but had programming gathered less momentum overseas, no doubt he would have been heard from again as time passed and opportunity offered.

The foregoing quotations are from the stenographic transcript of the presidential press conference June 26, 1947, on file in the Truman Library at Independence, Missouri.

[17] A remark made in December, 1955, three years after he left office, but not unrepresentative of views he expressed, on occasion, while he was President.

[18] This might also be taken as testimony to the political timidity of officials in the State Department and the Budget Bureau where that fear seems to have been strongest. However, conversations at the time with White House aides incline me to believe that there, too, interjection of the price issue was thought a gamble and a risk. For further comment see my "Congress and the Fair Deal: A Legislative Balance Sheet," *Public Policy,* Cambridge: Harvard University Press, 1954, Vol. 5, pp. 362–364.

Notes

CHAPTER 4

¹ Carl J. Friedrich, "Public Policy and the Nature of Administrative Responsibility," *Public Policy*, Vol. 1, Cambridge: Harvard University Press, 1940, pp. 3–24.

² Quotation from stenographic transcript of presidential press conference, July 12, 1951, on file in the Truman Library at Independence, Missouri.

³ For this account I am indebted to the technician in question.

⁴ Unfortunately at the time this was written, the debacle of budget presentation and related developments in 1957 had not been made the subject of an intensive case study published or in preparation by the usual university sources. Such a study is now planned by the Inter-University Case Program. Until its release, however, this is an instance in which I have had to break my general rule that the readers of this book should be able to lay hands readily upon another and more detailed treatment of its illustrative material.

In the absence of other treatments, these and succeeding observations rest, primarily, on interviews with a number of officials in the White House, the Executive Office agencies, and three of the executive departments. Various congressional assistants and committee staff members were interviewed, as well, along with several members of the Washington press corps. I am indebted to them all for my understanding as reflected in the text. These interviews were conducted in December 1956, in April, June, and October 1957, and in January, March, and April 1958. The *Congressional Record* and the *New York Times*, of course, provided an essential framework.

⁵ From the transcript of the President's remarks November 7, 1956, in *Public Papers of the Presidents: Dwight D. Eisenhower, 1956*, Washington: The National Archives, 1958, p. 1090.

⁶ *New York Times*, January 17, 1957. For the full text of the comments quoted in this news account see "The Budget for 1958," *Hearings*, U.S. House of Representatives, Committee on Appropriations, 85th Cong., 1st sess., Washington: 1957, pp. 5, 7, 14.

[7] Transcript of presidential press conference, January 23, 1957, in *Public Papers of the Presidents, 1957*, pp. 73–74.

[8] Paul H. Douglas, "A New Isolationism: Ripple or Tide?" *New York Times Magazine*, August 18, 1957, p. 10.

[9] *New York Times*, March 7, 1957.

[10] House Resolution 190, 85th Cong., 1st sess.

[11] Letter from the President to the Speaker of the House of Representatives, April 18, 1957, in *Public Papers of the Presidents, 1957*, p. 301.

[12] Transcript of presidential press conference, March 27, 1957, *ibid.*, p. 223.

[13] William S. White in the *New York Times*, March 28, 1957.

[14] On April 2 the President addressed the Washington Conference for the Advertising Council. On April 3 he spoke at the Fifth Annual Republican Women's National Conference. See texts in *Public Papers of the Presidents, 1957*, pp. 233–237, and pp. 256–259.

[15] Transcript of presidential press conference, May 15, 1957, *ibid.*, pp. 353, 355–356.

[16] Transcript of presidential press conference, May 22, 1957, *ibid.*, pp. 399–400.

[17] James Reston in the *New York Times*, May 23, 1957.

[18] Specifically, 203 Democrats and 39 Republicans voted against the increase; 140 Republicans and 11 Democrats voted for it. This vote was taken May 29, 1957.

[19] Letter from the President, June 25, 1957, to Representative Freylingheusen (R., N.J.) and comments of the latter as reported in the *New York Times*, June 26, 1957.

[20] For current reactions see the *Congressional Record*, 85th Cong., 1st sess., July 19, 1957, Vol. 103, pp. 12121–12122 and pp. 12136–12138. For retrospective comment see the *Congressional Record*, 85th Cong., 2d sess., April 17, 1958, Vol. 104, pp. 6666–6667.

[21] The parliamentary sequence was as follows: In the Committee of the Whole, a so-called "Powell-type" amendment, barring grants to states with segregated schools, was offered by a New York Republican and was adopted 136–105 (teller vote). A Wisconsin Republican then offered an amendment to strike grants-in-aid. Immediately, another amendment was offered by one of the bill's Republican supporters. This would have stricken the previously adopted anti-segregation proviso and at the same time made all grants-in-aid subject to the Administration's formula of "need." During the debate that followed, two of the Democratic members of the House Labor and Education Committee urged all proponents of the bill to support this last amendment. At that point, the Democratic Chairman of the House Rules Committee, Smith of Virginia, offered a motion to strike out everything but the enacting clause, which meant no bill at all. This motion was adopted 153–126 (teller vote). The House then confirmed that action by a roll-call vote of 208–203, with 111 Republicans and 97 Democrats supporting, 77 Republicans and 126 Democrats opposing.

[22] Transcript of presidential press conference, July 31, 1957, in *Public Papers of the Presidents, 1957*, p. 576.

[23] Transcript of presidential press conference, July 3, 1957, *ibid.*, p. 521.

The sentence order has been changed slightly for the sake of clarity. The provisions in question comprised Title III of the bill (HR 6127).

[24] As quoted in the *New York Times*, January 10, 1958. Eisenhower's address had been delivered January 9.

[25] William S. White in the *New York Times*, January 19, 1958.

[26] *Ibid.*

[27] Text of the President's State of the Union Message, January 9, 1958, in the *Public Papers of the Presidents, 1958*, pp. 2–15.

[28] Transcript of presidential press conference, January 15, 1958, in the *New York Times*, January 16, 1958. See also The Transcript in *Public Papers of the Presidents*, 1958, p. 92, where one phrase does not appear.

[29] Address by President Eisenhower to Republican rally in Chicago, January 20, 1958, as reported in the *New York Times*, January 21, 1958.

[30] Perhaps the classic instance was Eisenhower's stand in 1959 on the Development Loan Fund, which had been the central feature of his foreign aid program two years before. In 1957 the President had urged long-term financing for the Fund by borrowings from Treasury in lieu of annual appropriations. This recommendation was then rejected by Congress on economy grounds, and the Fund was established with appropriated funds. In 1959, however, the Senate Foreign Relations Committee prepared to shift the Fund's financing; this was considered indispensable by most committee members if the Fund were to achieve its purposes, and for various reasons 1959 seemed a propitious year to make the change. When the committee bill reached the floor, however, the Republican leadership speaking for Eisenhower opposed the change on economy grounds. The President now urged financing through appropriations. The Senate ultimately acted as he recommended. The comments of the Foreign Relations Committee Chairman, Fulbright of Arkansas, make instructive reading. See *Congressional Record*, 86th Congress, 1st sess., July 1, 1959, Vol. 105, no. 110, pp. 11316 ff., and July 2, 1959, Vol. 105, no. 111, pp. 11426 ff.

[31] See my "Presidency and Legislation: The Growth of Central Clearance," *American Political Science Review*, Vol. 48, no. 3 (September, 1954), p. 656.

Notes

CHAPTER 5

[1] See Pendleton Herring, *Presidential Leadership*, New York: Rinehart, 1940, especially pp. 52–72.

[2] For detailed discussion see Paul Hammond's study "Super-Carriers and B-36 Bombers: Appropriations, Strategy, and Politics," in the forthcoming case book on civil-military relations prepared for the Twentieth Century Fund under the editorial direction of Harold Stein.

[3] The Army's line on that occasion was set by General Ridgway, then Chief of Staff. For details see his *Soldier: The Memoirs of Matthew B. Ridgway*, New York: Harper, 1956, pp. 286 ff., and Glenn Snyder's case study on the origins of the "New Look" in the forthcoming case book on civil-military relations prepared for the Columbia University Institute of War and Peace Studies under the editorial direction of W. T. R. Fox.

[4] Early in January 1958 Lieutenant General James Gavin, then chief of Army missile research, requested retirement, effective March 31, 1958, avowedly in order to fight the Army's case from the outside, a procedure scorned by Navy leaders when Truman occupied the White House.

[5] Just before his death in 1956, Anthony Leviero of the *New York Times*, one of the ablest Pentagon reporters, told me that in his judgment no Chief of Staff could have resisted service pressure from below for public "revolt" against the "New Look" in 1954, had anyone of lesser military reputation then been President. It must be added, though, that General Ridgway might have tried to smother a revolt in any case. For Ridgway was that relative rarity among the Chiefs of recent years, a "professional" in the sense of Samuel Huntington's ideal-type.

[6] Louis Harris, "How Voters Feel About Ike's Health," *Collier's*, July 20, 1956, Vol. 138, p. 17 ff.

[7] As reported in the *New York Times*, April 14, 1945.

[8] For further comment which seems sound to me, see Elmo Roper, *You and Your Leaders*, New York: Morrow, 1957, pp. 139–144.

[9] These and all following "approval" and "disapproval" figures are taken from the records of the Gallup Poll through the courtesy of Dr. George

Gallup, director of the American Institute of Public Opinion, Princeton, N.J. Great care must be taken in using these data. I have suggested their leading limitations in the text. But there is very little else available which attempts to measure what I call "prestige." And Gallup's figures have one great advantage: they have been compiled by the same source, in much the same way, for over 20 years. For present purposes they have a second great advantage: they are very widely read in Washington. Despite disclaimers, they are widely taken to approximate reality.

[10] For whatever it is worth, Truman's previous "low" had been 32 per cent, recorded in the two months of October and November 1946, hard upon that year's beef shortage and mid-term elections. His next lowest approval figure, 36 per cent, was recorded in April 1948, the month of final action on the Marshall Plan, two months after his civil rights message to Congress and the unrelated bolt of Henry Wallace from the Democratic Party. Between these two low points of 1946 and 1948, the Gallup figures would suggest that Truman's "borrowing" of prestige during 1947 (as described in Chapter 3) boosted his own to a marked degree. Gallup's "approval" questions for the months of February, March, June, July, and October 1947 elicited a favorable response in the following proportions: 48, 60, 57, 54, and 55 per cent. The March "high" coincided with announcement of the Truman Doctrine shortly after a display of presidential firmness on a coal strike. As indicators of a *relatively* lasting *upward* shift of range, these figures illustrate the obverse of examples cited in my text. Truman, of course, looked far less partisan and far less like a candidate in 1947 than in 1948. Approval tumbled at the start of the latter year. It rose again, after his surprise election, to 69 per cent in January 1949. In all these instances, the indicated months are the months when surveys were made.

[11] For whatever it is worth, Eisenhower's first term "low" was 57 per cent, recorded in November 1954. This coincided with the mid-term elections and a critical stage of the first Quemoy-Matsu crisis. It is the only recorded instance in his first five years where approval dropped below 60 per cent. Indeed, two months later, in January 1955, the figure was 69 per cent. His 1958 "low" of 49 per cent in April coincided with what turned out to be the bottom of the 1958 recession. His 1958 "high" of 58 per cent in August followed close upon the unopposed landing of troops in Lebanon and the easing of tension in the Middle East. These conjunctions are in terms of dates when surveys were made, not necessarily of the release dates for results.

[12] Through 1959, up to the time of writing, Eisenhower's record of approval in these polls has been 58 per cent in February, 59 per cent in March, 60 per cent in April, 61 per cent in May, and 62 per cent in June.

[13] Lest any reader be misled, let me note that I would not pose these questions in this fashion if I thought the *second* term, as such, a dominant factor shaping the dimensions of those particular losses of prestige. I do not. Had the events of 1957–1958 or those of 1950–1951 occurred four years earlier, I know no reason to suppose the results for prestige would have been very different.

Gallup's data do suggest, however, that *some* down-trend in "approval" and *some* lessening of variations upward *may* be characteristic in second terms. Other things aside, a "boredom" factor may have played a part in Truman's case and Eisenhower's. There is, of course, no guarding against boredom unless, as in the case of F.D.R., one gets involved in a new play like his "War Presidency."

[14] It is suggestive, though of course not proof of anything, that "approval" of Eisenhower in the Gallup Poll was at a low for 1958 in April when opinion leaders were the loudest in their criticism of his "inactivity" or "indecision" on antirecession measures, and reached its high, that year, in August after he had intervened dramatically in Lebanon, an "active" and "decisive" move by which, as matters stood, no one was being hurt.

[15] These appearances are Gallup's again. "Approval" of Eisenhower, as measured by the Gallup Poll, reached a first term "high" of 79 per cent in August 1955, compared with two secondary highs of 75 per cent in September 1953 and in December 1955. Excluding the three highs, approval in these polls during his first three years averaged approximately 67 per cent. As has been noted previously, his all-time "low," up to the time of writing, was 49 per cent in April 1958. During the twelve months of 1957 his average had been approximately 65 per cent. Averages, of course, will have the least significance of any figures of this sort. I note them here only to give a crude frame of reference for the high and low results.

[16] See note 11, chap. 3.

[17] For what it may be worth, a Gallup Poll taken in May, 1951 showed approval of Truman only one percentage point above his all-time low of 23 per cent. That low was reached just six months later, amidst charges of corruption and a stalemate in Korean truce talks.

[18] From the summer of 1945 to late autumn 1946, Truman's approval, as measured by the Gallup Poll, dropped continuously and precipitously from 87 to 32 per cent. Early in his third year it rose as high as 60 per cent, and after temporary stabilization in the "fifties," dropped to 36 per cent early in 1948; it climbed steeply, again, late in the year. In Eisenhower's case, the comparable figures show a mild down-trend, broken by many upward variations, from an early high of 75 per cent to a low of 57 per cent in late autumn 1954. An upward trend appears immediately after, with approval at 69 per cent in January 1955, and at 79 per cent in August, amidst the "Geneva spirit." Thereafter, there was temporary stabilization in the middle of the seventies, followed by a mild slump to a "low" of 67 per cent in 1956, with a sharp move up again by the end of the year to 79 per cent in January 1957.

[19] In most of Roosevelt's years and most of Truman's, C. E. Hooper's rating service reigned supreme in radio. Hooper ratings were expressed as proportions of "actual" to "potential" audience among radio users in homes, based on a sampling of "radio-homes" with telephones in 36 cities. A multiplier of approximately 1.3 was used to convert sets into listeners. Not every presidential address received a Hooper rating in those years, but virtually all major addresses were rated through April 1948. The termination of these ratings could be due, I assume, to someone's loss of interest at the networks or in the White House. From 1935 to 1939 most addresses were also rated by another service, the Cooperative Association of Broadcasters (CAB), then maintained jointly by the networks.

Television began to be a presidential medium in Truman's second term. As its use spread, three different commercial rating services developed, each determining its ratings in a different and noncomparable way (and each, of course, excluding radio). Trendex ratings are based on a sampling of "television homes" with telephones in fifteen major urban areas across the country. Results are compiled on all viewing hours, but coverage is limited to one week out of four. Nielsen and ARB ratings are drawn from a national sample of all "television homes" (the data are obtained in different ways), but results are regularly compiled only on commercial programs in the case of Nielsen.

The data-gathering techniques of these three television services are such as to render their results, when and as available, noncomparable across service lines or with the older Hooper ratings. Moreover, in earlier years it was customary to pre-empt *all* networks for live coverage of major presidential addresses; this is no longer current practice with respect to either medium. In consequence, only the older radio ratings provide an internally consistent measure of presidential audiences for comparable addresses when network listeners were left no option but to listen or turn off their sets. To the extent that I have relied upon such data for the purpose of relative comparisons, only Hooper ratings have been used.

[20] These and other radio and television ratings cited in this chapter were furnished through the courtesy of Jay Eliasberg and Rose Marie O'Reilly of the Columbia Broadcasting System. CBS compilations of Hooper and CAB ratings on presidential addresses are acknowledged with particular gratitude.

[21] The dates, days, times, subjects, and ratings of these eight evening addresses are as follows:

Date	Day	Eastern Time	Subject	Rating
10/30/45	Tues.	10 P.M.	Wage and price policy	43.8
1/ 3/46	Thurs.	Same	Program for the year ahead	49.4
5/24/46	Fri.	11 P.M.	Railroad strike	34.4
6/29/46	Sat.	10 P.M.	Veto of price control bill	31.8
10/14/46	Mon.	Same	Lifting of controls on meat	57.6
6/20/47	Fri.	Same	Taft-Hartley veto	30.7
10/24/47	Fri.	Same	Special session of Congress	34.3
3/17/48	Wed.	10:30 P.M.	Foreign policy and defense	31.0

[22] For a brief indication of the steps leading toward beef decontrol, see Memoirs by Harry S. Truman, Vol. 1, *Year of Decisions*, Garden City: Doubleday, 1955, copr. 1955 Time Inc., pp. 488–491. For a quick review of the economic and political setting see Eric Goldman, *The Crucial Decade*, New York: Knopf, 1956, chap. 3.

[23] The dates, days, times, subjects, and ratings of these six Roosevelt addresses are as follows:

Date	Day	Eastern Time	Subject	Rating
5/27/41	Tues.	10:30 P.M.	Unlimited emergency	69.8
9/11/41	Thurs.	10 P.M.	"Shoot first" naval policy	67.0
12/ 9/41	Tues.	Same	Report on Pearl Harbor	79.0
2/23/42	Mon.	Same	Report on the war	78.1
4/28/42	Tues.	Same	Economic policy	61.8
10/12/42	Mon.	Same	Report on the war	58.9

[24] Unfortunately, no one of the television services has compiled ratings on all the Eisenhower "fireside chats" in 1957 and 1958, the two years checked for purposes of this study. Or, more precisely, if any of the services *has* rated them all, my inquiries have not produced its findings. (The White House may know more than I have found.) Moreover, in his second term, Eisenhower ceased pre-empting all the networks for his evening addresses; on some occasions he was carried "live" by two, on most by one. This is a tribute, I would gather, to television economics and to White House fear of viewers' anger at no choice. In consequence, at this time, I have been unable to assemble Eisenhower ratings in a reasonably complete, consistent series, on the order of those readily obtainable from radio ratings of Roosevelt and of Truman in the 1940's.

[25] For details on the staging which preceded presentation of the legislative program for 1954, see my "Presidency and Legislation: Planning the President's Program," *American Political Science Review*, Vol. 49, no. 4 (December 1955), especially pp. 980–996.

[26] The reference is to Eisenhower's "fireside chat" of January 4, 1954, when he discussed his legislative program in general terms on the eve of his State of the Union address to Congress. His Trendex rating on that occasion was 73.1 per cent, compared with equivalent ratings of 50.7 per cent for his fireside chat of June 3, 1953, and of 52.5 per cent for that of April 5, 1954. All three addresses were carried live by all networks.

[27] Franklin D. Roosevelt to Ray Stannard Baker, March 20, 1935. This letter is included in the Roosevelt Library collection at Hyde Park, New York.

[28] These attributions of intent to Truman, as well as comments on advice received by him, are drawn from notes made at the time. But they can be inferred from his own words. See especially: his message to Congress of July 19, 1950, outlining his post-Korean legislative proposals; his subsequent letters of August 1 and 18, 1950, concerning the addition of price controls; and his press conference of June 29, 1950, in which, among other things, he accepted a reporter's characterization of Korea as a "police action." See also the press conference of July 27, 1950, in which he distinguished the then situation from "all-out mobilization."

[29] Woodrow Wilson, *Constitutional Government in the United States*, New York: Columbia University Press, 1908, p. 81.

[30] For revealing comment see Robert Sherwood, *Roosevelt and Hopkins*, New York: Harper, 1948, pp. 428–438.

Notes

CHAPTER 6

[1] Transcript of presidential press conference, January 23, 1957 in *Public Papers of the Presidents: Dwight D. Eisenhower, 1957*, Washington: The National Archives, 1958, p. 73.

[2] This and subsequent references to Cabinet discussions on the January 1957 budget are drawn from interviews with two participants and with five responsible officials or consultants who were briefed by participants immediately after. The persons contributing these recollections at first or second hand were members, respectively, of the White House staff, the Bureau of the Budget, the Council of Economic Advisers, and three Cabinet departments, including Treasury. These interviews were conducted in February and March, 1957, and in February, 1958. I found no substantial differences in the accounts from these various sources. Even a year later, the incidents described were remembered vividly by those consulted; it is easy to see why.

[3] Report of Secretary Humphrey's press conference, *New York Times*, January 17, 1957. For the full text of the Secretary's statement see "The Budget for 1958," *Hearings*, U.S. House of Representatives, Committee on Appropriations, 85th Cong., 1st sess., Washington: 1957, pp. 1–3.

[4] Budget Message in *Public Papers of the Presidents: 1957*, pp. 40 ff.

[5] For details see Warner Schilling's forthcoming case study, "Fiscal 1950," now in preparation for the Columbia University Institute of War and Peace Studies, under the editorial direction of William T. R. Fox. For highlights see my "Presidency and Legislation: Planning the President's Program," *American Political Science Review*, Vol. 49, no. 4 (December, 1955); especially pp. 1005 ff.

[6] *Addresses of the President of the United States and the Director of the Bureau of the Budget at the Eleventh Regular Metting of the Business Organization of the Government*, Washington: Government Printing Office, 1926, p. 8.

[7] Transcript of presidential press conference, March 3, 1957 in *Public Papers of the Presidents, 1957*, p. 222.

[8] Harold Stassen, then Special Assistant to the President for Disarmament, a post he would retain for one more year, was a regular attender at Eisen-

hower's Cabinet meetings. From his specialized and institutionally insecure position Stassen tended to be free with his advice on matters of domestic policy, where almost always he appeared well-briefed, articulate, and "liberal." Add these "sins" to his well-known differences with Dulles and to his ill-fated "dump Nixon" move in 1956, and it is not surprising that in the words of one very close observer:

> Nothing probably shook the President's confidence so much, or did more to confirm Humphrey's faith in his own opinion, than hearing Stassen argue that the budget as it stood was both good economics and good politics . . . . As a matter of fact, his exposition was first-rate, forceful and clear, which probably made things worse . . . . Certainly nothing could have made the budget's other friends more cautious in their good words for it . . . they were embarrassed, naturally; they had to keep their standing in the club, which was hard enough in that atmosphere without being classed with Stassen, so to speak.

One of my informants goes so far as to assert that this single factor holds the key to the whole episode of presidential sanction for the Humphrey press conference.

⁹ The limitations native to such meetings are discussed at length in Richard F. Fenno, Jr., *The President's Cabinet*, Cambridge: Harvard University Press, 1959. See especially chaps. 3 and 4.

¹⁰ The reference is to House Resolution 190, mentioned in Chapter 4, *supra* p. 68.

Although there were obvious risks in disciplining Humphrey, I have found no indication that these weighed heavily with Eisenhower, personally, when he made his public response to the former's press remarks. However, one cannot be certain from outside.

¹¹ In addition to the incidents described in this chapter, indications of a President's dependence on himself will be found in each of the three cases of "command" presented earlier. For other instances not treated in this book, the reader is referred to the various case studies cited in these notes.

¹² In preparing this account of Korean developments during the fall of 1950 I have relied, in part, on notes of my own made at this time, on interviews with former President Truman, and on interviews with five former officials then at key staff levels in the State and Defense Departments, and the White House. These interviews were conducted in August and December 1954, in June and December 1955, and in January 1956, in February 1958, and in May 1959. Except where otherwise noted, quotations in this account of Korean developments during the fall of 1950 are taken from Memoirs by Harry S. Truman, Vol. 2, *Years of Trial and Hope*, Garden City: Doubleday, 1956, copr. 1956 Time Inc., chaps. 22–24. Except where otherwise noted, dates and similar specific references have been drawn from three sources: from testimony and appendices in "The Military Situation in the Far East," *Hearings*, U.S. Senate Foreign Relations and Armed Services Committee, 82d Cong., 1st sess., Washington: 1951, parts 1–5 (referred to hereafter as the *MacArthur Hearings*); from the *Department of State Bulletin*, Vol. 23, nos. 576–597, July 17–December 11, 1950; and from the United Nations General

Assembly, *Official Records*, Fifth Session, First Committee. 346th–353rd meetings, September 30–October 4, 1950. All dates are given as of Washington, not Korea.

For a more detailed account of these developments which puts them in the context of the war's whole course from its inception to the start of truce negotiations in July 1951, the reader is referred to Martin Lichterman's penetrating case study "To the Yalu and Back," prepared for the Twentieth Century Fund under Harold Stein's editorial direction and now in press. A less detailed treatment which differs somewhat in interpretation both from Lichterman's and from my own is found in Walter Millis's section of *Arms and the State*, New York: Twentieth Century Fund, 1958, chap. 7.

[13] For a chronological account of the decision to intervene in Korea (which was really a succession of decisions taken between June 26 and June 30, 1950), see Beverly Smith, "The White House Story: Why We Went to War in Korea," *Saturday Evening Post*, Vol. 224, no. 19 (November 10, 1951), pp. 22 ff. A very useful comment on the notions in the minds of those who counseled intervention—notions which also were to affect the choices of September and October, 1950—will be found in Alexander L. George's "American Policy-Making and the North Korean Aggression," *World Politics*, Vol. 7, no. 2 (January, 1955), pp. 209–232.

[14] Truman *Memoirs*, Vol. 2, p. 341.

[15] Truman spoke in San Francisco October 17, 1950. The preceding May he had traveled by train, in leisurely fashion, to and from a dedication of Grand Coulee Dam, a tour reflecting his apparent hope to raise the strength and change the mix of Democrats in Congress at the mid-term elections. (In effect, this was a hope to match the precedent of 1934 with roughly the results of 1958.) The hope was not realized, of course, though Democratic losses in both Houses were less, proportionately and absolutely, than in the three preceding off-year elections.

[16] Truman *Memoirs*, Vol. 2, p. 359.

[17] *Ibid.*, p. 360.

[18] At the time, United Kingdom, Australian and Philippine ground forces were serving under MacArthur; Turkish and Thai contingents were en route; a Canadian contingent was in formation. Next to the Americans, the Commonwealth—and in the Commonwealth, the UK—gave the principal outside assistance to the South Koreans; hence the emphasis on British views in this account. The ratio of Commonwealth to U.S. participation is suggested by the fact that (as of October) *one* Commonwealth and *seven* American divisions were engaged. I surmise that in November another Commonwealth division would have more than doubled British influence with Washington, but Atlee chose to strip his garrisons no further.

[19] Transcript of presidential press conference, September 21, 1950, on file in the Truman Library at Independence. It should be noted that as early as September 1, the President virtually had pledged some sort of UN action—without specifying UN *means*—by stating in a fireside address to the country that "Under the direction and guidance of the UN, we, with others, will do our part to help them [the Koreans] enjoy . . . free, independent, and united [government] . . . ." This theme, "the UN will

decide," also had been sounded before Inchon in some public statements by other American officials, especially by Acheson and by Phillip Jessup. State's Ambassador-at-Large. For occasions and texts see *Department of State Bulletin*, Vol. 23, nos. 583, 584, and 585, September 4, 11, and 18, 1950.

[20] The resolution was proposed to the Political (First) Committee on September 30 by Australia, Brazil, Cuba, the Netherlands, Norway, Pakistan, the Philippines, and the United Kingdom; a sponsorship designed to emphasize its international character. But drafting and negotiation of this sponsorship were largely in the hands of the State Department and the U.S. delegation.

[21] The text of the October 7 resolution on which I have relied is found in the *MacArthur Hearings*, Part 3, pp. 2436–2437. Alternatively, see *Department of State Bulletin*. Vol. 23, no. 590, October 23, 1950.

[22] The abstainers were Egypt, India, Lebanon, Saudi Arabia, Syria, Yemen, and Yugoslavia. The negative votes were cast by the Soviet Union (3), Poland, and Czechoslovakia.

[23] On September 24 the Indian Ambassador at Peking reported having had disturbing conversations with a Chinese military source. See K. M. Panikkar, *In Two Chinas: Memoirs of a Diplomat*, London: Allen and Unwin, 1955, p. 108. On September 30, the Chinese Foreign Minister, in a speech to a committee of the People's Political Consultative Conference, said, according to news reports, that Peking "could not supinely tolerate the crossing of the parallel," and "could not stand aside." Far more specific threats had been made far more formally about Formosa for months past, yet in that quarter Peking had remained supine. To allied foreign offices this apparently seemed more of the same in a minor key. Ninety miles of open water and an American fleet separated Formosa from mainland China; no such barrier divided China from North Korea. The difference does not seem to have made much impression upon allied diplomats in September, 1950.

[24] Truman *Memoirs*, Vol. 2, p. 362. See also, Panikkar, *Memoirs*, pp. 109–110.

[25] Leland Goodrich, *Korea: A Study of U.S. Policy in the United Nations*, New York: Council on Foreign Relations, 1956, p. 136.

[26] Marshall had succeeded Louis Johnson as Defense Secretary on September 21, in time to share, in form at least, in post-Inchon decisions.

[27] Truman *Memoirs*, Vol. 2, p. 362.

[28] *Ibid.*, p. 373.

[29] See *ibid.*, pp. 373–380 for texts of MacArthur cables November 4, 6, and 7 and for account of following action in Washington.

[30] *Ibid.*, p. 380.

[31] *Ibid.*, pp. 378–379.

[32] S. L. A. Marshall, *The River and the Gauntlet*, New York: Morrow, 1953, p. 1.

[33] For further detail see the Lichterman study cited in note 12.

[34] On November 28, coincidentally, John Hersey was at the White House and attended Truman's usual morning staff meeting in preparation for his memorable "Profile" published serially by *The New Yorker* the following spring. Hersey's account of Truman's announcement to his staff that the Chinese had intervened full-force sheds considerable light on the motiva-

tions and responses of this President. **See John** Hersey, "Mr. President, II—Ten O'Clock Meeting," *The New Yorker,* April 14, 1951, pp. 38 ff. In general, it can be said that Hersey's series is the most enlightening single source as yet available on Truman as President and on the daily tasks of being President in our time. It is superb reporting.

Notes

CHAPTER 7

[1] The reference is to the *Report of the President's Committee on Administrative Management*, Washington: Government Printing Office, 1937. For background see the second volume of reminiscences by the Committee's chairman, Louis Brownlow, *A Passion for Anonymity*, Chicago: University of Chicago Press, 1958, chaps. 28, 30, 31, and 33.

[2] These so-called "staff" facilities around the President are actually an odd assortment of personal and institutional staffs and of interagency committees. Their development has never been traced satisfactorily, nor their operations analyzed in depth, by any single source. Indeed, some of these facilities have yet to be discussed in any depth by any source. There is now underway a study of the institutionalized Presidency by Rowland Egger. When published, his work should do a great deal to further understanding of the Presidency as an institution.

[3] Clinton Rossiter, *The American Presidency*, New York: Harcourt Brace, 1956, p. 104.

[4] Exposure to detail can be carried too far, of course. Herbert Hoover is perhaps the classic instance of a man who went too far. For example, Hoover personally read and approved every letter sent by the Budget Bureau to executive agencies "clearing" their individual replies to congressional inquiries on legislation. In suggesting that a President be his own staff director, I would not urge that he routinely do the work of the whole staff. One admires Hoover's industry but not his judgment of what to take upon himself and what to leave to others.

[5] Arthur M. Schlesinger, Jr., *The Age of Roosevelt*, Vol. 2, *The Coming of the New Deal*, Boston: Houghton Mifflin, 1959, pp. 522–523.

This and later quotations are drawn from Schlesinger's characterization of Roosevelt in his earlier years. It often is assumed that in his last years, during the Second World War, Roosevelt was a "changed man"; that in his handling of military strategy and foreign policy, then his prime concerns, he became virtually the creature of his Chiefs of Staff. What his biographers will make of this, I do not know. But it is clear that they will deal with contradictory evidence. For a suggestive reading which discounts the "change" see William Emerson, "Franklin Roosevelt as Commander in Chief in World War II," *Military Affairs*, Vol. 22, no. 4 (Winter, 1958–1959), pp. 181 ff. See also Harvey Mansfield with Harold Stein, *Arms and the State*, New York: Twentieth Century Fund, 1959, Part one, chap. 3.

For a detailed case study of Roosevelt in action toward the end, see Paul Hammond's "Directives for the Occupation of Germany: The Washington Controversy," prepared for the Twentieth Century Fund under the editorial direction of Harold Stein and now in press. This shows Roosevelt a tired man indeed, whose foot slipped now and then, as at Quebec, but by no means a "changed" one. It also shows what I suspect may be the key to understanding F.D.R.'s War Presidency: that his personal perspective often coincided with the judgments of his military advisers, *but not for their reasons.* His personal, political judgment *may* have failed to keep pace with events, as Emerson suggests, although the evidence is inconclusive. But this is not to say that he failed to consult—and to inform—himself as politician, in much the same way he always had. And judging from what I have learned about his final conversations just before his death, it may be that he was fast catching up with events or was abreast of them; if so he was ahead of most of his advisers. At least it can be said that he was in the process of evaluating Soviet-American relations and that no one can claim certain knowledge of the way his mind was moving on the problems his successor shortly faced. The man whose mind remained unfathomed by associates was scarcely a changed man.

[6] Schlesinger, *Roosevelt*, Vol. 2, p. 528.

[7] *Ibid.*, p. 528.

[8] The classic instances of miscalculation on Roosevelt's part would seem to be his initial presentation of Supreme Court reform in 1937 and his careless choice of objects and of tactics for his party "purge," so-called, in 1938. See James M. Burns, *Roosevelt: The Lion and the Fox*, New York: Harcourt Brace, 1956, especially pp. 291 ff. and pp. 358 ff.

Many writers regard as a third such instance the "unconditional surrender" formula of 1943. I wonder. From a President's perspective that formula in that year may have been, among other things, a way to keep doors open rather than a way to slam them shut, at a time when the "balance of administrative power," in Arthur Schlesinger's phrase, remained indeterminate at home and abroad. Winston Churchill's comments are worth noting in this connection; see his *The Hinge of Fate*, Boston: Houghton Mifflin, 1950, pp. 685–691.

[9] These general observations on the workings of the Eisenhower "staff system" are drawn from periodic interviews with staff officials in the White House and with certain others whose work kept them in close contact with the White House. Fifteen individuals were interviewed at least once; three in the White House and four outside were interviewed three times or more, at intervals, constituting a rough sort of "panel." These interviews were conducted in January and June 1954, in April, June, and December 1955, in June 1956, in April and October 1957, in January, February, March, and April 1958, and in April 1959.

[10] This comment, made in personal conversation, dates from January 1958, three years before the close of Eisenhower's term.

[11] See Robert J. Donovan, *Eisenhower: The Inside Story*, New York: Harper, 1956, chaps. 2, 4, 6, 10, 23, 25.

[12] *Ibid.*, p. 357.

[13] For a summary of Eisenhower's political involvement as a potential candidate from 1947 on see Marquis Childs, *Eisenhower: Captive Hero*, New York: Harcourt Brace, 1958, chaps. 6–7.

[14] *Ibid.*, p. 117.

[15] Transcript of presidential press conference, May 31, 1955, as reported in the *New York Times*, June 1, 1955.

[16] The quotations are from Robert Donovan's account of Eisenhower's conference with twelve close associates in January 1956, on the question of a second term. See Donovan, *Eisenhower*, pp. 394–395.

[17] *Ibid.*, p. 402.

[18] See Memoirs by Harry S. Truman, Vol. 1, *Year of Decisions*, Garden City: Doubleday, 1955, copr. 1955 Time Inc., for example, pp. 328–329.

[19] I am indebted to former President Truman for permitting me to read his photostatic copy of the portion of the Harold Smith diary that covers the first fifteen months of Mr. Truman's Presidency. Smith, who had been Budget Director since 1939 resigned in July 1946.

[20] Transcript of Presidential press conference for the American Society of Newspaper Editors, April 17, 1952, on file in the Truman Library at Independence, Missouri.

[21] Jack Redding, *Inside the Democratic Party*, Indianapolis and New York: Bobbs-Merrill, 1958, p. 133. Reprinted by permission of the Bobbs-Merrill Company, Inc.

[22] For further discussion see my "Congress and the Fair Deal: A Legislative Balance Sheet," *Public Policy*, Vol. 5, Cambridge: Harvard University Press, 1954, especially pp. 374–378.

Notes

CHAPTER 8

[1] Arthur M. Schlesinger, Jr., *The Age of Roosevelt*, Vol. 2, *The Coming of the New Deal*, Boston: Houghton Mifflin, 1959, p. 529.

[2] See Chapter 7, p. 158.

[3] Edward S. Corwin, *The President: Office and Powers*, 4th ed., New York: New York University Press, 1957, p. 312.

[4] Woodrow Wilson, *Constitutional Government in the United States*, New York: Columbia University Press, 1908, pp. 79–80.

Notes

[1] What follows first appeared in the French edition of this book published in 1968. It represents an adaptation and enlargement of testimony before the Senate Subcommittee on National Security Staffing and Operations, March 25, 1963 (see "Administration of National Security," *Hearings*, U. S. Senate Committee on Operations, 88th Congress, 1st Sess., Washington: 1963, Part 1, pp. 74–84), together with enlargement of an article, "Kennedy in the Presidency," *Political Science Quarterly*, Vol. LXXIX, No. 3, September 1964.

Index

Acheson, Dean, 48, 124, 140f., 145
"Action making for enlightenment," 106, 125, *see also* Teaching
Adams, Sherman, 41f., 73, 98, 159ff., 205n
"Administrative power," balance of, 158, 184, 221n
Alsop, Joseph, 203
American government, structure of, 33, 39f., 186f., 191
"Anticipated reactions," laws of, 59
Army response to budget cuts, 1954–1958, 87ff., 210n
Arnall, Ellis, 14, 15, 24f., 36, 40, 45, 57, 59
Ashmore, Harry S., 21, 203n
Atomic Energy Act, 6

Bagehot, Walter, 34
Ballot-splitting, 4, 187
Bargaining advantages, presidential, 36ff., 39, 46, 54ff., 60, 112, 187, *see also* Vantage points
Barkley, Alben, 205n
Bay of Pigs, 202, 205, 207
"Belief system," American, 97, *see also* Politics
Berlin crisis, 1959, 83, 97; 1961, 200f.; 203
Bevin, Ernest, 48, 50
Blossom, Virgil T., 203n
Bradley, Omar, 126, 138, 141f., 145
Bridges, Styles, 71
British policy in Korean War, 124, 127f., 132, 144, 217n

British political system, 187, 193f.
Brownlow, Louis, 220n
Brownlow Committee, *see* President's Committee
Brundage, Percival, 66, 68, 74f., 109, 119, 153f., 161
Budget, Eisenhower's, 1957 (Fiscal 1958), 65ff., 70ff., 73, 74f., 76, 108ff.
  1958 (Fiscal 1959), 78f.
  1959 (Fiscal 1960), 82f.
Budget Bureau, 53, 66, 68, 113, 117, 153, 206n
Budget planning, 1956, 116f.
Burns, James M., 221n
Byrd, Harry F., 70

Cabinet, presidential, 23, 34, 39ff., 66, 109ff., 117, 153, *see also* President
Cater, Douglass, 33, 204n
Central High School, *see* Little Rock
Chamberlain, Neville, 194
Chiang Kai-shek, 11
Childs, Marquis, 165, 222n
Chinese intervention in Korean War, 12, 125ff., 135, 139ff., 143, 218n
Choice-making, presidential, 56f., 84, 107, 120f., 129, 146f., 148, 154, 179f.
Choices, presidential, defined, 56
Chou En-lai, 135, 218n
Churchill, Winston, 149, 157, 221n
Civil rights, 200f., 203, 204f.
Civil rights legislation, 1957, 76

Clayton, Will, 48
Clerkship, presidential, 6, 84, 112, 152, 185, 201, 213; *see also* Deadlines
Cleveland, Grover, 3
Cohn, Roy, 111
Command, costs of, 30ff.
    limits of, 19ff., 27ff., 201
Commitment, presidential, 196f., 200ff.
Compliance with presidential orders, factors favoring, 19ff., *see also* Orders, self-executing
Confidence, presidential, 161f., 163, 166f., 175ff., 180, 182f., 207
Congress, *see* President
Constituencies, presidential, 7, 183
Coolidge, Calvin, 3, 115
Corwin, Edward S., 193, 223n
Courts, Federal, 10, 15ff., 23, 31, 90
Crisis consensus, 4, 107, 186, 191
Cuban confrontation of 1962, 197ff.
Cuban missile crisis, 200f., 203f., 206, 210ff.
Cycle, presidential, rhythm of, 198f.
Czech *coup d'etat*, 1948, 51

Daniels, Jonathan, 94, 205n
Dawes, Charles G., 39
Deadlines, 155f.
Decision-making, *see* Choice-making
Defense appropriations, 1957–1958, 72ff., 79, 117
    1949, 87
Defense Production Act, 14, 60, 104f.
Defense reorganization, 1958, 79
Development Loan Fund, 72, 209n
Diem, Ngo Dinh, 204, 209, *see also* Vietnam War
Disarmament negotiations, 1957, 168
Donovan, Robert J., 9, 163, 165, 168, 202n, 222n
Douglas, Paul H., 208n
Dulles, John Foster, 72, 159f., 168

Eccles, Marriner S., 206n
Economic myths, combatting, 198, 201
Eden, Anthony, 194

Egger, Rowland, 220n
Eisenhower, Dwight D., 3, 9, 17f., 21, 28, 38, 64ff., 76f., 92f., 98f., 102f., 109ff., 114ff., 118, 120f., 127, 147ff., 153f., 158ff., 180, 194f., 196, 197f., 200, 205, 205n, 207, 210, 213; *see also* President; Presidential
    quoted, 28, 65, 66ff., 69, 70, 71, 72, 74, 75, 76, 79f., 108, 166
    the "new," 1959, 65, 82ff., 160, 169f.
Elections, congressional, 6, 47, 64, 79, 83, 92, 101, 112, 127, 211n, 217n
    presidential, 53, 64, 94f., 116f., 211n
Eliasberg, Jay, 213n
"Emergencies in policy with politics as usual," 3, 64, 191
Emerson, William, 221n
Employment Act, 5
European Recovery Program, *see* Marshall Plan
Events as conditioners of public attention, 100ff., 125f.
Executive branch, *see* President
Expectations as factors in persuasion, 59f., 71, 80
Expertise, presidential, 148f., 151, 179f., 181ff., 186, 192, 201

Fair Deal, 78, 84, 126, 205n
Faubus, Orval, 17, 21, 26, 28, 59
Fenno, Richard F., Jr., 216n
Folsom, Marion, 75, 80
Forrestal, James V., 48
Fox, William T. R., 210n, 215n
Friedel, Frank, 163
Friedrich, Carl J., 59, 207n
Fulbright, William, 209n

Gallup, George, 210n, 211n
Gallup Poll, results, 95ff., 194, 211n, 212n
Gavin, James, 210n
Geneva spirit, 1955, 98, 167f., 211n, 212n
George, Alexander L., 217n
Goldfine, Bernard, 42, 205n

Goldman, Eric, 213n
Goodrich, Leland, 218n
Government, American, structure of, 33, 39f., 186f., 191
Governmental energy, source of, 183, 185

Hall, Leonard, 205n
Hammond, Paul, 210n, 221n
Happenings, self-made, 102f.
Harding, Warren G., 182
Harriman, Averell, 52f., 55, 205n
Harris, Louis, 94, 210n
Hays, Brooks, 203n
Helium sales to Germany, 1938, 204n
Herring, Pendleton, 210n
Hersey, John, 219n
Herter, Christian A., 49, 205n
Hoffman, Paul, 53
Holmes, Oliver Wendell, Jr., 182
Hooper ratings, 100f., 213n, 214n
Hoover, Herbert, 102, 182, 220n
Humphrey, George M., 66ff., 76, 78, 80, 108ff., 113, 119f., 153, 161, 167, 169f., 198
Humphrey press conference, 1957, 66, 108, 110, 113, 148, 153f., 207n, 215n
Hundred Days of 1933, 37, 64, 87, 104
Hungarian revolt, 1956, 116, 167
Huntington, Samuel, 210n

Images of office, presidential, 162, 165f., 171, 175f., 178, 180, 185, *see also* Confidence
public, 95, 97, 171, *see also* Prestige
Indian diplomacy in Korean War, 134f., 218n
Inflation, 16, 53, 71, 104f., 114f., 116, 118, 126, 188f.
Influence, presidential, *see* Power
"Irreversibility become Irreparable," 198ff., 201
Issues, *see* Political issues

Jackson, C. D., 98
Johnson, Lyndon B., 77, 196f., 197f.,

200, 202f., 204, 208f., 213, *see also* President; Presidential; and Vietnam War
Joint Chiefs of Staff, 130f., 133, 137, 144f.
Jones, Joseph M., 206n

Kefauver, Estes, 205n
Kennan, George, 50
Kennedy, John F., Afterword, *passim; see also* President, Presidential
Kissinger, Henry A., 30, 203n
Knowland, William, 71, 131
Korean War, 10ff., 13ff., 27, 30, 40f., 97ff., 104f., 123–147, 176, 199, *see also* Defense Production Act; MacArthur; Panikkar; Price control; Steel; United Nations
Korean war aims, shift of, 1950, 123ff., 130f., 133f., 136ff., 140f., 144ff.
Krock, Arthur, 62
Krug, Julius, 52
Khrushchev, Nikita, 200, 203, 209, 213; *see also* Cuban Missile Crisis, Vienna meeting

Labor-Management Relations Act, *see* Taft-Hartley Act
Larsen, Arthur, 111
Lebanon, intervention in, 1958, 88, 97, 211n, 212n
Legislative program, 1954, staging of, 102f.
Leviero, Anthony, 210n
Lichterman, Martin, 217n, 218n
Lincoln, Abraham, 5, 182, 193, 198f.
Lippmann, Walter, 62
Little Rock, dispatch of troops to, 10, 16f., 21, 31, 76, 91f., 202n
Lovett, Robert, 48, 53
Lubell, Samuel, 3

MacArthur, Douglas, and Korean war aims, 1950, 12, 40f., 123, 125f., 127f., 129f., 132f., 137f., 140f., 143ff., 155, 204

dismissal of, 1951, 11ff., 18, 20f., 26ff., 30, 40, 44f., 59, 98, 202n
McCarthy, Joseph, 48, 82, 167
McConnell, Grant, 202n
MacDonald, Ramsay, 194
Mansfield, Harvey C., 202n, 221n
Marshall, George C., 27, 47, 48, 54ff., 59, 137, 145, 206n
Marshall Plan, campaign for, 1947–1948, 47ff., 176, 196, 206n, 211n
Marshall, S. L. A., 218n
Martin, Joseph, 13, 73
Mazo, Earl, 205n
Meat, decontrol of, 1946, 101
Methods of self-help, presidential, 153ff., 156ff., 159ff., 171ff., 177, 180
"Mid-century," 3f., 37, 39, 103, 106, 186ff., 191
Millis, Walter, 202n, 217n
Morganthau, Hans, 203

National Security Act, 6
National Security Council, 123, 130, 139f., 141f., 153
Navy "revolt" in 1949, 87, 89f.
Neustadt, Richard E., 206n, 209n, 214n, 215n, 222n
"New Look" of 1954, 87f., 210n
Newport conversation, 1957, 17, 21
News, presidential, 102, *see also* President; Press
Nixon, Richard M., 38, 170, 205n
Nominations for President and Congress 33f., 191
North Atlantic Treaty Organization, 77, 126f.
Nourse, Edwin G., 52
Nuclear miscalculation, fear of, 197, 200, 204, 210ff.; *see also* Cuban missile crisis

Orders, self-executing, 18, 31f., 43, 120, *see also* Command; Compliance
O'Reilly, Rose Marie, 213n

Panikkar, K. M., 135, 218n

Parallel, thirty-eighth, 123, 125, 127, 132, 135, 218n
Parties, political, structure of, 33f., 186ff.
Parties-in-electorate, realignment of, 187ff.
Party discipline, 33f., 37f., 187
Patterson, Robert B., 49f.
Perceptions, phenomenon of differing, 213
Performance, presidential appraisal of, 196f., 199
Persuasion, power of, 10, 32, 35ff., 55ff., 60
Policy, public, viability of, 183f., 192f., 199
Political issues in the Sixties, 188ff., 197
    disparate impacts of, 191
Political system, structure of, 33, 39f., 186ff., 191
Politics, party, presidential attitudes toward, 165, 167, 169, 171, 173f., 178f.
    public attitudes toward, 194f.
Polk, James K., 3
Poverty, War on, 202
Power, presidential, relationship to "powers," 7, 10, 34ff.
    relationship to choice-making, 57, 84, 107, 120, 154, 199f.
Power and "powers," distinction between, 204n
Power risks, presidential, 112, 119ff., 124ff., 129, 136ff., 144, 147ff., 201
Power-sense, presidential, 120f., 150f., 154, 161, 163ff., 171, 173f., 178, 180, 182, 185, 196f., 202ff.
Power-stakes, presidential, 57, 107, 109, 112f., 148ff., 151, *see also* Power risks
Presidency, institutionalized, 5f., 152f., 159f., 196, 203, 220n, *see also* Clerkship; President
    perspective of, 7f., 151, 183, 200
President, relations of, with allied governments, 12, 25, 38, 104, 127, 132, 134, 144
    with Congress, 6f., 31, 33f., 37,

46f., 49ff., 53f., 57, 66ff., 82ff., 88f., 92, 104f., 164f., 173f., 186f., 191, 204f., 213
with Executive officials, 7, 20ff., 34ff., 42f., 44f., 52ff., 57, 66ff., 109ff., 119, 145f., 156f., 173, 202f.
with party organizations, 37f., 74, 186f., 191, 205n
with press corps, 6, 58, 62, 80, 102f., 113, 134f., *see also* Press conferences; Reputation; Washington community
with public-at-large, 31, 53, 60, 71f., 89, 92, 100ff., 106ff., 125ff., 194f., 205ff.; *see also* Prestige; Teaching
with special publics, 17, 25, 37, 90ff.
with staff, 41f., 66ff., 80, 157f., 159f., 163, 172, 174, 220n
with state and local officials, 37, *see also* Faubus
President as expert, *see* Expertise
President as teacher, *see* Teaching
Presidential, *see* Choice-making; Confidence; Expertise; Images; Methods; Power; Prestige; Purpose; Time
President's Committee on Administrative Management, 152
Press as adviser to President, 134f., *see also* President
Press conferences, quotations from Eisenhower, 66f., 70, 71, 72, 75, 76, 108, 166
from Truman, 40, 60, 94, 132, 206n
Pressure, presidential stance under, 197, 206f.
Prestige, presidential, 54f., 58, 86ff., 90, 92, 93, 95ff., 125f., 142
Price, Harry Bayard, 206n
Price control legislation, 1950, 104f., *see also* Defense Production Act
Public image of President, 94f., 98, 171
of Presidency, 95, 97, 171
Public, presidential, defined, 86, *see also* Constituencies; Washington community

Public opinion, *see* Gallup; Images; Prestige; Teaching
Purpose, presidential sense of, 162, 167ff., 171, 178, 180, 185, 196

Quemoy-Matsu crises, 1954 and 1958, 97, 102f., 211n

Ratings, radio and television, 100ff., 212n, 213n, 214n
Rayburn, Sam, 68, 70, 78, 104, 194
Reagan, Michael L., 204n
Recession of 1958, 77, 82, 97ff., 211n
Redding, Jack, 176, 222n
Republicanism, modern, 65f., 111, 117, 148, 170
Reputation, professional, defined, 60, 62
Reputation building, 63, 64, 66ff., 80ff., 83f., 171
Reston, James, 62, 72, 208n
Rhee, Syngman, 133
Ridgway, Matthew B., 12, 210n
Rockefeller, Nelson A., 170
Rockefeller Brothers Fund, reports of, 170
Roosevelt, Franklin D., 3, 5, 38, 42, 63f., 87, 101, 103f., 106f., 156f., 160ff., 177f., 180, 182, 193, 198ff., 203, 205, 211, 220n, 221n, *see also* President; Presidential
Roosevelt, Theodore, 3, 5, 64, 106, 162
Roper, Elmo, 210n
Rossiter, Clinton, 152, 220n
Rostow, Elsbeth, 207
Rovere, Richard H., 62
Russell, Richard, 76

Sawyer, Charles S., 19, 22f., 34, 36, 45, 57, 203n
Schilling, Warner, 215n
Schine, David, 111
Schlesinger, Arthur M., Jr., 156ff., 163, 220n, 221n, 223n
School construction legislation, 1957–1958, 75f., 78, 208n
School integration, *see* Little Rock

"Separated institutions sharing powers," 33, 39, 186f.

Sherwood, Robert; 214n

Silverman, Corinne, 203n

Smith, Beverly, 217n

Smith, Harold D., 174, 222n

Snyder, Glenn, 210n

Snyder, John, 50, 55f., 206n

Sputniks, Soviet, 1957, 76ff., 97, 155

Staff, presidential, *see* Presidency; President

Staff system, Eisenhower, 159ff., 172

Stalin, Joseph, 48, 50f., 52

Stassen, Harold, 38, 118, 161, 168, 205n, 215n, 216n

Steel industry, seizure of, 1952, 13ff., 21ff., 24f., 25, 28f., 31, 57, 91f., 202n

Stein, Harold, 202n, 210n, 217n, 221n

Stevenson, Adlai E., 38, 59, 205n

Suez crisis, 1956, 38, 116, 167

Summary of analysis, chaps. 2–7, 179f.

Taft, Robert A., 47, 49, 51, 53

Taft-Hartley Act, 5, 15, 25, 203n, 206n

Teaching, presidential, 100, 103f., 105f., 125f., 129

Temperament, presidential, 162f., 182f., 195, 201

Time, President's use of, 155f., 158

Truman, David B., 204n

Truman Doctrine, 51

Truman, Harry S., 3, 9ff., 19ff., 27ff., 34, 38, 40f., 47f., 52ff., 59f., 78, 87f., 90, 92f., 95ff., 101, 104, 115, 124ff., 130ff., 137f., 145, 171ff., 176ff., 180, 196, 197ff., 198f., 202n, 205, 205n, 206n, 210ff., 213n, 216n, 217n, 218n, 222n, *see also* President; Presidential

quoted, 9f., 40, 123, 128, 130f., 132, 135, 137f., 141f., 177, 206n

Twenty-second Amendment, 83, 112

United Nations resolutions, 1950, 11, 123f., 127, 133f., 136, 217n, 218n

Vandenberg, Arthur H., 48f., 52ff., 55, 59

Vandenberg, Arthur H., Jr., 206n

Vantage points, presidential, 35ff., 60, 164, 169, *see also* Bargaining advantages

Veterans of Foreign Wars, 11, 203n

Veto, presidential, 33, 35, 47, 83f., 164

Vienna meeting, 1961, 200f.

Vietnam war, 196f., 200, 202, 204, 209f.

Voter alignments, instability of, 4, 187ff.

Wage Stabilization Board, 13ff., 16, 28, 57

Wake Island Conference, 12, 126, 136, 138

Washington, George, 166

"Washington community," 58, 62f., 65f., 72ff., 76, 78f., 85f., 89

Webb, James E., 52

Westin, Alan F., 202n

White, William S., 78f., 208n, 209n

Wiley, Alexander, 55

Wilhelm, Kaiser, 198

Willkie, Wendell, 194

Wilson, Charles E. (General Electric), 13ff., 16, 21f., 24f., 57, 59

Wilson, Charles E. (General Motors), 73ff., 185

Wilson, Woodrow, 5, 106f., 195, 208, 214n, 223n